total kabbalah

total kabbalah

Bring Balance and
Happiness into Your Life

MAGGY WHITEHOUSE

total kabbalah

Bring Balance and
Happiness into Your Life

MAGGY WHITEHOUSE

CHRONICLE BOOKS
SAN FRANCISCO

Library of Congress Cataloging-in-Publication Data available.

ISBN: 978-0-8118-6137-3

Manufactured in Thailand

This book was conceived, designed, and
produced by Ixos, an imprint of **Ivy Press**
Publisher David Alexander
Creative Director Peter Bridgewater
Art Director Sarah Howerd
Editorial Director Caroline Earle
Designer Ginny Zeal
Project Editor Stephanie Evans
Illustrators Ivan Hissey, John Woodcock
Picture research Katie Greenwood

10 9 8 7 6 5 4 3 2 1

Chronicle Books LLC
680 Second Street
San Francisco, California 94107

www.chroniclebooks.com

CONTENTS

INTRODUCTION

power. But understanding Kabbalah also requires great commitment. The casual seeker who wants

WHAT IS KABBALAH?
...ah is both a path of personal

✳ KABBALAH WAS ALWAYS INTENDED TO BE A LIVING TRADITION, NOT AN ARCHAIC, EXCLUSIVE FORM OF STUDY FOR MEN ALONE. IT BEGAN LONG BEFORE PEOPLE HAD BOOKS TO READ OR THEATERS TO VISIT, DURING A PERIOD WHEN THE VISIT OF A HOLY MAN OR WOMAN WAS AN EAGERLY ANTICIPATED EVENT. A HOLY PERSON COULD ANSWER THE QUESTIONS OF LIFE, THE UNIVERSE, AND THE NATURE OF DIVINITY.

Long before it was known as Kabbalah (meaning a "received tradition"), those who taught it were known as "The People Who Know." They passed it on to all who wished to understand the nature of life, but they mostly worked within the Jewish faith since it was one of the few monotheistic traditions in the world until the coming of Christianity. Although Kabbalah is traditionally believed to be the inner and mystical aspect of Judaism, it predates any known religion.

In order to be a living tradition that could be updated for each generation as human knowledge and experience grew, Kabbalah has always used two particular designs: the Tree of Life and Jacob's Ladder. The use of these designs within the tradition means that no matter how the external world changes, the heart of Kabbalah remains sound. Students could always check against them to ensure that they were still on the right path.

Kabbalah can be found within the inner teachings of all the world's religions as well as in the apparently disparate system of tarot, astrology, and chakras, though which run a common thread of universal wisdom. This is because it is not a religion in itself but a way of understanding the matrix of life.

Right: The Tree of Life is known in many traditions from Yggdrasil, the Nordic "World Tree," to the Bodhi Tree of Buddhism. Each one symbolizes the balance between Heaven and Earth.

Kabbalistic teaching incorporates reincarnation—the idea that all of us live different lives in order to achieve total joy. This doctrine has always been acknowledged in the inner, mystical beliefs of Judaism and Christianity. It is not the same as the Buddhist idea of transmigration, through which a soul can become an animal, insect, or plant. To the Kabbalist this would be against the natural law of the universe, according to which each individual species seeks to perfect itself. However, animal archetypes are to be seen in humanity, and a person could live the equivalent life of an ant as a slave to the workplace—or the life of a lion, ruling his or her territory.

JUST WHAT IS KABBALAH?

Kabbalah is both a path of personal development and a way of perceiving how the universe works. It aims to explain the relationship between God, the universe, and humanity, and the destiny of each human soul.

Kabbalah provides a structure for study, growth, belief, and self-realization rather than a form. Structure is like a skeleton. A skeleton is there to support the growth and development of a human being but it does not dictate the color of skin, hair, or eyes or the character of the person. Humans cannot grow without a skeleton, but with its support they can develop in whatever way is appropriate for them.

After the invention of the printing press in the 15th century, many complex and confusing books were published about Kabbalah. However, true Kabbalah continued underground by word of mouth through groups, known as schools of the soul, which had always been open to the serious seeker of enlightenment from any faith. In 12th-century Toledo in Spain, for example, Jews, Christians, and Muslims studied Kabbalah together.

The wide range of concepts embraced by Kabbalah over the years means that it sometimes appears contradictory, obscure, ridiculously complicated, and even incomprehensible. Each system stands on its own, but used together, the different interpretations are far too complex for the beginner to understand. Some of this complexity may have been intentional on the part of teachers down the ages, as the knowledge of the workings of the universe can confer great

power. But understanding Kabbalah also requires great commitment. The casual seeker who wants a "quick fix" will easily be put off by a system that is time-consuming and seems to require linguistic and mathematical knowledge.

Left: Kabbalah is as much an internal system as an external system. Experiencing the levels of creation within one's Self and rising to the levels of the archangels is a powerful way of understanding the tradition. (Illustration by Z'ev ben Shimon Halevi.)

Below: Kabbalah was at one time only available to certain Orthodox Jewish men who could read Hebrew. All this was to change in the mid-20th century with the rise of the Kabbalah Center.

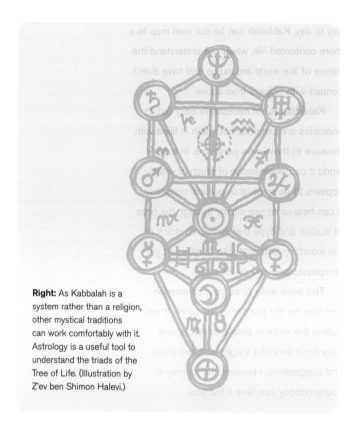

Right: As Kabbalah is a system rather than a religion, other mystical traditions can work comfortably with it. Astrology is a useful tool to understand the triads of the Tree of Life. (Illustration by Z'ev ben Shimon Halevi.)

Until the rise to prominence of the internationally known Kabbalah Center, the tradition was mostly believed to be available only to Orthodox Jewish men who were married, over the age of 40, and could read Hebrew. Some relatively public non-Jewish groups, such as The Golden Dawn, did exist in the late 19th and early 20th centuries but they focused on the magical tradition that was seen by many to be dangerous.

However, in the mid-20th century, when humanity began to feel safe in exploring spirituality outside of conventional religion, Kabbalah started to flourish openly. Its discipline and structure are important assets in a world where we have free rein to believe what we wish. It also offers very clear guidelines concerning magic, which are useful for those investigating the world's current openness toward the magical arts.

This book works primarily from one clear system of Kabbalah that is both the oldest available and the most recently updated. It is the easiest to understand for those who are not versed in ancient languages, deeply religious, or scholarly by nature. It is also the version most relevant to a generation that has learned of the power of positive thinking and has international media stars, such as Oprah Winfrey, promoting the idea that good thoughts create good things and that human free will is responsible for the good or bad situations that face us.

WHAT CAN KABBALAH DO FOR ME?

Kabbalah excels in the modern world in helping us to understand the psyche—our inner personalities and how they affect us and our ability to make free-will decisions.

To a Kabbalist, the diagram of the Tree of Life is a blueprint for each individual's psyche, personality, and self-development. The Tree of Life is generally viewed as representing the psychological world (known as Yezirah) where the human personality and soul reside. Once it is understood and experienced through exercises, such as following the design with your body or making a temple with chairs in a room, it can lead to great personal revelation and give clear indications of how life can be improved at all levels.

Kabbalah teaches that each human soul will eventually perfect itself through a series of journeys. Every one of us will achieve joy and union with the Divine, whether or not we believe in Kabbalah—or indeed in God Itself; the tradition is simply there as a tool to help us on those journeys.

The second of the Kabbalistic designs, Jacob's Ladder, shows the "invisible laws" that make life what it is, and explains the principles behind planets, angels and archangels, humanity, archetypes, animal and vegetable levels, and the great question of good and evil. It is believed to be the origin of the game of snakes and ladders, showing us where we are on our journey and what "snakes" might be lying ahead of us. The living tradition of Kabbalah can also make helpful, modern interpretations of the Bible that both adhere to ancient principles and fit perfectly with the lives of people today. Whether we are involved in competitive work, social and family pressures, mortgages, bills, global awareness, politics, or simply living from day to day, Kabbalah can be our road map to a more contented life, where we understand the nature of the world around us and have direct contact with helpers from above.

Kabbalah is not necessarily easy but its principles are simple and its path is filled with treasure to those who persevere. In today's world it can make sense of much of what appears to be spiritual or political nonsense. It can help us to see clearly through the haze of illusion and hype that surrounds much of the world's events and take a detached yet compassionate view of life today.

This book aims to be your companion and map for the journey of Kabbalah. It will outline the route in simple, practical, and easy-to-understand stages with exercises and suggestions. However, the journey is yours; nobody can take it but you.

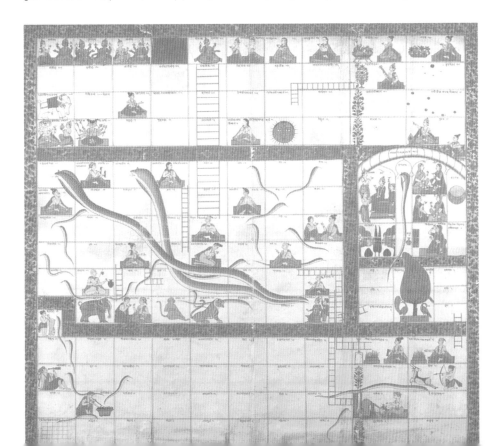

Left: The ancient game of snakes and ladders is said to be based on the Tree of Life. The paths lead to Paradise and the snakes to psychological Hell.

PART ONE

GENERAL PRINCIPLES

THE HEBREW WORD "KABBALAH" MEANS "TO RECEIVE." KABBALAH IS BOTH
A "RECEIVED WISDOM," HANDED DOWN DIRECTLY FROM THE HOLY ONE, AND
ONE THAT HAS BEEN PASSED ON BY WORD OF MOUTH FROM ONE GENERATION
TO ANOTHER FOR MORE THAN 4,000 YEARS. IT IS BASED ON TWO STRUCTURES:
THE TREE OF LIFE AND JACOB'S LADDER. THESE TWO STRUCTURES HAVE BEEN
USED THROUGHOUT THE CENTURIES TO ENSURE THAT THE HEART OF THE
TRADITION STAYED PURE—WHATEVER THE CUSTOMS AND TRADITIONS OF THE
DAY. IN ANCIENT TIMES, SINCE VERY FEW PEOPLE COULD READ OR WRITE,
KABBALAH WAS ALWAYS TRANSMITTED ORALLY. EVEN NOW, IT CAN ONLY BE
FULLY UNDERSTOOD IN THE CONTEXT OF DISCUSSION AND DEBATE BECAUSE IT
IS CONCERNED WITH THE DEVELOPMENT OF THE INDIVIDUAL. UNDERSTANDING
THE MEANING OF THE KABBALISTIC DIAGRAMS, AND HOW THEY ARE USED
ENABLES US TO MAKE MANY POSITIVE CHANGES IN LIFE.

CHAPTER ONE
FIRST STEPS

✳ ACCORDING TO LEGEND, KABBALAH IS THE KNOWLEDGE GIVEN TO ADAM AND EVE TO HELP HUMANITY FIND ITS WAY BACK TO EDEN. HAVING CHOSEN TO EAT FROM THE TREE OF KNOWLEDGE, THEY WERE FORCED TO LEAVE PARADISE FOR THIS WORLD WHERE THEY WOULD HAVE TO MAKE CHOICES FOR THE REST OF THEIR DAYS.

The first steps we take in life are much easier with a hand to hold. The teachings of Kabbalah are intended to be that hand; a way of showing us which steps are true and will take us forward and which are false and will make us stumble. The main Kabbalistic diagram is called the Tree of Life, to remind us of the other tree in the Garden of Eden that leads to the higher worlds. It is intended to be a design for living that works whatever our belief system. This is particularly useful in a time when open spirituality is increasingly more popular. Guidelines for happiness that do not specify that a particular belief system is required to achieve salvation are a very helpful tool in the modern world.

Kabbalah works on a basic structure of ten Sefirot, or circles, which depict ten aspects of God. These Sefirot are arranged in a particular pattern which, when understood, is like a language. They can be used to learn about the structure of the universe, our own psychological and physical makeup, the workings of angels and archangels, the pattern of the planets of the solar system—and the nature of God Itself. The first written evidence of the Sefirot is in the biblical Book of Exodus, where Moses is told to create the menorah, a seven-branched candlestick that symbolized cosmic law and how it operated through symbols and cycles of nature to a nation of people who could not read or write.

Hod   Nezach
Gevurah   Da'at
Binah   Tiferet
Keter   Yesod
Hokhmah   Malkhut
Hesed

Above: The seven-branched menorah. The branches and central column represent the Sefirot of the Tree of Life.

Right: Kabbalists believe that all of life can be demonstrated via the patterns made by the Sefirot in the Tree of Life. In the 11th century, the image was updated from the menorah to the Tree of Life that we now know in order to make it more accessible and understandable.

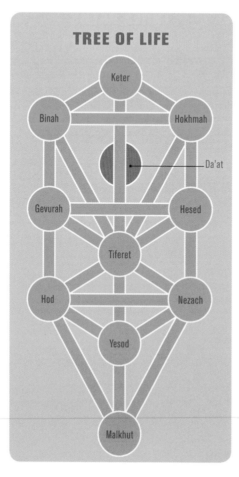

TREE OF LIFE

Keter

Binah   Hokhmah

Da'at

Gevurah   Hesed

Tiferet

Hod   Nezach

Yesod

Malkhut

THE ORAL TRADITION

Kabbalah is an oral tradition best taught in groups of people and passed on by word of mouth. This is so that it can be seen as pertinent to the life of each individual and also so that it can be updated constantly according to the era in which it is being studied.

An oral tradition enables the latest expansion of knowledge of the world, science, interfaith matters, and human perception to be placed on the Sefirot and the other aspects on the Tree of Life, to be understood in mystical terms. This keeps the tradition fresh and clear and continuously up-to-date.

There are many books containing knowledge about Kabbalah, dating as far back as the second century, but their accounts of the higher and hidden worlds are filled with allegory and metaphysical terms that are incomprehensible to us today. Many would-be students of Kabbalah have been put off by overcomplex archaic terminology. Even books written 50 years ago cannot assist the student wishing to examine the Internet or the advent of the New Age within the structure of the Tree.

The oral tradition teaches that there are three specific paths that can be taken: contemplation, devotion, and action. These equate to the three pillars that form the vertical structure of the Tree of Life. Contemplation is discussion, reading, or study of the tradition and would be placed on the left-hand, passive, column. Devotion is prayer or meditation in some form, and this is placed on the central pillar. Devotion can be either active or passive, such as singing on the one hand and sitting in silence and clearing the mind on the other. Action is either carrying out a specific exercise—such as creating a physical Tree of Life with chairs or stones, discussing what has been learned or what had been experienced through contemplation and devotion, and living the tradition in everyday life. This is placed on the right-hand, active, pillar.

Each of these practices is out of balance if carried out on its own; all three need to be used together. In an oral tradition in which people study, meditate, and talk together, each can be addressed in turn. Every student notes which one is the most pleasant and which the least comfortable, and examines how this might be reflected in the whole of his or her life.

THREE PATHS

Contemplation   Devotion   Action

Left: The Tree of Life is built around the three pillars, a vertical structure of Contemplation, Devotion, and Action.

THE DIVINE PLAN

✳ KABBALAH TEACHES THAT EVERY HUMAN BEING, REGARDLESS OF RACE, RELIGION, SOCIAL STATUS, OR QUALITY OF LIFE IS EQUALLY VALUED BY THE HOLY ONE. THE DIVINE PLAN IS FOR EACH ONE OF US TO PERFECT OURSELF OVER MANY LIVES SO THAT GOD MAY BEHOLD ITSELF IN US.

Right: The soul called to be a warrior may achieve that goal as a Samurai.

Every life offers us the chances we need to grow and, through a series of experiences, we will all reach what the Buddha called enlightenment. As each person's soul is different, we will all become perfect in different ways but we will all reach that goal, even the souls that may have the exact opposite in mind in their current lives. Even if it takes billions of years and just one soul is still resisting its own perfection, the divine plan will continue until the choice to experience total joy and union with the Holy One is made.

The soul who is called to be a soldier will perhaps become the perfect Samurai warrior, capable of complete detachment from anger, complete understanding of compassion, and able to judge exactly when action is needed and when it is not. The soul who is called to be a "Steward of the Earth" will perhaps become the wise one capable of living a life of example, not condemning those who do not understand but demonstrating simple and understandable ways of honoring the land. The soul who is called to be a Mother may be able to keep a perfect balance between discipline and love so that her children are always confident and joyful but understand the need for boundaries and mercy.

THE DIVINE MAN

Kabbalistic legend tells that each human being is one cell in a divine human being, known as Adam Kadmon. The word Adam comes from the Hebrew word "ha adamah" which means "of the Earth." The word is not gender-specific. "Kadmon" is Hebrew for primal or primordial, so Adam Kadmon is the primordial human being—the blueprint of the perfect human. In modern terms we could call him/her God's baby.

This being exists in potentiality only. It can only realize itself when all its soul-cells (us) have ourselves become enlightened. Then we will all become united in one image of God—and as an integral part of the divine baby be truly "born again," whatever our religious belief.

The existence of Adam Kadmon is the origin of the Biblical phrase "So God created man in his image, in the image of God created he him; male and female created he them" (Gen 1:26). This legend tells us that every one of us is a spark of God Itself—each a vital part of a divine baby that is destined to grow, develop, and eventually be fully realized. Adam Kadmon is also sometimes known as "son of man," (in Hebrew, "ben Adam") a term often given to Jesus of Nazareth as well as to the prophet Ezekiel, who was the first to write about Kabbalistic symbolism in the Bible. This would have been an acknowledgment of a human being who had reached such a high level of development that he or she might be seen as perfect.

In the case of the prophet, it was God who addressed him as "son of man," and the Bible implies that this is how God would address any one of us, seeing the real perfection potential within each soul.

FIERY MAN

Above: Adam Kadmon as the "fiery man." The figure is a vertical representation of the Holy Name JHVH (Yahweh) revealing a humanoid figure. (Calligraphy by Z'ev ben Shimon Halevi.)

HOW CREATION BEGAN

✳ KABBALISTIC LEGEND SAYS THAT GOD WISHED TO BEHOLD GOD. IN ESSENCE, GOD WISHED TO RECREATE ITSELF. HOWEVER, THAT POSED A PROBLEM BECAUSE FOR SOMETHING THAT WAS ABSOLUTE, OMNIPOTENT, OMNISCIENT, AND OMNIPRESENT TO CREATE "AN OTHER," IT FIRST HAD TO CREATE THE IDEA OF DUALITY.

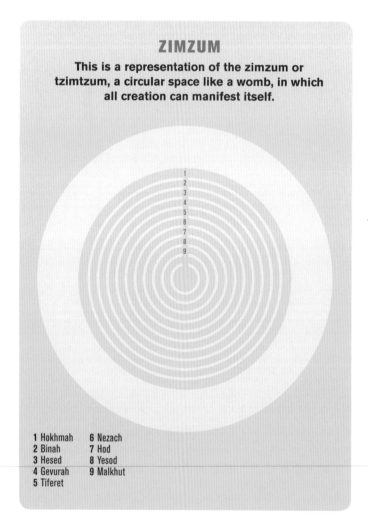

ZIMZUM

This is a representation of the zimzum or tzimtzum, a circular space like a womb, in which all creation can manifest itself.

1 Hokhmah	**6** Nezach
2 Binah	**7** Hod
3 Hesed	**8** Yesod
4 Gevurah	**9** Malkhut
5 Tiferet	

This is why humanity lives in a world of opposites—up, down; in, out; dark, light; male, female. It is also why there is such an extraordinary diversity throughout the universe. Duality evolved to create color, form, shape, size, sound—everything that we experience. The process that began creation itself is called zimzum, or tzimtzum, Hebrew for "contraction."

Legend has it that God conceived of different aspects of Itself beginning with Ain—"No thing" in Hebrew—meaning that God is beyond existence and comprehension, absolute nothing. From that, the Holy One made a contraction, the zimzum, which formed a space, like a womb, in which all of creation would manifest itself. This aspect of Divinity was known as Ain Sof (Hebrew for "without end") and was the first actual manifestation of separation between God and the universe. Into this space, God breathed Ain Sof Aur, "the endless light" that is the beginning of manifestation itself.

DIRECTING THE LIGHT

The endless light is the beginning of life, the creation of universes and different levels of reality. This light had to be directed so that it had boundaries and did not simply flow in one direction forever. Therefore, vessels were created to direct it into specific, mathematical patterns that would ensure that it was contained and could consolidate before moving on to continue the process of creation.

As each part of the journey taken by the light took it farther from its source, it became less refined, heavier, and more in need of regulation—in the same way that a mudflow is harder to direct down a water chute than clear water. The vessels were called Sefirot (single: Sefira). This is believed to come from the Hebrew root SFR. It is called a root because Hebrew did not have vowels in ancient times, so a word could be interpreted in many ways. SFR can mean "sapphire," "sefer" (book), "safar" (count), or "sifur" (say or speak). In ancient Greek, which has been used by Kabbalists for more than 2,000 years, Sefira means "sphere" or "circle."

A system of Kabbalah developed by a 16th-century mystic called Isaac Luria teaches that God made a mistake during the creation process and that the Sefirot, which had to contain the light, were too weak and shattered. However, more ancient forms of Kabbalah teach that the vessels were strong enough and held fast. The practice of Kabbalah is the same whether you choose to believe Luria's version— known as Lurianic Kabbalah—or the more ancient system, now known as Toledano Kabbalah. Either way, the process is to help God behold God by becoming perfect oneself. Lurianic Kabbalah says that this is to mend the shattered universe and Toledano Kabbalah says that the universe is already perfect; it is our perception and our actions that appear to make

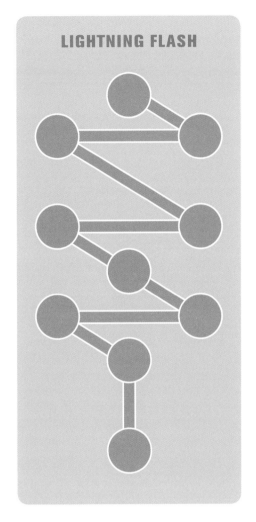

LIGHTNING FLASH

Left: The lightning flash of creation can be represented in the same way as the Tree of Life. It is perennial and can be seen as the growth of any living entity.

it seem any different. Whichever belief system is adopted, it is said that the endless light traveled in a lightning flash back and forward across the void, building the structure of creation. It began with the vibrational frequency of fire, became air, then water, and finally, earth. This lightning flash of creation is perennial and can be seen in the growth and birth of any living entity—after the first expansion of life, there must be consolidation of structure, such as bone and flesh, before further expansion can occur.

THE TEN SEFIROT

✳ THE TEN EMANATIONS OF CREATION, THE SEFIROT, ARE ALSO THE TEN ASPECTS OF GOD. NEWCOMERS ARE OFTEN CONFUSED ABOUT THE NUMBER OF NAMES THAT GOD APPEARS TO HAVE WITHIN THE TRADITION AND BY THE FACT THAT ORTHODOX JEWS NEVER PRONOUNCE THE ULTIMATE NAME OF GOD.

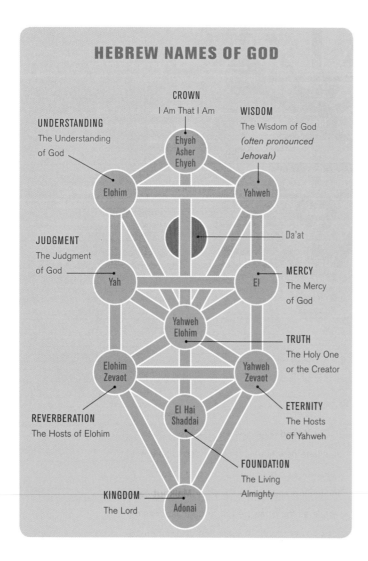

HEBREW NAMES OF GOD

CROWN
I Am That I Am
Ehyeh Asher Ehyeh

WISDOM
The Wisdom of God
(often pronounced Jehovah)
Yahweh

UNDERSTANDING
The Understanding of God
Elohim

Da'at

JUDGMENT
The Judgment of God
Yah

MERCY
The Mercy of God
El

Yahweh Elohim

TRUTH
The Holy One or the Creator
Yahweh Zevaot

REVERBERATION
The Hosts of Elohim
Elohim Zevaot

El Hai Shaddai

ETERNITY
The Hosts of Yahweh

FOUNDATION
The Living Almighty

KINGDOM
The Lord
Adonai

The simplest explanation is that as the ten emanations all require the tension of contact with each other, pronouncing one of the ten aspects of God alone could create a distorted image of the Holy One. The Hebrew root YHVH (Jehovah or Yahweh) is often used as it refers to the Wisdom of God. However, the "safest" terminology for God is generally seen as the word "Lord."

All the attributes of the names of God, with the exception of **Keter**, are capable of being either positive or negative. For example:

Our **Hokhmah** can be so concerned with receiving external inspiration that we never learn to think for ourselves nor how to live in the "real" world.

Our **Binah** can be so formulated that it never lets a good idea through, instead chewing it over until it is completely dissolved.

Our **Hesed** can be over-kind—to the extent that we destroy our own lives through constantly helping others.

Our **Gevurah** can either be too judgmental —even racist, bigoted, or prejudiced—or it can be so ineffectual that we never make decisions or learn the word "no."

NAMES OF GOD ATTRIBUTES

Each one of these attributes is also an aspect of the psyche of a human being.

KETER, THE CROWN, is the same as the human higher self—the aspect of us that is closest to God.

BINAH is our ability to understand and experience that wisdom—to process it and test its validity.

HOKHMAH is our ability to receive inspiration and wisdom from the higher worlds.

Keter

Binah

Hokhmah

Da'at

GEVURAH is our ability to be disciplined and discerning and make correct judgments.

Gevurah

Hesed

HESED is our capacity for love, kindness, and joy.

Tiferet

TIFERET is our real Self, the unique person who lives inside our personality.

Hod

Nezach

HOD is our intellectual processor, which gathers information and monitors and continues the projects begun by our Nezach.

Yesod

NEZACH combines our creative, artistic, and sexual impulses—the initiation of new projects, love affairs, or designs.

MALKHUT is our physical body, with its needs and its life force.

Malkhut

YESOD is our ego-consciousness, the foundation upon which we base most of our decisions, depending on our family, social, and educational training.

Our **Tiferet** can be weak or strong according to our ability to look at ourselves dispassionately. Two frequent weaknesses of Tiferet are pride or, alternatively, being too self-effacing (Who me? Oh no, I couldn't possibly…).

Our **Nezach** can lead us into a cycle of love affairs or new projects without finishing off old ones—adultery is a Nezachian principle. Finally, our **Hod** can overintellectualize to the point of

paralysis. We may keep seeking more information and never act on what has already been read. It can also become totally stuck in one viewpoint.

Our **Yesod**—the Ego—is reactive; it does not initiate new things. It can refuse to take a wider view and become entrenched in social conditioning and habit. Finally, our **Malkhut** can overrule all the other Sefirot through laziness or physical overactivity. It is also the place of greed.

CHAPTER TWO
FOUR WORLDS

✳ AS THE GRAND DESIGN OF CREATION UNFOLDED, THE QUALITY OF LIGHT CHANGED. IT EMANATED THROUGH THE WORLD OF ADAM KADMON, EXPRESSING ITSELF AS PURE FIRE. AS IT FLOWED FARTHER, CONSTRUCTING THE WORLD OF SPIRIT WHERE THE ARCHANGELS EXIST, IT BECAME AIR. AS IT FORMED THE WORLD OF IMAGES, ANGELS, AND EMOTIONS IT BECAME WATER. FINALLY, AS IT COMPLETED ITS JOURNEY, IT MADE EARTH.

Understanding the flow of creation is integral to understanding our world and ourselves. It is also helpful in interpreting the biblical book of Genesis, which appears to repeat itself but is actually detailing the flow of light through the different levels.

The Genesis story begins with the second world—Beriah, the world of Spirit. Tradition says that this is because the impulse for the biblical story of creation flows from the aspects of the Absolute that already exist in Azilut, the name that is given to the fiery world of Adam Kadmon.

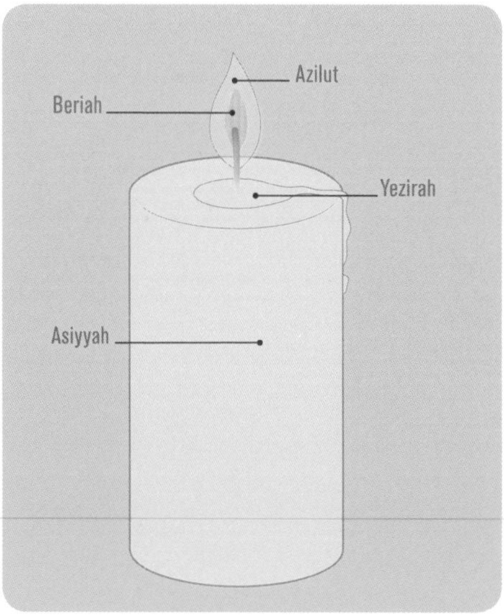

What we could call "relative existence" begins in Beriah—this is where time first exists together with the cosmic principles of creation and destruction. Both principles are necessary; the sun rising represents creation, while the sun setting stands for destruction. Without the two opposites, reality cannot exist.

The four worlds can be seen most clearly in a lighted candle. The golden flame is the fiery world of Azilut, and the darker color, around the wick (which is blue-black when observed clearly) is air that draws up the liquid of the wax and vaporizes it. This is the Beriatic world that is inextricably linked to the fiery world and to the liquid world of Yezirah. It is the fire of Azilut that heats the air of Beriah to vaporize the liquid of Yezirah. The solid wax of the candle represents the physical world, Asiyyah: it too is inextricably linked to the other worlds through the heat that permeates down from the flame through the air and liquid wax to also heat the solid wax. Eastern philosophies speak of a fifth element. To a Kabbalist this would be a central path linking the

Candle diagram with labels: Beriah, Azilut, Yezirah, Asiyyah

Right: A lighted candle is one of the world's perennial symbols of spirituality, and here represents the four worlds of Kabbalah.

Above: Air dividing from Fire at the beginning of creation is shown in this 19th-century image from *Bank's Bible*. Each star and planet is said to have its own spiritual entity, or angel, which is the creative force that maintains it.

crown of crowns of the fiery world of Azilut to the base of bases of the earthly world of Asiyyah. In a candle, this would be the wick itself.

Kabbalah teaches that humanity is unique among God's creation for its ability to access all four levels consciously. Angels exist only in the world of Yezirah. Although they permeate that entire world and therefore can link with both Spirit (Beriah) and Earth (Asiyyah) and communicate with both levels, they cannot exist physically in a body. Animals have physical bodies and basic psychological (Yeziratic) consciousness but are not spiritual beings. Humans on the other hand are physically existent, psychologically aware, and capable both of understanding spiritual concepts and of experiencing Divinity.

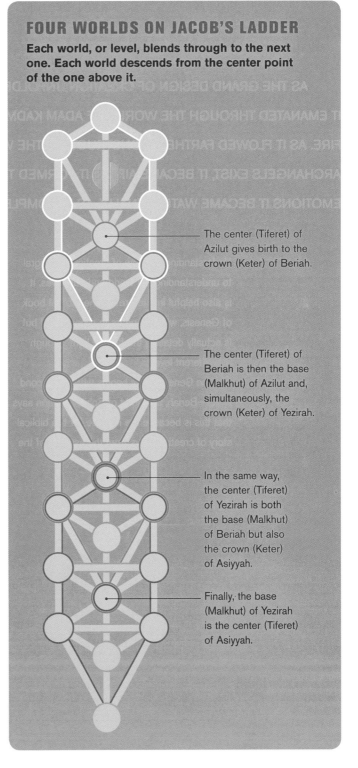

FOUR WORLDS ON JACOB'S LADDER

Each world, or level, blends through to the next one. Each world descends from the center point of the one above it.

The center (Tiferet) of Azilut gives birth to the crown (Keter) of Beriah.

The center (Tiferet) of Beriah is then the base (Malkhut) of Azilut and, simultaneously, the crown (Keter) of Yezirah.

In the same way, the center (Tiferet) of Yezirah is both the base (Malkhut) of Beriah but also the crown (Keter) of Asiyyah.

Finally, the base (Malkhut) of Yezirah is the center (Tiferet) of Asiyyah.

THE FOUR WORLDS IN NATURE

✳ IN AN ANIMAL OR HUMAN BEING THE FOUR LEVELS OF EARTH, WATER, AIR, AND FIRE AND THE WAY THEY MERGE WITH EACH OTHER CAN BE SEEN CLEARLY IN THE PHYSICAL BODY.

Right: The study of the Earth, the universe and the elements became science as we know it today. However, ancient scholars believed the mystical element was equally as important as physical reality.

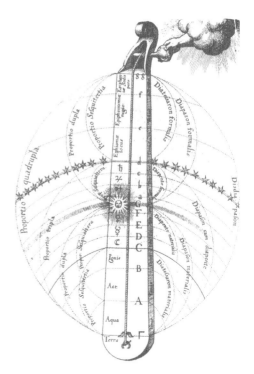

Earth is represented by bones, muscles, organs, and skin, all of which are infused with liquids. Water is represented by our blood, lymph, saliva, digestive juices, urine, and sweat. These liquids are filled with air—the life-giving oxygen in our breath that reaches every single cell in the body.

Fire is represented by the life force and through the heat of our bodies. A person who is filled with joy or awareness is often referred to as "radiant," and our less frequently observed electromagnetic fields are vibrations of light.

Healers and mystics say that the electromagnetic field, or aura, contains the soul and spirit of a human being. This vibrational energy field permeates our bodies on several levels and disconnects on physical death. In this way, the human essence returns to the heavenly realms; not being physical, our soul and spirit cannot experience literal death.

Our universe also works through these four basic elements. Our ancestors worshipped the sun for its life-giving force; it was an elemental god. The sun's heat and light permeated everything and, although our predecessors might not have realized it, it is the sun's light that even illuminates the night, reflected from the moon. The light of the sun shines through the air, which thickens through our atmosphere and becomes

Above: The structure of the Earth corresponds to the four elements, with fire at the very core of the planet producing fiery gases and liquids.

impregnated by water vapor, often appearing as clouds. The majority of the Earth itself is covered with water and it is only deep within the planet's crust that the liquids—including oil—dry out. The core of the Earth is filled with molten rock, re-creating the fire of Azilut.

According to Kabbalistic tradition there is a cycle of life: the end of all things (i.e., the core of the Earth) is also the beginning. This is similar to the Christian view of the Alpha and Omega. Kabbalah would equate the fifth element of Metal (as in the Chinese Five Elements tradition), with the great heat of the center of Earth because metal is made from heating rock. This molten center is also the path that links directly from the Keter of Keters in Azilut to the Malkhut of Malkhuts in Asiyyah—the highest of the high to the lowest of the low.

The power of each level and its absolute importance to life is demonstrated by how long we could live without each level. Without the physical sustenance that we eat, a human being could live for a couple of months, as long as there was water to drink. Without water, a human could live for about three days. However, without air we could survive only for about five minutes. If the Sun died, all living things on the surface of the Earth would freeze to death in seconds.

Above: This 19th-century *Bank's Bible* image shows Spirit (Beriah) forming the concepts of liquid and solid to enable the planet Earth to be formed (Yezirah) and made (Asiyyah).

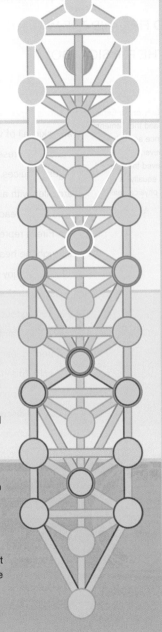

HOW THE FOUR ELEMENTS CONNECT
All four elements are interdependent.

AZILUT As each world merges with the next, transformation takes place. The world of Azilut is unchanging without time, space, or form. It represents the sense of sight.

BERIAH The "kite" shape between Azilut and Beriah is "the breath of God" or "the Word" (as in St. John's Gospel) which begins creation. It is the heart of the oral tradition and represents the sense of hearing.

YEZIRAH Between Beriah and Yezirah humanity can touch the world of Spirit. It equates to the sense of smell, which requires air and water. The lower "kite" represents the sense of taste—water and solids.

ASIYYAH The world of Earth equates to the sense of touch. It is the only world that has no direct contact with Azilut and is consequently the coarsest and the most fragile of the worlds. Only in this world do we experience death.

THE FOUR WORLDS IN US

✳ KABBALAH TEACHES THAT EACH HUMAN BEING CONTAINS THE FOUR BASIC ELEMENTS OF EARTH, WATER, AIR, AND FIRE. EARTH IS OUR BONES, MUSCLES, ORGANS, SKIN, AND HAIR. WATER IS THE BLOOD, LYMPH, AND OTHER LIQUIDS SUCH AS SALIVA AND DIGESTIVE JUICES. AIR IS THE BREATH WITHIN US AND THE GASES PRODUCED BY THE BODY, AND FIRE IS THE WARMTH THAT SIGNIFIES LIFE IN US.

THE FOUR ELEMENTS IN THE HUMAN BEING

Of the four elements, fire is the most powerful energy we have and can be used to create or destroy. We have harnessed it through electricity, gas, and nuclear fission but we will never fully control it.

In the human, the element of fire is focused in the "core star," located about one and a half inches above the navel, right in the center of the body. In healing, this can be seen as a bright light, the essence of Divinity in the individual. In Kabbalah the core star is the place where the three lower worlds meet and humanity can consciously experience Divinity.

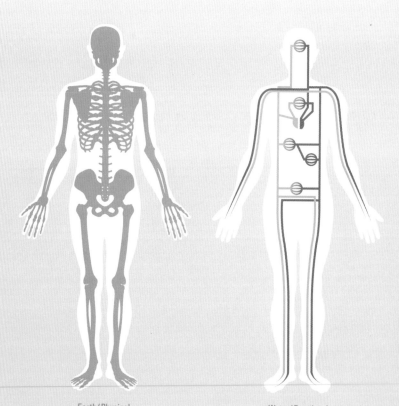

Earth/Physical

Water/Emotional

However, this is only viewing the elements from a physical standpoint. Kabbalah also suggests that water represents our emotional lives—our feelings and moods. The Moon, which is known to affect the tides on Earth is also the origin of the term "lunatic" from the theory that psychiatric patients who suffer from emotional disorders are often more disturbed around the time of a full Moon.

Air represents our spiritual level and the realm of pure thought. It is interesting that the Internet, faxes, and telephones that transmit our thoughts and words around the world are essentially transmitting through air. The renowned native American teacher Brooke Medicine Eagle, author of *Buffalo Woman Comes Singing* (Ballantine Books, 1991), tells of how until the mid-20th century, native American elders were able to contact one another over hundreds of miles by telepathic thought alone—and the messages passed between them were able to be verified as fact. However, once the tribes had television and wired communications, they lost the ability to use their minds alone for communication.

Fire represents the Divine. This is based on the ancient belief that all life comes from the light of the Sun.

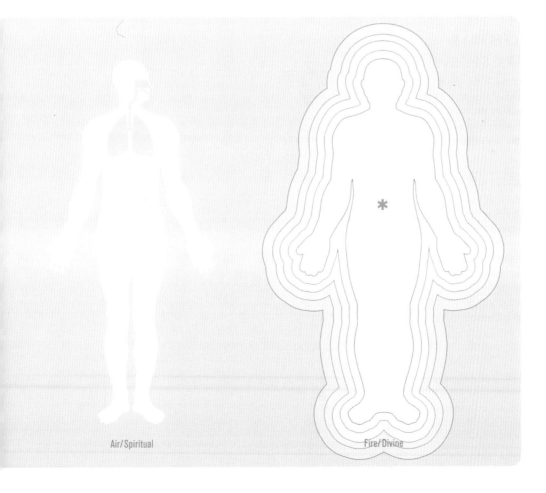

Air/Spiritual

Fire/Divine

SCIENCE, THE BIG BANG, THE FOUR WORLDS, AND DNA

✳ SCIENCE AND RELIGION ARE OFTEN SEEN AS HAVING VERY DIFFERENT POINTS OF VIEW ABOUT CREATION AND HUMAN EVOLUTION. SCIENCE AND KABBALAH, HOWEVER, ARE FAR MORE COMFORTABLE WITH EACH OTHER. THE CONCEPT OF THE "BIG BANG" AND THE DISCOVERY OF DNA ARE BOTH COMPLETELY COMPATIBLE WITH KABBALISTIC TEACHING.

Above: According to science, physical existence came into being with a sudden burst of Light from no known source.

Dr. Gerald Schroeder, author of *Genesis and the Big Bang, the Discovery of Harmony between Modern Science and the Torah* (Bantam Doubleday, 1991) was one of the first modern scientists to link Kabbalah with cosmology. He teaches that Kabbalistic interpretation of the book of Genesis sets forth a clear description of what is now called the Big Bang explanation for the origin of the universe.

The evidence Schroeder presents is two-fold. Firstly, that the Hebrew word for "the first day" in Genesis is really "day one," and this allows not only for the Big Bang's 15 billion-year odyssey, but also allows Einstein's Theory of Relativity in all of its hypotheses of space, matter, and time.

Dr. Schroeder quotes the 16th-century Kabbalist Nachmanides, who lived in the Spanish city of Gerona, saying that though the days in Genesis Chapter One are 24 hours each, they contain "*kol yemot ha olam*"—all the ages and all the secrets of the world.

Nachmanides also taught that creation was, firstly, a tiny speck but in that speck was all the raw material that was needed to make everything else. As this speck expanded out—through the lower worlds—this substance turned into matter as we know it. And the moment that matter formed from this substance, time began.

Einstein's formula $E = MC^2$, tells us that energy transforms into matter. And once it begins to change, time begins.

DNA AND KABBALAH

Science now teaches that the blueprint of life is deoxyribonucleic acid—DNA. This is a large molecule structured from chains of repeating units of a sugar called deoxyribose and a phosphate linked to four different bases abbreviated to the letters A, T, G, and C.

Our genetic makeup is composed of DNA chains, which in turn are made up from hundreds or thousands of simple molecules. The order in which those molecules are linked determines the information contained in the DNA and it is the sequence of those molecules that molecular biologists are now trying to decode.

The structure of DNA contains the information for specifying the proteins that allow life. Proteins include everything, from hormones such as insulin, which regulates our blood-sugar levels, to enzymes, which help us digest our food. Each protein affects others in a great chain. Understanding the structure of the DNA chain was a scientific triumph, though now there is another, tantalizing, theory: that the structure itself is evolving—from two to four strands—echoing the four dependent bases or worlds of Kabbalah.

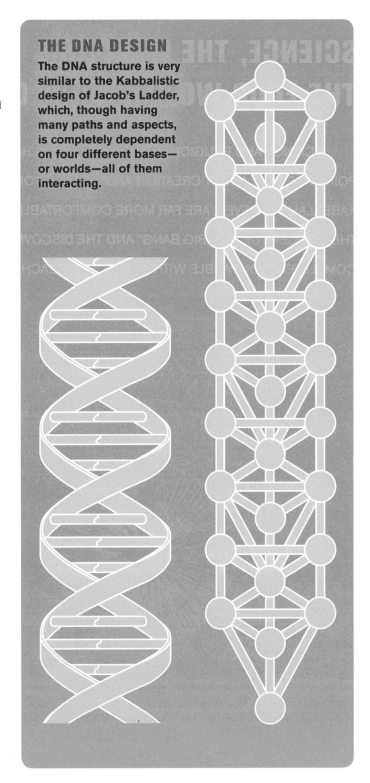

THE DNA DESIGN

The DNA structure is very similar to the Kabbalistic design of Jacob's Ladder, which, though having many paths and aspects, is completely dependent on four different bases— or worlds—all of them interacting.

PART TWO

TOOLS OF KABBALAH

THE PRIMARY TOOL OF KABBALAH IS THE TREE OF LIFE. THIS DESIGN CONTAINS

ALL OF REALITY WITHIN IT, AND TO UNDERSTAND IT IS LIKE BEING ABLE TO

SPEAK THE LANGUAGE OF THE COSMOS. THE TREE IS REPEATED FOUR TIMES

VERTICALLY TO MAKE JACOB'S LADDER, WHICH IS THE BLUEPRINT FOR THE

DESIGN OF ALL CREATION. WHEN PEOPLE REFER TO THE TREE OF LIFE, THEY

USUALLY MEAN THE PARTICULAR TREE THAT REPRESENTS THE HUMAN PSYCHE.

IN ADDITION TO THE TREE OF LIFE AND JACOB'S LADDER, KABBALAH IS

STRONGLY LINKED WITH ASTROLOGY. THE ZODIAC AND ITS STAR SIGNS ALSO

RELATE TO THE PSYCHOLOGICAL, YEZIRATIC WORLD OF THE TREE OF LIFE.

KABBALAH IS CLEAR THAT IT IS THROUGH THE USE OF ALL FOUR WORLDS—

FIRE, AIR, WATER, AND EARTH—THAT HUMANITY WILL FULLY REALIZE ITSELF.

KABBALAH ALSO HAS A WRITTEN TRADITION OF SACRED TEXTS, BEGINNING

WITH THE *TORAH*, THE FIRST FIVE BOOKS OF THE BIBLE.

CHAPTER THREE
UNDERSTANDING SACRED TEXTS

✴ THE MAJORITY OF THE SACRED TEXTS OF KABBALAH ARE 2,000 YEARS OLD, ALTHOUGH THERE IS DISAGREEMENT ABOUT THE DATE OF THE MOST FAMOUS OF THEM, THE *ZOHAR*. IN THE LAST HUNDRED YEARS, AUTHORS HAVE WRITTEN MORE SIMPLE GUIDES TO THE TRADITION THAT CAN BE UNDERSTOOD WITHOUT KNOWLEDGE OF HEBREW, COMPLEX SYMBOLOGY, OR RELIGIOUS TEXTS.

Until the invention of the printing press, the majority of Kabbalists could work only with the original tools of the Tree of Life and Jacob's Ladder. Previously, sacred texts were written by hand and kept secret from the general public. However, once the written word was available to all, the tradition appears to have become much more complex. Numerous non-Jews discovered it and wrote down their own interpretations according to their location and religion. Many Kabbalists were strongly influenced by the works of Aristotle, Plato, and Plotinus. There is a long-standing connection with the ancient Greek system known as Hermeticism, based on the Emerald Tablet and other writings of the legendary Hermes Trismegistus.

Kabbalah is the inner tradition that underlies the Jewish faith and its teachings are laced throughout the Bible, particularly the *Torah*, which is the foundation of Jewish belief.

Left: *Portae Lucis* ("doors of light") by Paolus Ricius Augusta (1516) is the earliest-known representation of the Sefirot in print. The Latin text reads: "doors of light, this is the door of the holy name, the righteous ones will enter it."

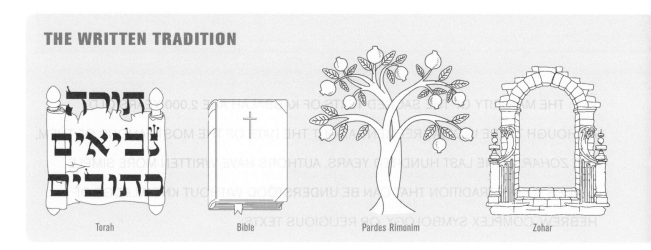

THE WRITTEN TRADITION

Torah   Bible   Pardes Rimonim   Zohar

However, there is strong evidence that the writers of the New Testament also understood Kabbalistic principles, especially the authors of the four Gospels that make up the accepted Canon of the Christian faith. St. Paul also claimed to have been the student of a known Kabbalist, Rabbi Gamaliel.

SIGNIFICANT KABBALISTIC TEXTS

The *Zohar*, or "Book of Splendor," is an incredibly complex book in 23 volumes that currently retails at approximately $400. It is believed to be based on discussions by an esoteric group led by Rabbi Simeon ben Yohai in Palestine during the second century CE. The discussions demonstrate how the Tree of Life is used as a special language between members of the group in order to understand the *Torah*.

The book itself is controversial. No one knows whether it was written in the second century and rediscovered by a 13th-century Spanish Jew, Moses de Léon, or whether de Léon himself wrote it. If the latter is correct, it is still valuable as an insight into a Kabbalistic group at work, and it demonstrates great knowledge on his part. However, most Kabbalists believe that it is a genuine document from the second century CE.

The *Sefer Yezirah*, "Book of Formation," similarly has a disputed authorship. Probably written in the first century CE, it is a textbook on Kabbalistic theory—a metaphysical primer. It is the first text to describe the Lightning Flash: "the appearance of Ten Sefirot out of Nothing as a Lightning Flash, or glittering flame without Beginning or End. The Word of God is with them as they go forth and return."

Another great Kabbalistic text, though one from hundreds of years later, is the 16th-century *Pardes Rimonim*, "The Garden of Pomegranates," by Moses Cordovero, the leader of a Kabbalistic group in Safed, Palestine. The *Pardes Rimonim* synthesizes all Kabbalistic thought up to that time in an orderly, philosophical system, reconciling various different schools of Kabbalah with the conceptual teachings of the *Zohar* in order to demonstrate their essential unity.

Above: All the written Kabbalistic texts are valuable sources of information, but each needs to be read with full understanding of the traditions and social lore of the times in which they were written. It should also be remembered that the oral tradition included teaching by and for women, while the written tradition was a masculine domain.

HOW KABBALAH WAS TAUGHT THROUGH STORIES

✳ IN THE DAYS WHEN KABBALAH WAS FIRST TAUGHT, VERY FEW PEOPLE COULD READ OR WRITE, AND EVEN THE BIBLE HAD NOT YET BEEN COLLATED INTO ONE BOOK. THE KNOWLEDGE WAS PASSED ON IN STORIES TOLD AROUND THE FIRE AT NIGHT.

Right: The stories told in ancient times were structured according to universal principles observed through the movement of the stars. Here, an astrologer casts a chart to answer a particular question according to the placement of the planets at the time of asking.

ALLEGORY

The stories of the great characters of the Bible are also told as allegories of aspects of human development.

Stories based on Kabbalah still exist today—even in fairytales such as Cinderella. This tells the story of a Soul that has lost its Father (the link to the Divine) and is confined by its Ego (the Wicked Stepmother), not allowed to reach its own potential but forced to work at a lower level (the kitchen). The Soul's true Self (Fairy Godmother) thinks of a plan to link the Soul (Cinderella) with the higher world of Spirit (the Prince). The plan is almost spoiled by the Stepmother and the Soul's baser instincts of laziness and willfulness (Ugly Sisters), dressed up in the finery of the Persona (the mask we present to the world).

The Soul's vegetable and animal levels of basic life (see chapter 6) are transformed into a coach and horses to take Cinderella to the ball, where her true beauty is obvious, and Soul and Spirit are united. The Ego and lower personality traits continue to oppose this sacred match but are overcome by Spirit's deeper connection with the Soul, which enables him to find and claim her.

During those times, extended families lived together in one house, and a storyteller in the family was considered a great asset. Even better, a traveling holy man telling new stories was as exciting a prospect as a visit to the theater would be for subsequent generations.

READING THE *TORAH* ON FOUR LEVELS

The *Torah*, along with most of the rest of the Bible, can be divided into four categories of comprehension. These are the literal, the allegorical, the metaphysical, and the mystical. The origins of the first three levels of perception are based on our senses of feeling and thought. In most people, one of these aspects is usually stronger than the others. A mainly instinctive person will see the world through the senses, a feeling type through symbology and moods, and a thinker through ideas. Generally, the fourth mystical view is not perceived by any of the other senses and requires a distinct shift of consciousness.

The Bible can therefore be seen as a literal history, an allegory or series of stories that demonstrate which kinds of behavior are productive in our lives, a system of abstract ideas, or an example of the spiritual development of humanity through multiple lives. It also contains a mystical element that speaks directly to the heart, soul, and spirit of the seeker.

ADAM AND EVE: A STORY ON FOUR LEVELS

✳ ADAM AND EVE, THE FIRST CREATED MAN AND WOMAN IN THE BIBLICAL STORY OF GENESIS, LIVED IN THE GARDEN OF EDEN. KABBALAH TEACHES THAT THIS GARDEN WAS A WORLD OF POTENTIAL NOT A PHYSICAL REALITY. IT EXISTED ONLY IN THE WORLD OF THE PSYCHE—YEZIRAH.

Below: Adam and Eve were not physical beings during the time they spent in the Garden of Eden; it was only after they began to make their own choices that they could incarnate on Earth.

Adam and Eve were not able to rise up to the higher world of Spirit, and nor could they descend to the lower world of matter, because they did not know how to make choices. There was also no death because there was no physical life.

Kabbalah teaches that God had to create a situation in which choice was required in order for the first humans to begin the process of the four journeys and start using their unique facility of free will.

To begin the journey of life, God told the couple that there was one thing they should never do—eat from the Tree of Knowledge of Good and Evil. Eve disobeyed and Adam then followed. The couple then awoke to the possibility of choice, to their own sexual differences and to their nakedness. The Bible says that when God discovered what they had done, He banished them from Eden to a life of toil, pain, and death.

Kabbalah teaches that all this was "set up" so that humanity would begin to make its own choices, and that it was necessary for the divine baby, Adam Kadmon, to begin its growth. Eve, therefore, was the first to demonstrate the willingness to accept consequence as a result of choice.

THE DESCENT TO ASIYYAH

The descent to Asiyyah, the physical world, brought the experience of reproduction, with the associated pain and the hard work of

QUEST FOR THE HOLY GRAIL

In the anonymously written 13th-century "Quest for the Holy Grail," Eve is said to have plucked a twig of the Tree of Knowledge and planted it outside Eden to remind the couple of the journey back to Paradise.

According to legend, wood from the descendants of that tree appear in many mystical stories, including that relating to the staff of Moses, which was known as the "staff of sapphires." The Hebrew root word for sapphire is "SFR," the same as for Sefira.

The fantasy novels of C.S. Lewis, *Chronicles of Narnia,* also tell the story of a magical tree which is a doorway to other worlds. Wood from this tree became the famous wardrobe that enabled the Pevensie children to travel into the land of Narnia.

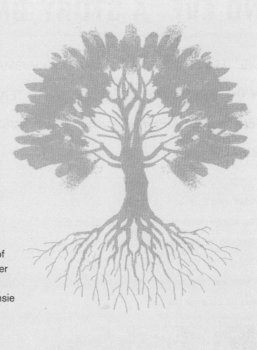

Below: The serpent is not always seen as an evil symbol. Mucalinda, the king of snakes, shielded Buddha from the elements as he sat in meditation. In the Aboriginal myth of the Dreamtime the great serpent played a major part in the process of creation.

living off the land. The literal story tells of disobedience and its result; the allegorical one of the importance of making decisions and learning from the consequences. The metaphysical story describes the beginning of the journey of humanity, and why we have a yearning to return. A mystical interpretation is that this situation was God's own choice, that children are bound to wish to explore, and that blame is inappropriate.

The descent from Yezirah to Asiyyah is the allegorical, metaphysical, and mystical interpretation of the Biblical phrase "Unto Adam also and to his wife did the LORD God make coats of skins" (Gen 3:21). Only in the literal form would it mean that the couple put on animal skins to keep them warm.

Kabbalistic legend says that if Adam and Eve had been allowed to remain in Eden, their new knowledge would have enabled them to realize that the other tree there, the Tree of Life, was the pathway to Divinity itself. The reason why the Kabbalistic diagram is called the Tree of Life is that it has always been associated with the way back to the higher worlds.

Legend also has it that Kabbalah was first given to Adam and Eve, at God's instigation, by the archangel Raziel (whose name means "secrets of God"). Once they were safely on Earth, it was good for them to know the secrets of the Tree of Life so that they would wish to begin the journey home.

CHOICE AND CONSEQUENCE

✳ KABBALAH TEACHES THAT ALL OF LIFE IS ABOUT CHOICE. EVERY DECISION WE MAKE HAS A CONSEQUENCE AND, JUST AS IMPORTANTLY, WE ALSO HAVE A CHOICE AS TO HOW TO VIEW THAT CONSEQUENCE. IF SOMEONE IS ARRESTED FOR BAD DRIVING AND FINED, HE OR SHE CAN SEE THE PENALTY FOR THIS BEHAVIOR EITHER AS BEING UNFAIR, TOTALLY JUST, OR SIMPLY THE PROCESS OF LAW.

Right: Since Eve, woman has been seen as a temptress. It is often easier to blame others for our actions instead of making conscious choices.

Some people would take the situation described here personally, while others would regard it simply as a minor inconvenience. Both of these reactions are choices; they are not imposed upon us.

In the case of the narrative about Adam and Eve, for example, we can make choices about how we view the biblical story. We can consider it as evidence of the way women are constantly and unfairly judged to be inferior to men, or we could use the story as a weapon for blaming women—especially if we acknowledge that the written tradition was rarely presented from the woman's perspective. We may see it as a terrible thing that humanity was forced to leave the Garden of Eden and as evidence that God is cruel and unforgiving. Alternatively, we may perceive Adam and Eve as innocent children who made a choice out of curiosity and a desire to learn, and who meant no harm. Or, we might decide that their being banished from Eden was the best thing that could have happened for the subsequent development of humanity.

CHOICES AND RULES

✡ In ancient times when people lived in tribes, they learned that the choices they made every day could mean the difference between survival or death. Eat this and you will thrive; eat that and you will die. Nowadays, in a world where we purchase food that has been prepared for us under specific rules and regulations, we do not have to make as many vital choices; instead we may find ourselves choosing between 30 different possible lunches in just one shop! Many of us no longer realize how important every single choice might be.

✡ Whether we like it or not, the modern human being is expected to follow certain rules, such as driving a car on the correct side of the road and paying for heating and lighting in the home. Not following the rules leads to unpleasant consequences. It is the same with Cosmic Law, the laws that govern this universe. These include understandable rules, such as gravity and the cycles of day, night, and time. They also include what is nowadays called the Law of Attraction—that like attracts like.

✡ Kabbalah teaches that the Ten Commandments from the Book of Exodus form a God-given system for understanding the Law of Attraction, or Karma. The commandments are the clearest guidance system we have for assessing which choices will help us to live happily and which will not. Importantly, Karma is not always negative. Today we can understand the Law of Attraction through techniques such as "Cosmic Ordering," where we focus on a thought for good and see that manifest in our emotional and physical lives.

Below: This 16th-century woodcut of the Tree of Life demonstrates that every choice we make leads to further choices—but that the farther we go along one path the more difficult it is to turn back and choose again.

HUMAN NATURE

It is obvious to any parent that if he or she left a two-year-old child in a room alone for half an hour after giving permission to do anything except touch the wooden box on the table, the child would head straight for the box as soon as the door was closed. In exactly the same way, rules and regulations that forbid children to smoke cigarettes, see adult-rated movies, or drink under age are flouted worldwide. It is the nature of humanity to choose to seek adventure and push boundaries.

MOSES: THE SPIRITUAL JOURNEY

✳ THE JEWISH NATION CELEBRATES THE BIBLICAL STORY OF THE EXODUS FROM EGYPT AS THE FESTIVAL OF PASSOVER, OR PESACH. THIS WAS THE FESTIVAL JESUS WAS CELEBRATING AT THE LAST SUPPER BEFORE HIS CRUCIFIXION. THE STORY OF THE EXODUS IS FILLED WITH KABBALISTIC SYMBOLISM, BUT THE CRUX OF IT IS THE ESCAPE FROM SLAVERY.

This is an allegory of the soul's escape from the slavery of social and economic rules to a higher level of living. The Israelites had moved to Egypt during the time of Joseph, when there was a famine in their homeland. At first they were content, but after Joseph died, they became enslaved by the Egyptians. This is symbolic of the human Ego ruling the Self in everyday life. (It is worth mentioning that according to mystical traditions, the word Israelite means "one who struggles with God" and is not necessarily associated with the Jewish nation.)

Moses was born at a time when the Egyptian Pharaoh had ruled that all Hebrew boy babies were to be killed at birth. In order to save Moses, his mother and sister hid him in a basket of rushes and floated him down the river Nile, where he was rescued by a princess of Egypt. This represents the need for the Soul to be sent out from its natural home in the

Right: This depiction of the Tabernacle in the desert shows a huge and complicated structure. But the secret of Kabbalah is that once you understand the workings of Jacob's Ladder, all that you need can be carried within your mind and heart.

higher worlds in order to be raised in an appropriate environment to fulfill its destiny.

As a man, Moses killed an Egyptian who was beating a Hebrew slave. The Egyptian represents an aspect of Moses' psyche that he realized was evil and had to be overcome. A similar "wake-up call" is experienced by many people who face a serious physical or psychological challenge or the death of a loved one. Once Moses had committed this act he ran away from Egypt and from all he had known. This is the journey of the Self to the Soul level, seeking a new life that will have meaning. After a series of challenges, Moses found a teacher, Jethro, and married his daughter Zipporah. Once he was trained in the discipline of serving Jethro and had learned the trade of a shepherd, he was called by God to return to Egypt to set the Israelites free.

ESCAPE FROM EGYPT

Moses' battle with the Pharaoh is legendary for the ten plagues that beset Egypt. Each one represents a negative aspect of one of the ten Sefirot of the Tree of Life. After the killing of the firstborn sons of Egypt, the Pharaoh allowed the Hebrews to leave and they entered the wilderness, where they lived for 40 years. Forty is an important Biblical number, representing four tens—the four worlds, which each contain ten Sefirot. It represents a total cleansing of the whole human being, from the Divine to the physical.

At the beginning of the Exodus, the Israelites had to cross the Red Sea. The Self had to commit itself to the new life and spiritual journey by placing its trust in Providence and drowning out the call of the Ego for it to return. The Israelites then received the Ten Commandments—again representing the ten Sefirot of the Tree of Life.

At the end of the journey to the Promised Land, all the original Israelites, including Moses, had died. It was up to one of the new generation—Joshua—to lead his people to the "Land of Milk and Honey." This represents the need for every old habit to be overcome in order to reach enlightenment and it is an allegory that is repeated in different ways throughout the Old Testament.

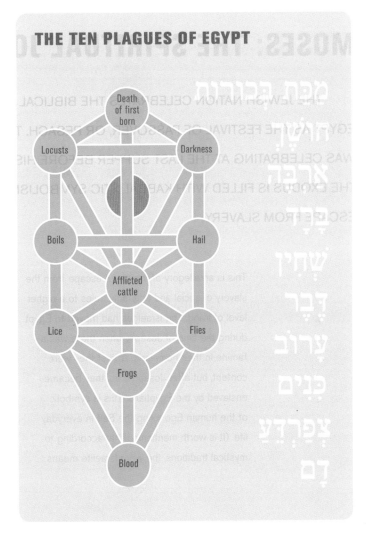

THE TEN PLAGUES OF EGYPT

Death of first born

Locusts

Darkness

Boils

Hail

Afflicted cattle

Lice

Flies

Frogs

Blood

Above: The ten plagues (also in Hebrew script) that Moses brought upon Egypt each represent a negative aspect of the ten Sefirot.

THE BURNING BUSH AND THE CHAKRA SYSTEM

✳ MOSES' DESTINY WAS REVEALED TO HIM IN THE STORY OF THE BURNING BUSH IN CHAPTER THREE OF EXODUS. THIS IS AN ALLEGORY FOR HOW EACH OF US CAN EXPERIENCE THE DIVINE THROUGH OUR DIFFERENT SENSES, AND THE STORY CAN BE INTERPRETED THROUGH MORE THAN ONE MYSTICAL TRADITION.

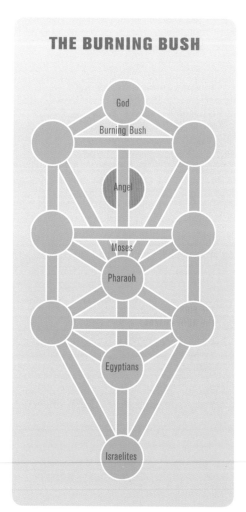

THE BURNING BUSH

- God
- Burning Bush
- Angel
- Moses
- Pharaoh
- Egyptians
- Israelites

Moses saw and heard an angel in the middle of a flaming bush that was not being consumed by the fire. He turned aside to look at this wonder, and the Lord God spoke to him from the bush, calling his name. Moses answered, and God told him that his task was to return to Egypt to rescue his people from the Pharaoh and slavery.

This story fits onto the Tree of Life. The burning bush is Azilut, the divine world from which the Holy One himself emanates at the place of Keter, the crown of the Tree of Life. The presence of the angel represents the non-Sefira of Da'at, the doorway between worlds and the place of the Archangel Gabriel, the messenger of God. Moses is positioned in what is known as the soul triad between Gevurah, Hesed, and Tiferet, where he acknowledges his true Self to God. The Pharaoh represents the false pride of Tiferet, the Self, while his people, the Egyptians, represent Yesod, the Ego-mind that is enslaving the Israelite people who are placed at Malkhut.

A more mystical interpretation would expand the story as a psychological journey for us. We are Moses receiving a "wake-up" call from Spirit to realize that we have a false view of

Above: A "burning bush experience" is one where we have a sudden realization that we are being called to perform some kind of service in life. Usually it is impossible to explain such a revelation to others, as it appears so unlikely, but it makes a mark on our soul that cannot be eradicated.

ourselves, and that we are enslaved by our inner personalities and old habits and routines. We are being called to stand up for what we truly believe in, and live an authentic life instead of one ruled by social convention.

The fact that Kabbalah equates so easily with the chakra system—modern interpretations of the Tree of Life color it with the colors associated with the chakras—demonstrates that Kabbalah is a universal system that can be used by people of different faiths without requiring them to change their belief system.

THE SEVEN CHAKRAS

Another method of interpreting the story is through the Hindu system of chakras, or energy wheels. These are energetic interpretations of the seven major nerve ganglia in the body. The angel (throat chakra) spoke to Moses, who perceived the angel and the divine fire through his insight (third eye chakra). God (crown chakra) asked Moses to identify his real Self and have compassion on his people (heart chakra). The Pharaoh represents the solar plexus chakra, the misguided, prideful Self, and the Egyptians are the sacral chakra, ruled by habit and control. The Israelites fighting for survival in Egypt form the base chakra.

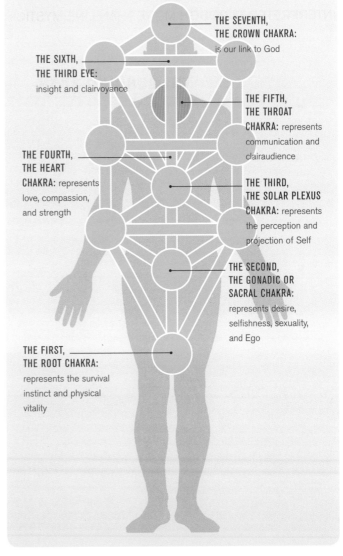

THE SEVENTH, THE CROWN CHAKRA: is our link to God

THE SIXTH, THE THIRD EYE: insight and clairvoyance

THE FIFTH, THE THROAT CHAKRA: represents communication and clairaudience

THE FOURTH, THE HEART CHAKRA: represents love, compassion, and strength

THE THIRD, THE SOLAR PLEXUS CHAKRA: represents the perception and projection of Self

THE SECOND, THE GONADIC OR SACRAL CHAKRA: represents desire, selfishness, sexuality, and Ego

THE FIRST, THE ROOT CHAKRA: represents the survival instinct and physical vitality

MERKABAH—CHARIOT RIDERS

✳ THE FIRST WRITTEN EVIDENCE OF KABBALISTIC RITUAL DATES BACK TO THE SECOND CENTURY CE WHEN WE HEAR OF SAGES AND MYSTICS "RIDING THE CHARIOT." THIS IS A MEDITATIVE PRACTICE BASED ON A VISION DESCRIBED IN THE BIBLICAL BOOK OF EZEKIEL, AND IT GAVE RISE TO THE FIRST "OFFICIAL" NAME GIVEN TO KABBALAH.

Until that time, people who studied the oral tradition had been known as "the people who know" or "the teachers of the line," and it was not until the Middle Ages that the word Kabbalah became widely known.

Merkabah, or "chariot riding," is a way of making an internal journey of meditation and visualization through the four worlds to gain direct experience of the Divine Presence. It was named for the Hebrew word for chariot, because it was based on the prophet Ezekiel's vision of "the appearance of the likeness of the glory of Yahweh" (Eze 1:28). In this image, the Lord appeared on a throne carried by four part-human creatures. God spoke directly to Ezekiel, who had experienced great tragedy in his life, referring to him as "son of man." In this way, God acknowledged the perfection within his creation—regardless of how imperfect Ezekiel might have thought himself to be. Chariot riding lifts our souls to the level where we can experience God's love for our perfect selves, and each journey, taken with guidance from others, can reveal and confirm our destiny, as well as being an experience of joy and great bliss.

The description from the Book of Ezekiel is used to create meditations for ascending through the worlds, although the practice has always been shrouded in secrecy because it can be dangerous if undertaken by anyone who is not solidly grounded in reality.

Modern Kabbalists have developed simple, introductory meditation techniques that can offer a glimpse of the work of the Chariot and which are safe to use. These involve awareness of the four worlds in the physical body to balance it and draw divine energy down to Asiyyah before attempting the ascent through Yezirah and Beriah to the base of Azilut.

A CAUTIONARY LEGEND

Four rabbis attempted the ascent. One experienced the Divine Presence and died. The second saw the Divine and went mad. The third saw but did not believe, lost his faith, and became a heretic. The fourth, Rabbi Akiva, experienced the vision in peace and lived ever after in peace. The tale is a warning for those who are not mentally and emotionally balanced or who use mind-altering drugs to experience higher levels. Drugs can and do take the user to other worlds but without the protection of a guided, disciplined ascent. Some energies in the higher worlds can damage the human psyche if approached in ignorance.

The undisciplined seeker can easily have an unpleasant, frightening experience and be put off spiritual work if attempting to attain too much knowledge too soon.

SIMPLE MERKABAH MEDITATION

The best way to experience a guided meditation is through hearing it. If you can, record these words and play them back to yourself as you sit in a quiet room. Ensure that you have no interruptions and, if it helps you focus, it is a good idea to add some soft, soothing music in the background.

1 Sit comfortably and consciously relax your body, from the skin at the back of your head and on your face, to your shoulders. Spend a few minutes doing this until you feel heavy.

2 Experience, consciously, the weight of your physical body and how it is being pulled down by gravity. Focus on the word Asiyyah, focus on the physical world: the solidity of your bones, your muscles, your organs, your skin.

3 Widen your experience to feel the steady beat of your heart, pumping the life-giving blood around your body. Sense the flow of Yezirah, the watery world of the psyche around your body. Feel the liquid that makes up more than 90 percent of you, the saliva, the lymph, the intestinal fluids. Feel the liquid in your eyes, your ears, your mouth, and the flow of life throughout your body.

4 Concentrate on your breath, drawing in the oxygen with deep, slow breaths. This is carried in your bloodstream to every cell of your body. Sense the lightening effect of the spiritual world of Beriah as it infuses every molecule within you.

5 Feel the heat within your body and the radiance around you—the electro-magnetic life force that is the heart of your being. You are a living being, a physical

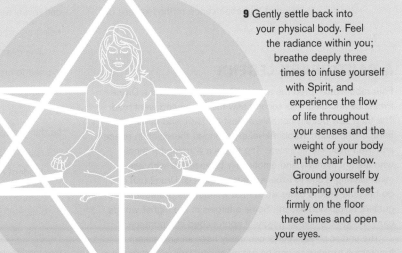

creature, a person with emotions and thoughts, a soul with a lightness of heart, and a child of the Divine.

6 Imagine the light around you expanding up above you and being met by a greater light from another reality. Feel yourself being drawn up through space into a huge void where you can hear the beating of great wings and the celestial music of the spheres. All that you are is expanding in joy and awareness.

7 Time has stopped; space is no more; you are in the midst of a great light; in the presence of holiness. Your name is called, and you are immersed in radiance. If you have a question, ask it now and listen for the reply.

8 Now feel yourself peacefully withdrawing from the light. Celestial beings guide you lovingly back down through the worlds, their wings brushing against you and drawing your awareness back to the worlds of space, time, and reality.

9 Gently settle back into your physical body. Feel the radiance within you; breathe deeply three times to infuse yourself with Spirit, and experience the flow of life throughout your senses and the weight of your body in the chair below. Ground yourself by stamping your feet firmly on the floor three times and open your eyes.

THE NEW TESTAMENT: FOUR GOSPELS, FOUR WORLDS

✳ CHRISTIANITY WEAVES ALL FOUR GOSPELS OF THE NEW TESTAMENT INTO ONE NARRATIVE, AS IN A NATIVITY PLAY WITH THE SHEPHERDS AND THE MAGI IN THE SAME STORY. YET TO A KABBALIST, THE FOUR GOSPELS TELL JESUS' STORY AT THE FOUR DIFFERENT LEVELS OF THE FOUR WORLDS. JESUS' OWN TEACHINGS SHOW STRONG SIGNS OF KABBALISTIC KNOWLEDGE.

MATTHEW AND ASIYYAH

Matthew writes of the Asiyyatic world: earthly power, tribe, leadership, and the importance of the bloodline. He highlights the physical challenges of life on earth and Jesus' physical kingship as Messiah. Jesus' birth is told with the emphasis on Joseph, on the visit of the Magi with their gifts, and King Herod's fears over the birth of a physical King of the Jews. The temptations before Jesus in the desert are all physical: to turn stones into food, to prove that God would save him if he jumped, and the offer of the kingship of the world.

MARK AND YEZIRAH

Mark represents the Yeziratic world. At this soul level humanity can choose to be separate from animals (the "wild beasts" in Mark's temptation story) and become aware of free will. It is through the soul that we decide to act for good or for evil. Jesus' temptation in Mark is a choice between his baser self and a higher level of consciousness where he may be in touch with angels.

LUKE AND BERIAH

Luke writes of the Beriatic, spiritual world. His Gospel features Jesus' mother and his female friends. This is the spiritual perception of life: women's place was deemed unimportant in the physical view of the Jewish, Roman, and Greek

Right: The four Gospels are also represented by the four creatures that are mentioned in Ezekiel's vision. The bull represents Matthew, the physical world; the lion, Mark, the psychological world; the eagle, Luke, the spiritual world of air; and the human, John, the divine world of Azilut.

THE PASSION

✡ **For Matthew and Mark** the crucifixion is full of anguish. Luke and John focus on the mystery of a divinely inspired right of passage. In the lower worlds of Matthew and Mark (body and psyche), Jesus cries out at his pain:
"My God, my God, why hast thou forsaken me?" (MATT 27:46, MARK 15:34).

✡ **In Luke,** Jesus is able to see his crucifixion as impersonal. There is no judgment of it or of people's behavior:
"Father, forgive them; for they know not what they do ... into thy hands I commend my spirit" (LUKE 23:34, 23:46).

✡ **In John,** the crucifixion is shown simply as a necessary evil on the way to new life. Without Jesus' acceptance and acknowledgment of death, resurrection cannot occur. Jesus gives completion to his mother by giving her into John's care and gives himself willingly to death purely as the next stage of his development as a divine being:
"It is finished" (JOHN 19:30).

worlds of Jesus' time, but at the spiritual level, the feminine in Judaism was deeply respected. The Gospel's emphasis is on family, companionship, and communication, and it works in tandem with Matthew, balancing masculine with feminine. In Matthew, Jesus replies to Satan's temptations with answers from the written (physical) law but in Luke he replies with God's own authority at the spiritual level.

JOHN AND AZILUT

John's Gospel is the divine world of Azilut. It tells of direct experience of God. There are no parables, similes, or allegories: it is Jesus telling us straight.

THE GOSPELS ON JACOB'S LADDER

In Kabbalah, the Gospels tell Jesus' story on the four levels of the four worlds.

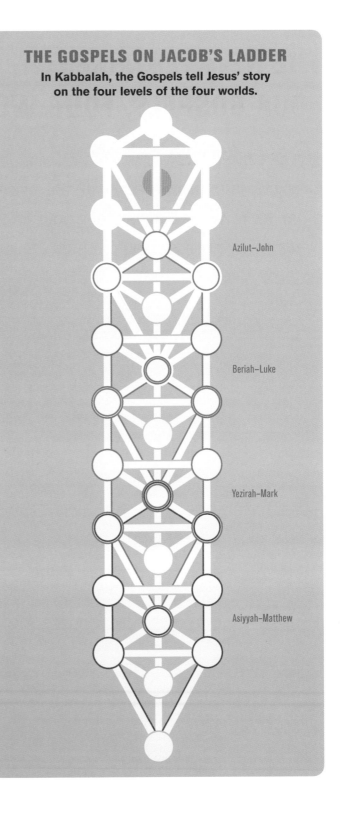

Azilut–John

Beriah–Luke

Yezirah–Mark

Asiyyah–Matthew

CHAPTER FOUR
SACRED DESIGNS

✳ THE TREE OF LIFE DIAGRAM IS BASED ON THE SEVEN-BRANCHED CANDLESTICK CALLED THE MENORAH. WE FIRST HEAR OF THIS SYMBOL IN THE BIBLICAL BOOK OF EXODUS, WHEN GOD TELLS MOSES TO MAKE A TABERNACLE. THIS WAS A TEMPLE FOR WORSHIP THAT COULD BE TRANSPORTED BY THE ISRAELITES AFTER THEY LEFT EGYPT AND TRAVELED THROUGH THE WILDERNESS TOWARD THE PROMISED LAND.

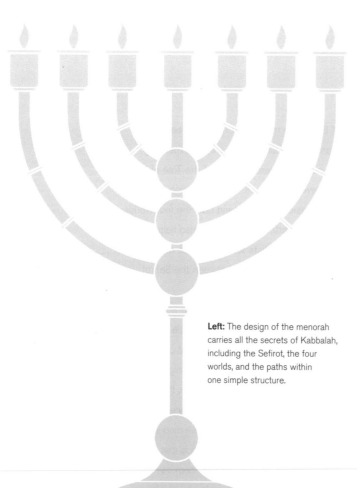

Left: The design of the menorah carries all the secrets of Kabbalah, including the Sefirot, the four worlds, and the paths within one simple structure.

The instructions for both the menorah and the Tabernacle are detailed very precisely in Exodus, Chapters 25–27. The menorah was to be made out of one piece of gold with ten specific buds, knops (ornamental knobs), or bulbs (as they are variously known in different translations of the Hebrew). These express the ten Sefirot, or principles, by which the world came into existence. The three buds on the right are the active Sefirot and the three on the left the passive. Where their branches join on the central stem and foot of the menorah are the Sefirot of the middle pillar of equilibrium.

In all, ten menorot were made and placed in the sanctuary of the Tabernacle, each one representing one Sefira of the divine world of Azilut. The reason for ten menorot to represent one world came from the belief that each single Sefira contained its own Tree of Life. This was an indication of the eternity of life and the repetition of sacred patterns from the design of the universe to molecular structure.

The idea behind a specific design that demonstrated the "matrix" of all life was to give the Israelites a structure on which to base their

THE STAR OF DAVID

Also known as "Magen David" (shield of David), this six-pointed star is deeply associated with Judaism, although it is known to have been used back to the Bronze Age as a universal mystical symbol. Jews in Nazi Germany were made to wear a yellow Star of David on their clothes to show their Jewish faith.

It is believed that its six points represent the six days of creation, and the inner space represents the Sabbath or seventh day. These in turn correspond to the seven lower Sefirot of the Tree of Life and seven "righteous men" of the *Torah*: Abraham, Isaac, Jacob, Moses, Aaron, Joseph, and David. As King David is the seventh soul that completes the image it is known as his Star.

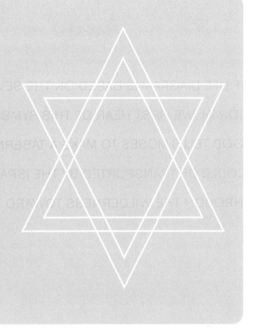

belief, so that they could be confident of keeping focused in an unfamiliar world. Similar to the way that Catholics use the rosary to pray, Kabbalists can try to ensure that every action they undertake is perfectly balanced by taking the aspects of all the Sefirot into consideration. To do so is a great challenge but, if achieved, it leads to a life of spiritual awareness and abundance.

ISAAC THE BLIND

The design of the menorah was updated in the early 13th century by a rabbi called Isaac the Blind, who lived in the French/Spanish border town of Posquières. It is not known whether Isaac truly was blind since he also had the Aramaic nickname "Saggi Nehor," meaning "of much light"—in the sense of having extremely good eyesight. It could be that he was physically blind but had vision through his intuition. He may have created the new design as a kind

of Braille—a model that he could feel rather than see—or simply as a way of expanding the possible interpretations of the Tree of Life. Whatever the reason, the new design made it much easier to understand how the four worlds of creation fitted together and also helped medieval Kabbalists to examine the meaning of the triads (triangles) between the Sefirot and the paths that linked them.

The beauty of the "new" design was that while it appeared complex, just a little study would reveal repeating patterns that could be equated with the movement of the night skies, the process of conception and birth, the turning of the seasons, and many other processes of which we are far less aware in the modern world. However, the beauty of Kabbalah is that the Sefirot and the designs around them can also be used to develop a business plan, build a house, write a book, or construct a spiritual service.

THE TEN SEFIROT AND THE TEN COMMANDMENTS

✳ EACH ONE OF THE TEN SEFIROT REPRESENTS ONE OF THE TEN COMMANDMENTS AS GIVEN TO MOSES AT MOUNT SINAI. IN THE BIBLE, WE ARE TOLD THAT THE COMMANDMENTS WERE GIVEN TWICE: THE FIRST TIME ORALLY, IN EXODUS 20, AND THE SECOND, WRITTEN IN STONE, IN EXODUS 34. THIS WAS TO DEMONSTRATE THAT THE COMMANDMENTS HAVE INNER (ESOTERIC) AND OUTER (EXOTERIC) MEANINGS.

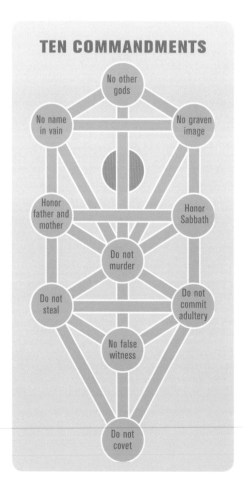

TEN COMMANDMENTS

- No other gods
- No name in vain
- No graven image
- Honor father and mother
- Honor Sabbath
- Do not murder
- Do not steal
- Do not commit adultery
- No false witness
- Do not covet

TEN COMMANDMENTS: ESOTERIC MEANING

No other gods This does not mean that there are no other gods but that putting lesser gods such as fame, money, sex, or power before the Holy One means that Grace cannot be received.

No graven image This is not that we may not make images or paintings but that they should not be "set in stone" as the only correct image. The image of God as an old man in the sky is a graven image because it excludes other interpretations. A ruling that a human "should" look a certain way or be a certain color—or otherwise be judged as inhuman—is also a graven image.

Do not take the name in vain This is a warning that using one divine name, calling on only one aspect of God—God's judgment or mercy but not both—is dangerous. The ultimate name of God is "I am," so to take His name in vain is to say "I am stupid," or "I am ugly." We are a part of the Holy One and denial of our Divinity is the worst kind of self-harm.

Remember the Sabbath and keep it holy
This is an injunction to rest, relax, and remember who we are. Constant influxes of stressful energy not only harm us but the environments we work and live in. Buildings need rest as well as living organisms.

Honor thy father and mother This is an injunction to remember both the sacred masculine and feminine and also to honor the tradition of your birth. We were all born into a specific time and belief system and our task is to make peace with that system even if we do not wish to embrace it.

Do not murder "Do not kill" is a mistranslation dating back to St. Jerome's Bible translation in the fourth century CE. "Murder" includes destroying your own emotional or spiritual life as well as that of other people.

Do not commit adultery This means not mixing two things that harm each other. Marital infidelity is included, but it applies also to two people who damage each other mentally and spiritually and yet remain in this relationship.

Do not steal This includes theft of ideas, reputation, or taking up so much of someone's life that nothing remains.

No false witness This is broadcasting information that destroys good opinion or inaccurately creates a high opinion of someone or something.

THE TEN COMMANDMENTS (EXOTERIC MEANING):

✡ Thou shalt have no other gods before me.
✡ Thou shalt not make unto thee any graven image.
✡ Thou shalt not take the name of the Lord thy God in vain.
✡ Remember the Sabbath day, to keep it holy.
✡ Honor thy father and thy mother.
✡ Thou shalt not commit murder.
✡ Thou shalt not commit adultery.
✡ Thou shalt not steal.
✡ Thou shalt not bear false witness.
✡ Thou shalt not covet.

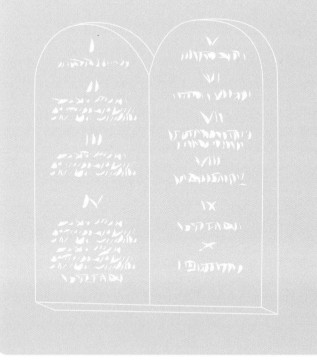

Do not covet This is advice to be grateful for what you have so that it can increase. To focus on someone else's good luck creates resentment that brings increasing feelings of lack and unhappiness.

JACOB'S LADDER

✳ JACOB'S LADDER IS A DESIGN OF HOW THE UNIVERSE WORKS, WITH ONE LEVEL BLENDING SEAMLESSLY THROUGH TO ANOTHER. THE DESIGN FOR THE LADDER IS GIVEN IN THE INSTRUCTIONS FOR THE TABERNACLE IN THE BOOK OF EXODUS. EVEN THE COLORS ARE SPECIFIED: WHITE OR GOLD FOR AZILUT, BLUE FOR BERIAH, PURPLE FOR YEZIRAH, AND RED FOR ASIYYAH.

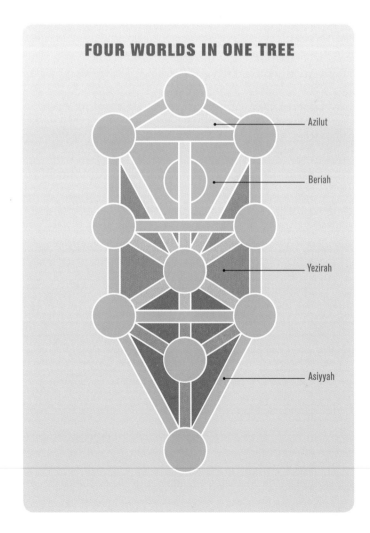

FOUR WORLDS IN ONE TREE

Azilut

Beriah

Yezirah

Asiyyah

At the top of the ladder is Azilut, the world that was called forth out of "no-thingness" by the Ten Utterances of God. As this world emerged from Ayn Sof Aur, so the lower worlds emanated from Azilut.

Directly from the divine level comes the world of Beriah, which manifests diagrammatically as a sub-tree emerging from the midst of the Azilutic tree. The impulse then continues: from the center of Beriah emerges the Tree of Yezirah, the World of Formation.

All three of these worlds are directly connected to Azilut. The final world, however, the physical world of Asiyyah, is connected only to Yezirah and Beriah. This makes it much coarser and more easily broken or damaged.

Because Kabbalah works on a system of "wheels within wheels," there are also said to be four worlds contained within the one world of Azilut.

Throughout Kabbalistic literature there are various differing models of the four worlds and their relationships to one another. These are all both correct and incorrect because they are all subjective views of an objective world.

Each level has quite a different outlook. For the purposes of this book, the simplest and most practical system has been adopted.

Every human being embraces the entire ladder from crown to base; at some point on our journey we will have access to each point. Our role is to begin our own existence in Azilut, descend to Asiyyah, and find our way home over a series of lifetimes. While the design as laid out here is geometrical and perfect, the ladder of an average human is much more fluid. Over centuries we may strengthen the right-hand pillar of the ladder through many lives filled with action but may neglect the left-hand column of study, receptiveness, and discernment. Our own "personal" ladder would then appear bent or misshapen. Drawing or painting a Tree of Life or Jacob's Ladder (instructions are given on page 120) can often demonstrate how we have slipped out of balance both in this life and numerous others. The magic of the designs lies in the way that they enable our subconscious to speak to us about what is going on inside our spiritual, psychological, and physical bodies.

A strongly intellectual human might be able to draw the upper worlds clearly but make errors in Yezirah and Asiyyah and miss a vital pathway from the right-hand side of the ladder. Someone focused on physical, social, and political life might paint over the triad relating to soul development, and someone who is physically disabled might smudge the aspect of Asiyyah where the physical problem lies—or not fill in a part of Yezirah that might demonstrate a psychological reason for the physical issue. By amending errors on the ladder and making it perfect, we make a divinely understood commitment towards healing those imbalances within ourselves.

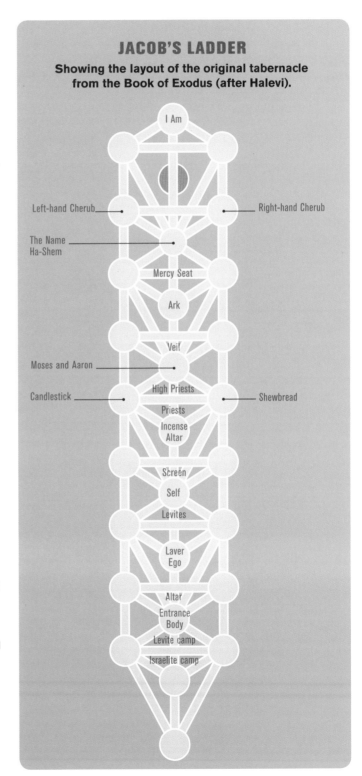

JACOB'S LADDER
Showing the layout of the original tabernacle from the Book of Exodus (after Halevi).

I Am

Left-hand Cherub

Right-hand Cherub

The Name Ha-Shem

Mercy Seat

Ark

Veil

Moses and Aaron

Candlestick

High Priests

Shewbread

Priests

Incense Altar

Screen

Self

Levites

Laver Ego

Altar

Entrance Body

Levite camp

Israelite camp

KETER, THE CROWN OF THE TREE OF LIFE

✳ KETER IS THE CROWN OF EXISTENCE, THE SOURCE OF BLISS, AND THE PLACE WHERE OUR PSYCHE EXPERIENCES DIRECT CONTACT WITH GOD. THERE ARE FOUR KETERS ON JACOB'S LADDER, JUST AS THERE ARE FOUR OF ALL THE SEFIROT, ONE IN EACH WORLD. PERHAPS THE MOST USEFUL FOR THE STUDENT OF KABBALAH TO OBSERVE INITIALLY ARE THE TWO LOWER KETERS, BEGINNING WITH THE KETER OF YEZIRAH, OUR HUMAN HIGHER SELF.

Above: Neptune rules visionaries, and those who are glamorous and charismatic. It represents spirituality, mysticism, and ideals. Neptune's trident is a cross piercing a crescent, the cross representing matter, the crescent representing personality which is released to a higher level than personal Ego.

THE KETER OF YEZIRAH

The Keter of Yezirah is the crown of the psyche, also the Malkhut (base/kingdom) of the divine world, and the Tiferet (center/Self) of the spiritual world. This is our psyche's place of contact with Divinity, variously known as Shekhinah ("the presence of God" or "the feminine aspect of God"), Adonai ("the Lord"), and as the place of the Messiah. This is the level of consciousness reached by someone of the high order of Jesus of Nazareth, Buddha, and other enlightened beings.

For most of us, the experience of Keter is fleeting and hard to define. We can all touch this aspect of ourselves, but normally we experience it via being centered in the lower Sefira of Tiferet. When we are balanced at Tiferet, we can receive impulses and experiences from Keter.

All the Sefirot on the Yeziratic Tree of Life are linked to one of the planets of the solar system. Keter represents Neptune. Before this outer planet was discovered, Kabbalists referred to Keter as "the first swirlings"—meaning the creative force that formed the known solar system.

THE KETER OF ASIYYAH

The Keter of Asiyyah, the physical world, is the place of physical perfection. An animal or human being that is superbly fit and head of its pack, or winner of a particular race, is operating from this point. It is linked with the Tiferet of Yezirah, the place of awakening consciousness, and with the Malkhut of Beriah, the place of awareness of a higher world. Therefore, it often follows that a strong and powerful human, having reached his or her physical goal, finds that he or she changes levels, and wishes to help others through teaching or example. However, this aspect of power can become a negative wish to control or hurt others physically. Without the important balance between the three worlds, the physical superiority in an individual is ultimately an empty experience. This can be seen in those who become famous through their physical beauty or their ability to perform but who have no altruistic aspects. They often seek a kind of parallel higher world through alcohol or drugs but this is destructive to both the psyche and the spirit.

KETER

Keter represents omnipotence, omnipresence, and omniscience.

Keter of Azilut

Keter of Beriah

Keter of Yezirah

Keter of Asiyyah

TOUCHING KETER: POSITIVE

This is the place reached in deep meditation. You are still aware of your body but all is still, silent, and clear; time appears to have stopped. There is deep contentment, love, and communion. While the feeling is peaceful, it is also fiercely joyful. There is often a sensation of very bright light.

TOUCHING KETER: NEGATIVE

A strong sense of self-satisfaction, and the wish to teach others so that they may look up to you and see your inherent wisdom and holiness.

NEPTUNE

Neptune is the outermost planet of our solar system. It is named for the Greek god of the sea, and Neptune is the ruler of the watery world of Yezirah. Astrologically, Neptune represents all things mysterious, undefined, and non-material as well as sensitivity, suffering, and illusion. Neptune rules Pisces, the sign of compassion. It is also a force of delusion; many seekers think they have reached enlightenment but are only fooling themselves. Because Neptune takes 165 years to circle the Sun and approximately thirteen and a half years to change zodiac signs, its influence affects whole generations.

HOKHMAH

✳ HOKHMAH IS THE PLACE OF INSPIRATION. IT IS TRADITIONALLY CALLED "WISDOM" BUT IT COULD JUST AS ACCURATELY BE CALLED "THE PLACE OF LATERAL THINKING." HOKHMAH ON THE YEZIRATIC TREE IS ALSO THE NEZACH OF THE SPIRITUAL TREE OF BINAH, SO IT IS INFLUENCED BY THE ATTRIBUTES OF THAT HIGHER WORLD THROUGH VIVID IMAGES AND COLORS.

Right: In Kabbalah, Hokhmah is linked with the astrological sign of Aquarius and the planet Uranus. Influenced by Aquarius, Uranian energy is inspirational and associated with unexpected events.

Hokhmah is also the place of the "third eye" of the human energy field and of clairvoyance—the ability to see non-physical reality. Hokhmah is the first impulse to create, both for God and for humanity. It is the flash of inspiration or intuition that comes before any conscious thought. As it is the first Sefira on one of the side pillars of the Tree of Life, it is associated with duality, whereas Keter, on the central column, represents unity. Hokhmah is like the sperm that will impregnate the egg of Binah on the opposing column. Together, they form the first step in the creative process. Without the balance of Binah, Hokhmah would be as destructive as a lightning bolt.

This Sefira is associated with the planet Uranus, but before Uranus was discovered, Hokhmah represented the whole of the zodiac, that is the 12 astrological signs of Aries, Taurus, Gemini, Cancer, Leo, Virgo, Libra, Scorpio, Sagittarius, Capricorn, Aquarius, and Pisces. Uranus is linked with Aquarius, a sign that is both revolutionary and fixed. So Uranian energy is unexpected and stubborn, and can be dangerous. Uranus is the inspired thought or action that can overturn a government, reveal a new impulse for religion, or invent a new kind of transport. Equally, Uranus can provoke someone to change career, redesign a house, or paint a picture. It is an energy that cannot be anticipated and is difficult to control.

TOUCHING HOKHMAH: POSITIVE

This is the flash of inspiration that you receive when trying to sort out a thorny problem; it's clear, it's brilliant, it's unexpected—and it's probably outrageous. It is also the sudden knowledge that something is either right or wrong. That something is simply "known" with surprising authority.

HOKHMAH

Hokhmah is the first masculine principle.

- Hokhmah of Azilut
- Hokhmah of Beriah
- Hokhmah of Yezirah
- Hokhmah of Asiyyah

TOUCHING HOKHMAH: NEGATIVE

This inspiration is impossible or just out of reach so that you spend so long trying to catch it and identify it that you lose touch with reality. Many people seek inspiration and the excitement it offers without grounding the energy. This can lead to feeling very spaced out. It can also be dark—an impulse to hurt or destroy either yourself or someone else and be contradictory just for the sake of it.

BIBLE CHARACTER

Adam, the first man who experienced all of life as revelation.

URANUS

Uranus is blue-green, mostly hydrogen, and swathed in fierce winds that go in opposing directions according to their location on the planet. The series of rings around it are composed mostly of ice boulders. Uranus was discovered in 1781, at the time of the French and American revolutions, and the Industrial Revolution in England. It is named for the Greek word for sky, Ouranos, a god who was husband to Gaia, the Earth. Uranus takes 84 years to circle the sun and seven years to change zodiac signs.

BINAH

✳ IF HOKHMAH IS THE FIRST ACTIVE OR MASCULINE IMPULSE ON THE TREE OF LIFE, THEN BINAH IS THE FIRST RECEPTIVE OR FEMININE IMPULSE. EACH IS WORTHLESS WITHOUT THE OTHER. BINAH IS THE SEFIRA OF UNDERSTANDING; THE VOICE OF GOOD SENSE TO HOKHMAH'S CRAZY VISION. TOGETHER THEY CAN MAKE A WORKABLE PLAN.

Right: Saturn is often seen as being a malefic or negative planet because it is the agent of Karma, bringing loss and sorrow. It is also the great teacher—and it repays with interest whatever it has taken once we have learned its lessons.

Binah is all about boundaries, limits, and structure. It is associated with the planet Saturn (the farthest of the planets visible with the naked eye from Earth). Together they focus on rules and regulations: the responsibilities, restrictions, and limitations we encounter throughout life. Binah tempers imagination, inspiration, and spirituality, and it ensures that any good fortune is lasting rather than a "flash-in-the pan."

But its Saturnine influence also hands out Karmic lessons, such as prosperity and relationship issues that have to be addressed.

The Binah of Yezirah is also the Hod of Beriah, the spiritual world. Hod is the Sefira of intellect or information. Binah draws on the world of Spirit to give us a level of true understanding rather than just psychological intellect or judgment. It draws together all the information available, blends it with experience, and makes considered decisions.

Keter, Hokhmah, and Binah together make up what is called the "supernal triad"—the level of human spiritual awareness. The seven Sefirot below them are more concerned with physical and psychological life. In ancient days, human beings were only expected to work with the supernal triad when reaching old age, after they had raised their children and made a secure home. In modern civilization, however, we have the advantages of leisure time, heat, light during the hours of darkness, and access to teachings through books, television, theater, movies, and the Internet. So it is easier to work with these levels at a young age.

BINAH

Binah represents the mother of the seven lower Sefirot.

Binah of Azilut

Binah of Beriah

Binah of Yezirah

Binah of Asiyyah

TOUCHING BINAH: POSITIVE

To be in Binah is like being the wise grandparent who knows what will work and what will not and has both the kindness and the discipline to sit down with a child to help him or her build a perfect model. Binah is about perseverance and strength.

TOUCHING BINAH: NEGATIVE

Negative is just the word: Binah can say "no" to absolutely anything, implying it is too difficult, complicated, or just newfangled. Being in negative Binah is to refuse to address anything new, not to be interested in anything outside of one's own experience, and to complain about how the world has gone to pieces "since my day."

BIBLE CHARACTER

Eve, the first to embrace knowledge, with the joy and pain that that brings.

SATURN

Named for the eponymous Roman god, Saturn's Greek counterpart is Chronos, god of time. Saturn is a gas giant with colored rings, formed mostly of ice. It spends around two and a half years in each astrological sign, taking about 29 years on its journey around the Sun. Each "Saturn Return" is astrologically a significant time of transition. At the age of 29 we move from youth to maturity, at 58 from maturity to wisdom and, at 86, with the third Saturn return, a spiritual or earthly transformation—or a return to childhood mentality.

DA'AT

✳ BETWEEN BINAH AND THE NEXT SEFIRA OF HESED IS THE MYSTERIOUS NON-SEFIRA OF DA'AT. IT IS CALLED A NON-SEFIRA BECAUSE IT HAS NO ATTRIBUTES OF ITS OWN; RATHER, IT IS THE LINKING POINT BETWEEN WORLDS. THE DA'AT OF YEZIRAH IS LIKE AN UMBILICAL CORD TO SPIRIT. INFORMATION FROM THE FOUNDATION (YESOD) OF BERIAH IS CHANNELED THROUGH IT TO THE LOWER WORLD.

Above: Pluto represents what is deep within each of us and its energy is the most intense and potent there is. It symbolizes death, rebirth, sex, evolution, degeneration and regeneration. Pluto's glyph or symbol is the circle of spirit over the crescent of personality pierced by the cross of matter.

Da'at's effect on us is profound and sometimes unnerving. Our prayers or affirmations rise up to Spirit—and through Spirit to the Divine—through the Da'ats of Yezirah and Beriah. And Grace descends through them.

The lightning flash of creation passes across Da'at from Binah to Hesed, but there is no path for it to follow as there is between all the other Sefirot. This is the black hole, where things that cannot survive in the lower worlds are lost or destroyed. If an impulse, whether it is a thought or a developing fetus, is not strong enough to make the leap of faith across Da'at, it will die. Most of us have had what seemed to be a brilliant idea in the night only to find in the morning that it has either vanished or has lost all relevance. That is the effect of Da'at.

The Da'at of the lower world of Asiyyah has the same link with the foundation of Yezirah and it is through this channel that we perceive that all may not be well with our body, for example, that it is tired, cold, or sick. It is also where our body picks up signals of what we want it to do: run, jump, stretch, or lie down. So, Da'at is a communication system—but not one that is given to gentle chat or gossip. It is more like a wormhole in space where you can be tossed and turned and tumbled through to another universe.

Da'at is ruled by Pluto—or, perhaps more accurately nowadays, by the series of planetoids in the same Kuiper cosmic belt. Astronomers say that Pluto is too small to be a planet and too erratic because it orbits both inside and outside of Neptune, but this does not inhibit it from representing Da'at. The more mysterious Pluto and its fellow planetoids become, the more appropriate they are!

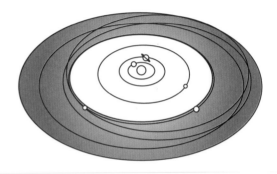

Above: Pluto's orbit around the Sun takes it inside and outside the orbit of Neptune, the planet of Keter. This represents Da'at's ability to take us to different dimensions.

DA'AT

The window of Da'at acts as a wormhole between levels of reality.

Da'at of Azilut

Da'at of Beriah

Da'at of Yezirah

Da'at of Asiyyah

TOUCHING DA'AT: POSITIVE

Da'at has no characteristics of its own, but a positive Da'at experience is insight into spiritual truth, a feeling of transformation, and the knowledge of the interconnectedness of all things.

TOUCHING DA'AT: NEGATIVE

This is the long, dark night of the soul. To be in a negative space in Da'at is to be spiraling into a void, a "bad trip" on drugs, or a living hell.

BIBLE CHARACTER

The Archangel Gabriel, bringer of messages between God and humanity.

PLUTO

Pluto is named for the Roman god of the Underworld. It takes 248 years to orbit the Sun and, due to its eccentric orbit, 12–32 years to pass through each zodiac sign. Since it was discovered only in 1930, we can only speculate on its astrological effect, but it is certainly generational. When Pluto was in Libra (relationships), humanity began to see acceptance of homosexuality and divorce. When Pluto was in Scorpio (sex and death), the Aids epidemic began. Pluto rules Scorpio, previously assigned to Mars. Before its discovery, Kabbalists did not place any planet or representational form at Da'at, regarding it as a place of passage and transformation rather than a Sefira with its own attributes.

HESED

✳ HESED IS THE SEFIRA OF UNCONDITIONAL LOVE, MERCY, KINDNESS, AND JOY. JUST AS HOKHMAH IS OUT OF BALANCE WITHOUT BINAH, HESED NEEDS ITS COUNTERWEIGHT OF GEVURAH, THE SEFIRA ON THE OTHER PILLAR OF THE TREE OF LIFE AT THE SAME LEVEL. HESED IS PLACED ON THE ACTIVE PILLAR. IT IS A SEFIRA OF EXPANSION AND IS THE DRIVING FORCE FOR ANY IMPULSE THAT SURVIVES THE "BLACK HOLE" OF DA'AT.

Below: The name of the supreme god was adopted for the planet. Jupiter is protective and was once believed to be charged with cosmic justice. Jupiter's symbol is the crescent of personality uplifted by the cross of matter.

Hesed is unlimited expansion. It is ruled by the planet Jupiter, which also controls tumors—growths that spiral out of control. Gevurah, its opposite, rules surgery and chemotherapy.

The joviality of Hesed can spiral out of balance, giving so much love and help that it ends up paralyzing others by leaving them nothing to do. They then do not learn how to help themselves. Giving too much and doing too much for other people may sometimes be a way of demanding love from others and can become controlling.

Hesed is the origin of the word Hasid, the name given to a branch of Orthodox Jewry that follows the teachings of the 18th-century eastern European mystic, the Ba'al Shem Tov (Hebrew for "Master of the Good Name"). The Ba'al Shem Tov was highly influential at a time of great unhappiness and persecution and he taught his followers to seek joy, to dance, and celebrate life in the midst of tragedy. Ironically, the Hasidim, while still great dancers, are now one of the most rule-bound sects within the Jewish faith.

Jupiter was the king of the gods, and student Kabbalists often wonder why this planet is placed at Hesed, which is not the ruler of the Tree of Life. The answer is that Hesed is the highest Sefira in the lower worlds, and Jupiter is the ruling planet of the lower worlds. If we return to the first of the commandments, "No other gods," we see that Jupiter is a lesser god than the great "I Am." It rules the world below the supernal triad of Divinity.

TOUCHING HESED: POSITIVE

Hesed is exciting, passionate, and vital. It is not a sexual feeling but it is invigorating and joyful. To touch Hesed is to drop all prejudices and constraints and expand into glorious, unconditional love. Everything is beautiful and perfect. The Sefira can be summed up by one word: "Yes!"

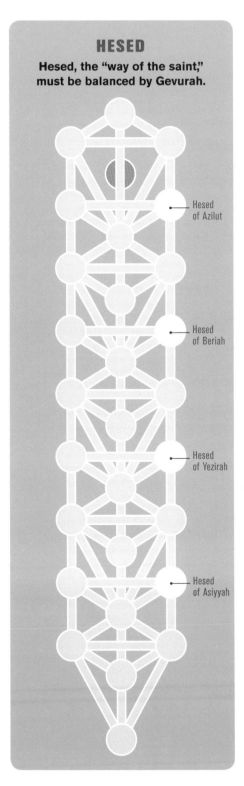

HESED

Hesed, the "way of the saint," must be balanced by Gevurah.

Hesed
of Azilut

Hesed
of Beriah

Hesed
of Yezirah

Hesed
of Asiyyah

TOUCHING HESED: NEGATIVE

Negative Hesed is run ragged with overactivity. It is a feeling of being under pressure, with too many things to do. Deep in the heart of all the giving is a steadily growing knot of resentment matched with a fear that stopping all the activity will make the world fall apart. Hesed is frantic acceleration heading straight for a brick wall.

BIBLE CHARACTER

Queen Esther, wife of the King of Persia, who realized her own true queenship and compassion in risking her own life to save her people.

JUPITER

Jupiter is a hydrogen giant and one of the three brightest lights in the night sky. Its surface is ravaged by great storms, including the great red spot, which is known to have been raging since the 17th century. It is at least two and a half times as large as all the other planets in the solar system combined and has more than 60 moons. Jupiter rules the astrological sign of Sagittarius, spends approximately a year in each sign of the zodiac, and takes about twelve years to circle the Sun. It is associated with good fortune, long-distance travel, and gambling.

GEVURAH

✳ GEVURAH MEANS "NO" IN ALL ITS ATTRIBUTES. THIS IS THE PLACE OF DISCERNMENT, JUDGMENT, DISCIPLINE, STRENGTH, AND DISCRIMINATION. AT ITS BEST IT IS PATIENCE AND AT ITS WORST IT IS CRUELTY. GEVURAH APPLIES "TOUGH LOVE" TO SITUATIONS AND TAKES NO PRISONERS.

Gevurah is the aspect of God that is most familiar to those with a basic knowledge of the Old Testament: the wrathful God of punishment. Without Gevurah, we would never have left Eden and our world would be so overflowing with divine love that we would never be able to develop our own will. Without Gevurah to amputate a diseased limb, the whole person would die from gangrene. Without Gevurah we would have no police force, no army, and no government.

Right: This early 16th-century woodcut shows the archetypes of the planets in the Zodiac with Mars in the ascendant. "Mars rising" in an individual's chart depicts a powerful person who may tend to be overjudgmental.

Together, Gevurah and Hesed balance and control human emotions, either consciously or unconsciously. Without Gevurah, Hesed would empty his pockets to a beggar and then starve and be evicted from his own home. Without Hesed, Gevurah would never leave the house, never smile, and never forgive. Working in tandem, they depict the moral qualities of a human being—integrity and the capacity for true love and courage. Together with the next Sefira, Tiferet, they form the human soul.

Gevurah is ruled by the planet Mars and the zodiac sign of Aries. It was associated with Scorpio before the discovery of Pluto and it contains many Scorpionic aspects. However, Scorpio is more concerned with darkness and transformation than Gevurah. Gevurah is the soldier, the tactician, and the peaceful warrior—but he uses a very sharp sword.

It is not Gevuric to attack repeatedly; that is an active principle, and Gevurah is placed on the passive pillar. Rather, Gevurah is the general who plans the battle carefully in the context of war. It is the principle of martial arts, using the energy of the opponent to overcome. Gevurah waits for the other side to attack and then strikes once, with devastating effect.

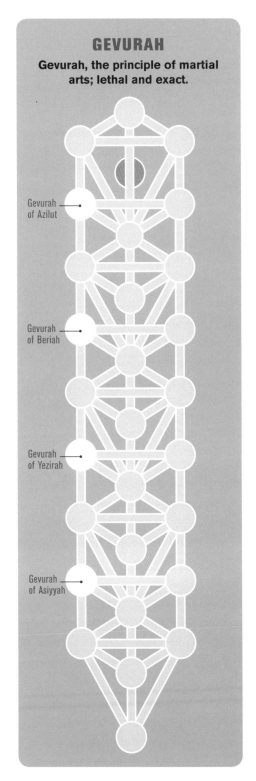

GEVURAH

Gevurah, the principle of martial arts; lethal and exact.

Gevurah of Azilut

Gevurah of Beriah

Gevurah of Yezirah

Gevurah of Asiyyah

TOUCHING GEVURAH: POSITIVE

Positive Gevurah is the ability to make sound decisions without emotional involvement. Gevurah is detached, impartial, sensible, and feels clear, true, and very powerful. Gevurah is infinite patience, one swift strike, and infinite patience again.

TOUCHING GEVURAH: NEGATIVE

Negative Gevurah feels mean, cruel, and judgmental. It is also passive aggressive; refusing to act, without caring what hurt it inflicts.

BIBLE CHARACTER

Deborah, one of the judges of Israel.

MARS

Mars is named for the Roman god of agriculture before he was associated with the Greek god of war, Ares. The farmer is an apt image for Gevurah, for he eliminates weeds and protects his land. However, the god of war is the image most people are familiar with. Martian energy is associated with sexual and aggressive urges, courage, and combativeness. But it is the energy behind our feelings, whatever they may be, and therefore it represents passion rather than actual sex, which is the province of Venus.

Mars is called the Red Planet because of the amount of iron oxide on the rocks on its surface. Its orbit takes just under two years and it changes astrological signs every 45 days or so.

TIFERET

✳ TIFERET IS HEBREW FOR BEAUTY OR TRUTH. THIS IS THE CENTRAL POINT OF THE TREE OF LIFE AND REPRESENTS OUR TRUE SELF. IT IS MOST EASILY VIEWED AS THE POINT WHERE WE CAN STAND AND BOTH DIRECT AND DRAW IN THE ENERGY OF ALL THE OTHER SEFIROT. IT IS LIKE A CAR DRIVER DECIDING WHERE HE OR SHE WANTS TO GO, AND WHETHER TO BRAKE, ACCELERATE, TURN LEFT, OR TURN RIGHT IN ORDER TO GET THERE.

Balanced Tiferet draws on the discernment of Gevurah and tempers it with the kindness of Hesed. It experiences the genuine understanding of Binah and the inspiration of Hokhmah; it receives Grace from Keter through Da'at. It also balances the intellectual processes of Hod and the impulses of Nezach while resting on the supporting foundation of Yesod and, through that, stand firmly and safely on the Earth.

Tiferet is where we all, at heart, want to be—confident and happy in who we really are. Below Tiferet, all the Sefirot are ruled by natural instincts such as sexuality, the need for food and shelter, and having to jostle for our place in the tribe. Tiferet is about becoming an individual rather than a herd creature. When we do that, our friends and family can sometimes find it threatening and, often, when seekers are moving toward "finding themselves," there is huge resistance from those around them. Tiferet is the point where a human can make conscious choices. However, this can turn against us if we become puffed up with self-importance, seeing ourselves as being superior.

TIFERET AND THE ZODIAC

Tiferet is ruled by the Sun in the astrological chart, and the proverb "there is nothing new under the Sun" is a Kabbalistic dictum. Indeed, there is nothing new below Tiferet because the lower Sefirot all repeat the cycles of nature and life. All original impulses come from the Sun and the Sefirot above it.

Tiferet is at the crown of the physical world, the center of the psychological world, and the base of the spiritual world. This is where you become the real you.

Many people say they are nothing like their astrological Sun sign, and they are speaking the truth. Most of humanity lives in its Moon sign— the Sefira of Yesod. It is part of our journey to move from the Moon to the Sun.

TOUCHING TIFERET: POSITIVE

You are in Tiferet when you can see any given situation dispassionately. Suddenly, everything makes sense and you can see through the illusions and maybe even the falsehoods. From here, clear decisions can be taken that take all aspects into account and are both fair and kind.

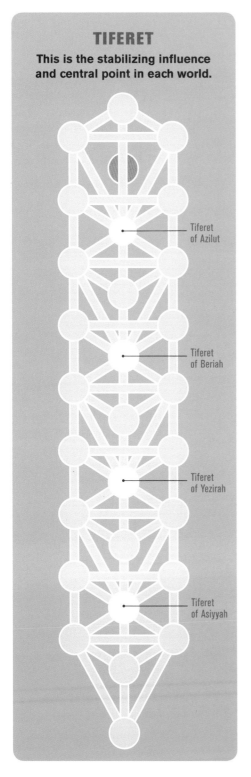

TIFERET

This is the stabilizing influence and central point in each world.

Tiferet of Azilut

Tiferet of Beriah

Tiferet of Yezirah

Tiferet of Asiyyah

TOUCHING TIFERET: NEGATIVE

Negative Tiferet is pride. It is the knowledge that you are the only one who can see things clearly, and using that power to control others. Since Tiferet is at the crown of the physical body, it can use that power to become immensely strong, and that power can be used either for good or for ill.

BIBLE CHARACTER

Ruth, who left her land and tribe because she found something greater that she believed in. She found love and became the ancestor of King David.

SUN GODS

The Sun in mythology represents both the Greek Sun god, Helios, and Apollo, the god of the light of the Sun. When Christianity began to spread across the world, images of Helios and Apollo were used for Jesus. Both gods were depicted with the sun's rays extending from their head, which explains why we see a halo on holy images. Mystically, it means that the person is in Tiferet and in touch with his or her real Self.

NEZACH

✱ NEZACH IS HEBREW FOR VICTORY OR ETERNITY AND IT IS THE SEFIRA OF THE FEELINGS AND POWERS THAT STIMULATE CREATIVITY. NEZACH CONTAINS WHAT PEOPLE USUALLY UNDERSTAND AS LOVE, EXCITEMENT, AND ART IN ALL ITS FORMS. IT IS ALSO THE HOKHMAH OF ASIYYAH, SO IT IS THE FIRST SEFIRA THAT CAN BE SEEN AT WORK IN THE PHYSICAL WORLD.

Below: Venus (or Aphrodite) symbolizes the force of attraction. Although Venus may seem less significant than other deities such as the sun god Apollo, her power over love influences many aspects of life.

Nezach is the driving force behind all vital functions, including our coronary, digestive, and autonomic systems, and all the processes that work in cycles. In nature, Nezach kickstarts each season, and its counterpart, Hod, maintains it until Nezach starts the following one.

In our psyches, we associate Nezach with love but this is sexual love not Hesedic unconditional love, With Nezach, all is instinctive. Without the balance of Hod, it can become overwhelming and even violent in its desire.

It is Nezach and Hod that power our everyday lives. That neither is conscious can be seen in the glazed expressions of people in the rush hour, going through the motions to get to their destination. Nezach is the continual daily effort to begin the repetitive actions of work, running a home, bringing up children, and socializing.

TOUCHING NEZACH: POSITIVE

If you have ever punched your arm in the air with the exhilarating feeling of having won or achieved something, then you will understand why Nezach is known as "Victory." It is also the tug of desire when you see a handsome man or a beautiful woman, or the perfect car, house, or piece of jewelry. It is what drives you to take the first step toward a goal.

TOUCHING NEZACH: NEGATIVE

Uncontrolled Nezach is one of the reasons for addiction; it is a craving for more and more. In sex this can lead to nymphomania or rape. Drug abuse is a Nezachian malfunction. Often, rock and movie stars get so high on Nezachian adrenalin that they get withdrawal symptoms when they are not adored. Drugs fill that gap temporarily but they damage the natural Hod–Nezach balance.

BIBLE CHARACTER

Rachel, the beautiful, much-loved wife of Jacob, so ruled by her need for a child that she embraced magic. She died in childbirth.

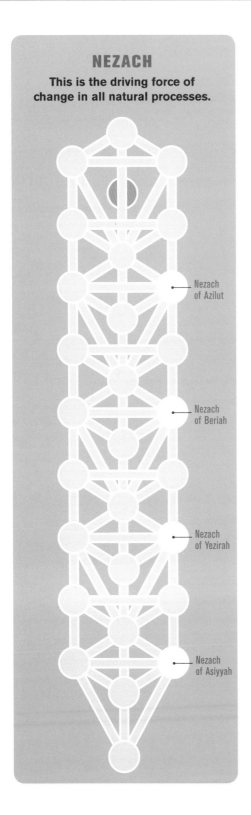

NEZACH

This is the driving force of change in all natural processes.

Nezach
of Azilut

Nezach
of Beriah

Nezach
of Yezirah

Nezach
of Asiyyah

VENUS

Nezach equates to the planet Venus, also known as the Morning or Evening Star. Astrologically, Venus rules the signs of Libra and Taurus. Both are deeply concerned with beauty, but in different ways, and it is through beauty that Nezach attracts. Interestingly, in the human race it is usually the female who displays her physical beauty, enhancing it with makeup (and nowadays, cosmetic surgery). In the animal world, it is the male that displays for the female.

Libra is about balance and ethereal beauty, and Taurus is about sensual beauty and comfort. The Roman goddess, Venus, and the Greek goddess, Aphrodite, were both associated with sexual love, and often with sexual excess. The origin of the word "venereal" refers to diseases of Venus. Venus also governs finances—love and money are humanity's primal driving forces.

A day on Venus—the time it takes the planet to turn once on its axis—is 243 Earth days. This is longer than a Venusian year, which is 225 Earth days long. Venus changes signs approximately every 25 days.

HOD

✳ HOD MEANS SPLENDOR OR REVERBERATION IN HEBREW. IT RECEIVES THE IMPULSE DIRECTED FROM NEZACH AND HONES IT. WHEN PEOPLE "COME TO THEIR SENSES," IT MEANS THEIR NEZACH IS BEING CONTROLLED BY THEIR HOD. THIS SEFIRA IS ALSO THE ASIYYATIC BINAH, SUPERVISING THE NERVOUS SYSTEM AND THE DIGESTIVE PROCESSES.

Above: Mercury, the messenger from god to man, is also the internal link between our soul and our personality, between the eternal and the mundane.

Hod is about thought and information. It gathers and disseminates. It is not knowledge itself —that is information mixed with experience. The Internet, the computer nerd, and the academic are primarily Hodian, but so are the wit and the raconteur. Hod loves to spread information and can be either an intellectually stunning wordsmith and comedian or a repetitive bore.

It is Hod that interprets and processes much of the information that comes in through our eyes. Continually sorting and filing impressions that come in, it directs our feet down the street so as to avoid lampposts, other people, traffic, and litter on the ground. All of this is automatic; only when something new and unknown occurs does it refer back to the consciousness of Tiferet. This is why we can reach a destination without having any idea how we arrived.

TOUCHING HOD: POSITIVE

It is positive Hod when you enthrall a group of people with your wit and intellect. Actors, presenters, and other communicators often have a strong Hod, and its "splendor" is demonstrated in public performance. It is also Hodian when you are enjoying a really good book, watching an informative program, or teaching with clarity. Positive Hod is a satisfying feeling of intelligence and the right placing of information. It is also clear Hod to perform magical tricks for amusement and tell jokes.

TOUCHING HOD: NEGATIVE

If you have ever lain restlessly in bed with thoughts going round and round in your head, preventing sleep, and driving you deeper into depression, then you have experienced negative Hod. In this mode, the Sefira is recycling the same, ultimately useless, information. It blocks out any new impulse from any of the Sefirot above and any excitement or impulse from Nezach, and so cannot lift itself out of depression. Negative Hod can also express itself in the continual search for more information. This is often used as an excuse for not acting to change a situation; the continual gathering of information causes paralysis. It becomes impossible to make a decision. Hod can also talk its way out of anything by using intellectual tricks and be extremely cruel, particularly with words.

HOD

Hod is associated with the mind, psychic ability, and prophesy.

Hod of Azilut

Hod of Beriah

Hod of Yezirah

Hod of Asiyyah

BIBLE CHARACTER

Leah, who tricked her husband into marrying her instead of her sister Rachel and continued to outwit her for all of their lives. Unlike Rachel, who is on the active right-hand column, Leah maintains and endures, becoming a respected wife if never loved.

MERCURY

Hod is ruled by the planet Mercury, the name given to the messenger of the gods. Mercury is the smallest of the planets and the closest to the sun, completing an orbit every 88 Earth days. Mercury, or Hermes, was the god of trade, commerce, communication, and thievery and has a reputation as a trickster.

Astrologically, Mercury rules the signs of Gemini and Virgo. Gemini is quicksilver and sharp, while Virgo edits and processes information, and it changes signs approximately once a month. However, between three or four times a year, Mercury goes retrograde, meaning that it appears to go backward in the sky. This is always a time when communications should be double checked, because misunderstandings are frequent.

Mercury in your chart indicates how you communicate, your ability to rationalize, whether you are a quick thinker, and how easy it is to learn. Nowadays, with the use of email at work, we often communicate with each other's Hod/Mercury before any other Sefira.

YESOD

✳ YESOD IS HEBREW FOR FOUNDATION. THIS IS THE HUMAN EGO, THE PART OF US THAT PRESENTS A PERSONA OR IMAGE TO THE WORLD AND HIDES OUR REAL SELF. THIS CAN BE BOTH GOOD AND BAD BECAUSE IT DISGUISES BOTH OUR STRENGTHS AND WEAKNESSES. THE EGO IS LIKE FIRE; A GOOD SERVANT BUT A BAD MASTER.

Yesod is intended to be the servant of the Self; a true foundation that takes care of everyday work so that the Self has time and opportunities to make conscious decisions. When a human being learns any new task, from riding a horse to making a cake or driving a car, full conscious attention is required. There may even be a feeling of fear or anticipation. But once that process is learnt, the consciousness of Tiferet hands over to Yesod to run on automatic. This is why we may be intending to go to one place to shop but find ourselves in another. Our automatic systems (this time Hod and Yesod together) took us to where we usually go. Yesod relates to the reticular activating system in the brain,

which filters the impressions that come to us through our senses. There are too many for us to be able to focus on all of them simultaneously, so a selection process has to take place. If you read "left foot," the reticular system immediately gives you access to how your left foot feels. Up until that moment, the information was irrelevant so the reticular system edited it out.

Yesod forms during the first seven years of our life, through repeating patterns. It learns that fire burns, how to cross the road safely, and other useful information. Yesod also learns our parents' attitudes toward love, money, and life, and what is acceptable behavior. The patterns learned by the age of seven will never change unless we reach consciousness at Tiferet and amend them through our own will.

Yesod is also the Da'at of Asiyyah and it is through this link that we experience pain or discomfort from our physical body.

TOUCHING YESOD: POSITIVE

Yesod is the ability to work on automatic so it can continue a task while the mind is totally engaged in something else. It feels comfortable, reassuring—as if everything is right with the world.

Left: Artemis is seen as the mother of all life but was "defeminized" to become Diana, goddess of the hunt. When Apollo became Sun god, Artemis was made the full Moon goddess but Kabbalah does not equate this association with femininity.

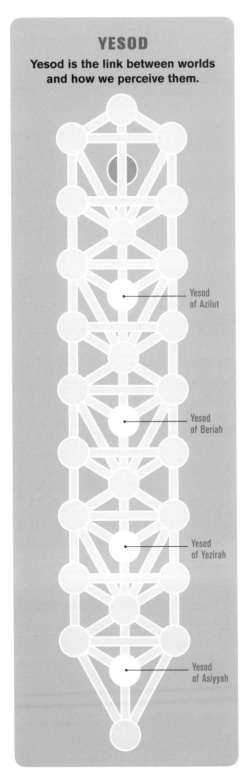

YESOD

Yesod is the link between worlds and how we perceive them.

Yesod of Azilut

Yesod of Beriah

Yesod of Yezirah

Yesod of Asiyyah

TOUCHING YESOD: NEGATIVE

Yesod dislikes anything new; it feels wrong and uncomfortable. Yesod is strongly resistant to change, particularly ones that might affect its standing with the family or social group. It often misses opportunities that would lead to transformation.

BIBLE CHARACTER

Joseph, with his coat of many colors that hid his true self and his arrogance, which caused him to be sold into slavery. He rose to great prominence in Egypt through understanding how to work the system.

YESOD AND THE MOON

Yesod is represented by the Moon, which changes signs every two and a half days and circles the Earth every 28 days, thus repeating its influences every month. The Moon affects the physical tides and all water on Earth, and its power over the human emotions is equally as strong. The Moon is associated with the astrological sign of Cancer. The crescent Moon goddess is Diana, the virgin huntress; the full Moon goddess is Artemis, the mother.

Most astrological traditions regard the Moon as feminine to the Sun's masculine: Kabbalah does not. As both Tiferet and Yesod are on the central column, they are regarded as asexual.

MALKHUT

✳ MALKHUT, THE BASE SEFIRA OF THE TREE OF LIFE, MEANS "KINGDOM" IN HEBREW. IT IS THE PLACE WHERE ALL THE OTHER SEFIROT BECOME MANIFEST. THE MALKHUT OF AZILUT, THE DIVINE WORLD, IS THE KINGDOM OF GOD WHERE DIVINITY MANIFESTS. THE MALKHUT OF BERIAH, THE SPIRITUAL WORLD, IS THE KINGDOM OF HEAVEN WHERE SPIRIT MANIFESTS. JESUS REFERS TO BOTH IN THE NEW TESTAMENT.

Above: In the Kabbalistic view, the pollution of the Earth is just as much a physical manifestation of the lack of care for our spirits and souls as it is of carbon emissions and litter.

The Malkhut of Yezirah is the Tiferet of Asiyyah, too, so it is the place where the psyche is fully linked with the physical body. At death, this is the first Sefira to disconnect from the physical body.

For us, Malkhut is how we experience the physical universe. No matter how we may enjoy looking at representations—images, photographs, and movies—there is nothing better than being in front of the real painting, in the real landscape, or meeting the real person. We are more comfortable with physical proof than we are with theories and suppositions. This is partly a deep-seated knowledge that the process of manifestation is completed in the physical world, but it can also be a denial of other possible realities.

Kabbalists say that Keter is in Malkhut and Malkhut is in Keter, referring to the completion of a full cycle in Jacob's Ladder. God is just as much in the physical manifestation of a rock as It is in the vastness of infinity.

The physical body of a human being, powered by the emotions and intelligence of the psyche, the ideas and inspiration of Spirit, and the initial life force of the Divine, is capable of achieving great things. The secret to happiness is to realize that all four worlds have a relevant part in that success. Twenty-first century humankind tends to worship Malkhut in the form of physical beauty and strength, preferring to recreate youth in the body rather than develop the soul.

THE EARTH

Malkhut is the Earth, also known in astrology as the ascendant, or rising sign. The rising sign is the sign of the zodiac that was coming over the horizon at dawn on the day of birth. The sign changes every hour or so as the Earth moves around the Sun. It is associated with our physical appearance and also with our own perception of our place in society and the world. Someone with a Cancerian ascendant usually has either a crescent-moon face and figure (slender and pale) or a full-moon face and figure (rounded and ample). He or she will have a deep inner need to nurture others.

The Earth goddess is known as Gaia or the Great Mother. As the Keter of Keters is the Great Father, he must be united with the Great Mother to be complete.

TOUCHING MALKHUT: POSITIVE

The phrase "to be grounded" refers to positive Malkhut. It is being solidly present on Earth and aware of all that is around you. You can then use this as a springboard to the rest of the Tree of Life.

TOUCHING MALKHUT: NEGATIVE

Negative Malkhut is when you simply cannot be bothered to get up off the couch and even picking up the TV remote to switch channels is too much of an effort. Alternatively, it can be the refusal to believe in anything without physical proof.

BIBLE CHARACTER:

Sarah, wife of Abraham and founding mother of Israel. Sarah is associated with Shekhinah, the presence or feminine aspect of God.

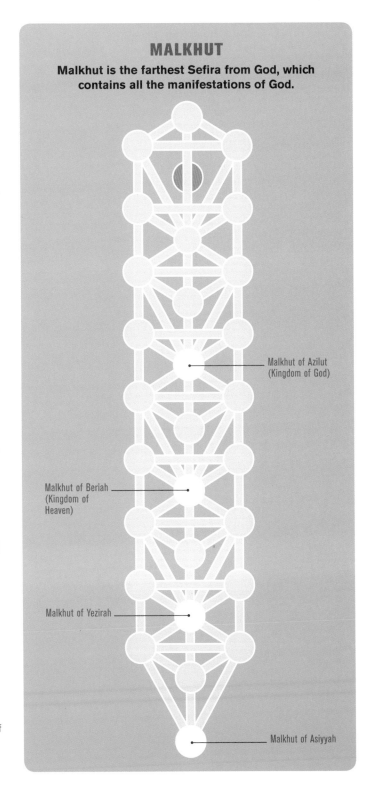

MALKHUT

Malkhut is the farthest Sefira from God, which contains all the manifestations of God.

Malkhut of Azilut (Kingdom of God)

Malkhut of Beriah (Kingdom of Heaven)

Malkhut of Yezirah

Malkhut of Asiyyah

PART THREE

TREE OF LIFE

THE TEN SEFIROT AND ONE NON-SEFIRA OF THE TREE OF LIFE ARE LINKED BY A

COMPLEX SYSTEM OF PATHS AND TRIANGLES, KNOWN AS TRIADS. THESE HELP

TO DEMONSTRATE THE UNIQUE BLUEPRINT FOR EACH OF US, DEPENDING ON

OUR PERSONAL ASTROLOGY, GENETIC STRUCTURE, AND TRAINING. KABBALISTS

OFTEN USE THE NAMES OF THE SEFIROT IN A KIND OF LANGUAGE, SPEAKING

OF SOMEONE AS BEING "VERY GEVURIC" (SEVERE), OR "HESEDIC" (OVER-

GENEROUS). THE TREE OF THE PSYCHE IS A TREE OF ARCHETYPES THAT

HOVERS BETWEEN THE SPIRITUAL AND PHYSICAL WORLDS. IT DEMONSTRATES

THE ISSUES WE ALL ENCOUNTER AND WHAT OPPOSES AND WHAT SUPPORTS

OUR DEVELOPMENT AS INDIVIDUALS.

BASIC KNOWLEDGE OF ASTROLOGY CAN HELP IN INTERPRETING HOW

THE SEFIROT AND TRIADS OPERATE TOGETHER, BUT GREAT SELF-AWARENESS

CAN BE ACHIEVED WITHOUT THIS KNOWLEDGE. LEARNING HOW YOUR OWN

TREE OF LIFE WORKS IS THE KEY TO FINDING YOUR DESTINY AND DISCOVERING

WHY SOME THINGS MAKE YOU HAPPY AND OTHERS UNCOMFORTABLE.

CHAPTER FIVE

KABBALAH AND PSYCHOLOGY

✱ IN EACH ONE OF US, THE TEN SEFIROT DANCE TOGETHER IN A GREAT BALLET OF LIFE. WHETHER THE MUSIC AND MOVEMENT ARE HARMONIOUS OR IN DISCORD IS TO DO WITH THE BASIC SETUP OF OUR TREE. EACH SEFIRA IS CODED ACCORDING TO OUR PARTICULAR BLUEPRINT. MORE IMPORTANT THAN WHAT WE HAVE BEEN GIVEN, HOWEVER, IS WHAT WE CHOOSE TO DO WITH IT.

Above: Leonardo da Vinci's interpretation of Roman architect Vitruvius' writing, which described the perfect human form in geometric terms, represents the perfect man at all levels.

A person with Sefirot that constantly challenge and pull against each other can, from the central point of consciousness, Tiferet, decide to use that contradictory power to become an innovator or pioneer in art or science, or a counselor who can help others with similar problems.

Alternatively, he or she can simply attempt to ride out the conflicting emotions by using a soporific such as work, shopping, sex, drugs, or food. Most of us manage a mixture of the two, controlling some aspects of our psyche and learning to live with others.

You may already have worked out with which Sefirot you resonate and which ones you dislike. Usually, you are repelled by the ones you do not use much in your own life—or perhaps you do not realize that you are using them in a harmful way.

The overkind person often has problems with the words "discipline" or "judgment," even thinking they are wrong. This individual may not be able to see that too much kindness is just as harmful to a child as too much discipline. Such people are frequently overjudgmental and harsh with themselves, withholding the pleasures that they work so hard to give to others.

The Tree of Life itself is an image of you from the back—as if you are looking away. Tradition says that this is because humanity cannot look upon the face of God and live

WHAT ARE YOU LIKE?

✡ **Are you a Hokhmah person**—constantly inspired but not achieving much?

✡ **Are you a Binah person**—wise and kindly but insisting on definite rules and regulations and good behavior?

✡ **Are you a Hesedic person**—constantly giving and doing things for others?

✡ **Are you a Gevuric person**—applying discipline, keeping order, and following rules?

✡ **Are you a Tiferet person**—an independent, strong person capable of seeing through the world's illusions but neither being judgmental nor soft?

✡ **Are you a Nezachian person**—artistic, creative, loving social life, romance, and shopping?

✡ **Are you a Hodian person**—intellectual, scientific, rational, and logical?

✡ **Are you a Yesodic person**—happy to go with the crowd and addicted to TV reality shows?

✡ **Are you a Malkhutian person**—a stay-at-home person who earns what you need in order to do nothing very much and lets the world pass you by?

(Exodus 33:20). As we are in the image of God, and the Tree of Life is our perfected image, it would be too bright and overwhelming for us to see without a filter.

As Kabbalah was disseminated around the world, this injunction was amended so that you can regard the Tree as your mirror image. However, it is just that: a mirror image of you. It is not an image of someone in front of you. This misconception has led to many images of the Tree being drawn showing a man facing forward. This places the Sefirot on the wrong side of the diagram and causes great confusion.

Whichever of the two ways you choose to view the Tree, the right-hand Sefirot of Hokhmah, Hesed, and Nezach should represent your right side and the left-hand Sefirot of Binah, Gevurah, and Hod should represent your left-hand side.

OTHER ARCHETYPES

Carl Jung identified a large number of archetypes. These are often linked to the main archetypes and may represent aspects of them. They overlap and many can appear in the same person. For example:

✡ **Family archetypes**
Father: Stern, powerful, controlling (Gevurah)
Mother: Feeding, nurturing, soothing (Hesed)
Child: Birth, beginnings, salvation (Tiferet)

✡ **Story archetypes**
Hero: Rescuer, champion (Tiferet)
Maiden: Purity, desire (Nezach)
Wise old man: Knowledge, guidance (Binah)
Magician: Mysterious, powerful (Hokhmah)
Earth mother: Nature (Malkhut)
Witch or sorceress: Dangerous (Yesod)
Trickster: Deceiving, hidden (Hod)

✡ **Animal archetypes**
Faithful dog: Unquestioning loyalty (Hod–Yesod–Nezach triad)
Enduring horse: Never giving up (Yesod–Nezach–Malkhut triad)
The devious cat: Self-serving (Hod–Yesod–Malkhut triad)

THE THREE PILLARS

✳ WE HAVE ALREADY LOOKED AT THE THREE COLUMNS OF THE TREE OF LIFE AS BEING ACTIVE, RECEPTIVE, AND DEVOTIONAL. EACH OF US FEELS A PULL TO ONE SIDE OR THE OTHER, BUT IT IS OUR LIFE'S WORK TO ACHIEVE A BALANCE ON THE CENTRAL COLUMN. THAT WAY WE ARE IN LINE WITH THE GRACE OF GOD, WHICH INCLUDES MIRACLES AND DIRECT ACCESS TO THE DIVINE.

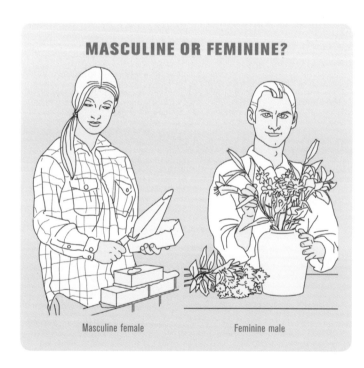

MASCULINE OR FEMININE?

Masculine female   Feminine male

Above: The reincarnation principle suggests that souls are predominantly born as one sex or the other. If we "change sex" we often demonstrate many characteristics of our previous incarnations in both lifestyle and sexual preference.

hand column is the pillar of severity or of form and is the feminine, or receptive, side of the Tree.

The common modern perception is that mercy and action are "good" or "strong" and that receptivity and severity are "bad" or "weak." This is a dangerous misconception and is the cause of much unhappiness. Many modern women reject the idea of receptivity and live lives of frantic action and giving in order to try to be effective both in the world and in their own lives.

FINDING THE BALANCE

One of the most important lessons that the Kabbalist can learn is that there must be balance between the masculine and feminine. Here, we are talking about masculine and feminine traits, not about men and women, and it is vital to understand that both sexes contain both aspects. In an ideal world, men are 51 percent masculine and 49 percent feminine, and women are 51 percent feminine and 49 percent masculine. To overbalance in either direction cuts us off from Grace, which can only come to us down the central column.

The central column is the one where we feel balanced and where we have the ability to be grounded and in direct contact with the higher worlds. This is known as the pillar of consciousness. The right-hand column is known as the pillar of mercy or force and is the masculine, or active, side of the Tree. The left-

Kabbalah views masculine and feminine as equally important. Without someone to receive, no one is able to give; without someone creating openness, no one can offer love. The power of the feminine is profound; in one way, all of life is feminine. Every second, we are all receiving the impulse of the creative force—from the higher worlds, from the sun, and from the air. Unless we took in that air and our skins absorbed that light, we would die. This is why God is so often seen as masculine—because It is the driving force of creation. As children of God we want to give in the same way—to give feels wonderful, but we have to remember to receive first.

THE FLOW OF LIGHT

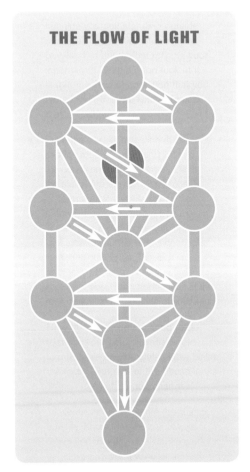

Great mystics and teachers all know how to receive through meditation. They become still and tune in to the creative force in order to receive inspiration. If we get that balance right, we become incredibly powerful; we both receive and give in equal measures.

If we give too soon, we go out of balance. When the lightning flash hit the Tree of Life, the light of creation flowed into each of the Sefirot in turn. The secret is that each Sefira must be filled—as in Psalm 23, "my cup runneth over." If it tries to feed the next Sefira before it, itself, is filled, then it never experiences the joy of complete communion with the Divine and what it gives is the lesser for it.

Above and left: Elements in Nature demonstrate that each Sefira must be filled before it overflows and fills the vessel below it. This creates essential balance between active and passive.

PILLAR OF FORM

✳ THE PILLAR OF SEVERITY, OR FORM, IS ALL ABOUT STRUCTURE AND BOUNDARIES. WHEN OUT OF BALANCE, IT ACTS AS AN IMMOVABLE OBJECT TO THE RIGHT-HAND PILLAR'S IRRESISTIBLE FORCE. IT IS LIKE A BRICK WALL, BUT BRICK WALLS PREVENT FLOODS AND FIRES AND KEEP US PROTECTED. THE LEFT-HAND PILLAR, WHEN BALANCED, ASSESSES, CONSIDERS, AND CONTEMPLATES—AND MAKES STRONG, SOUND, AND WISE DECISIONS.

Left: The child, the mature adult, and the elderly person represent the pillar of form.

The three Sefirot of the left-hand pillar are Hod, Gevurah, and Binah. Hod represents the child, Gevurah the adult, and Binah the elderly person. Children are an open book, eager to take in information, but they have little experience with which to assess whether the information is good and useful or not. They use repetition to learn, and once the information is learned, it is acted upon without much thought. By their adulthood, people have more experience of life and know how to interpret the information; they balance the inflow of data from Hod with what they know of pain and pleasure, fear, and love and make decisions based on those criteria. Elderly people have knowledge of whether or not good decisions were made previously and the results of those decisions. Ideally, they can apply that knowledge as well as drawing new information and new decisions from the two lower Sefirot in order to set strong but flexible boundaries.

All three Sefirot work together to make up the human decision-making process. A person with a strong Hod but a weak Gevurah is likely to seek more and more information without putting it to any good use. Constantly surfing the Internet to discover what diet is best is

ARE YOU OVERBALANCED ON THE LEFT PILLAR?

Anything that leads to paralysis is a symptom of an out-of-balance left pillar. Some of the issues listed appear to be active, but are symptoms of resistance to real progress. All are useless unless they achieve a result that can move you on to a different level.

You are overbalanced at one or more levels on the left-hand pillar if:

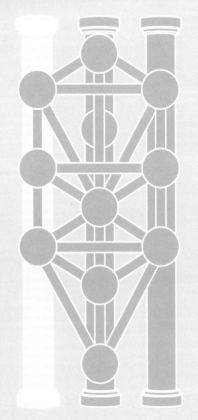

✡ You follow the letter of the law

✡ You always go for the same walk, to the same restaurant, or buy the same make of car, and find it hard to be spontaneous

✡ You seek reassurance from several different people before you make any decisions; you are constantly afraid

✡ You are an information junkie

✡ You cannot start your day before reading your emails and reacting to them

✡ Your search for spiritual knowledge means you change disciplines every six months

✡ You make life decisions based on information from your childhood

✡ You are often impatient

✡ You are judgmental of other people's decisions

✡ You have standard prejudices—all blondes are dumb; all dogs bite; all sports are boring

✡ You turn down opportunities because they are too scary

✡ You are often depressed and lethargic.

Hodian; actually choosing a diet and sticking to it is Gevurah. Assessing the effects of the diet and whether it is good for you is Binah. A person with a weak Hod but a strong Gevurah would make decisions based on very little information, but stick to them no matter what.

ASTROLOGICAL SIGNIFICANCE

The three planets that are associated with these Sefirot are, ironically, all masculine gods, but their rulerships are about powerful feminine attributes. Hod is Mercury, the messenger (*see page 69*). Mercury carried information but did not use it himself. Mars is the strategist using martial arts and the minimum of effort to win a conflict (*see page 62*); for example, the president of a country does not actually go to war—instead, he or she instructs others to do that. Saturn (*see page 56*) is the god associated with boundaries and time.

PILLAR OF FORCE

✳ THE PILLAR OF ACTION OR FORCE IS CONSTANT MOVEMENT AND FLEXIBILITY. WHEN IT IS OUT OF BALANCE, IT IS LIKE A BOLTING HORSE OR A RUNAWAY TRAIN. EXPANSION AND MOVEMENT ARE VITAL TO LIFE, AND IT IS THE POWER OF THE RIGHT-HAND PILLAR THAT MAKES A DANDELION FORCE ITS WAY THROUGH TARMAC. HOWEVER, A TUMOR IS THE RESULT OF UNSTOPPABLE GROWTH IN THE BODY.

Right: The teenager, late maturity, and extreme age represent the pillar of force.

The three Sefirot of the right-hand pillar are Nezach, Hesed, and Hokhmah. Nezach is the teenager, Hesed the middle-aged person, and Hokhmah the ancient mystic.

Nezach is awash with desires and hopes that are acted upon at every conceivable opportunity. This is the time when young people become slaves to fashion and the idea of wearing a new outfit for every social event. They have to have new and up-to-date accessories or they feel they will die. As innovators and artists, they break boundaries and shock people.

Middle-aged people can let go of the vagaries of fashion and give their time to protect, help, and guide others. They may do this as a mentor or boss; sometimes they over-organize and run other people's lives for them because they know they can do it better and faster.

Mystics have let go of everyday issues and may be truly in tune with the ways of the universe. They may be so unfocused on the physical that they forget to eat or take care of themselves.

All three work together to make things happen. They move the human race forward

ARE YOU OVERBALANCED ON THE RIGHT PILLAR?

Anything that requires constant impulse and action is evidence of an unbalanced right pillar. Although the idea of control appears passive, it is only maintained by continuous effort and takes up a huge amount of energy.

You are overbalanced at one level or more on the right-hand pillar if:

✡ You have to make new purchases every day/week to feel good; you are a fashion junkie

✡ You tidy your children's rooms instead of teaching them to do it

✡ You have to go out every night

✡ You feel resentful that nobody ever takes as much care of you as you do of them and you are overtired through doing too much

✡ You say, "Oh for God's sake, let me do it!" to anyone who's being too slow in your view

✡ You live in constant agitation and you are always rushed and late

✡ You have high blood pressure or you have tumors

✡ You constantly go to workshops but never achieve the qualifications

✡ You jump from relationship to relationship instead of working at the one you are in

✡ You find that you destroy relationships and things that you love without knowing how.

with creative vision and invention but can move too swiftly without focus or due consideration.

A person with a strong Nezach but weak Hesed might be a nymphomaniac and pursue pleasure for purely selfish reasons. One-night stands are very Nezachian. Such people might also create sensational art but it would be neither lasting nor inspirational. Someone having a strong Hesed but a weak Hokhmah could be so focused on others that he or she becomes a control-freak who never allows other people to make mistakes. This individual is unable to see that it might be for a higher good for people to learn lessons for themselves and is unable to rest or make space to enjoy his or her own life.

ASTROLOGICAL SIGNIFICANCE

The planet Venus represents Nezach (*see page 67*); this goddess is always acting to find passion. Hesed is Jupiter, the king of the gods, who always knows best for everyone whether they like it or not. Hokhmah is Uranus, the planet of revolution (*see page 54*).

PILLAR OF CONSCIOUSNESS

✱ THE CENTRAL COLUMN IS THE PLACE WHERE YOU CAN BE BOTH GROUNDED AND INSPIRED. THE SEFIROT HERE DRAW INFORMATION FROM BOTH SIDES OF THE TREE AND ARE AFFECTED BY THE SIDE THAT IS STRONGER. IF YOU ARE OUT OF BALANCE ON EITHER SIDE, IT IS VERY HARD TO FOCUS ON INNER WORK SUCH AS MEDITATION OR PRAYER.

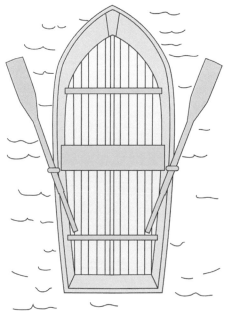

Right: The only position from which you can row a boat is the center, facing the stern. But this requires trust that you are going in the right direction.

The four Sefirot of the central column are Malkhut, Yesod, Tiferet, and Keter. The non-Sefira of Da'at is also placed here. On this column we need to be focused in Tiferet, otherwise we are likely to be spaced out (Da'at and Keter) or overattached to the physical world and social custom (Yesod and Malkhut).

A good way of experiencing the central column is to imagine that you are sitting alone in a rowing boat, facing the stern so you can only see where you have come from unless you make a conscious decision to turn around and look ahead.

Malkhut is the boat itself and you can only stay afloat if the craft is in good condition. Yesod is where you place your feet in order to balance yourself while you pull on the oars. Tiferet is where you sit and make the decisions as to where you want to go and at what pace. You would not want to sit at Yesod because that way you would tip the boat up and make it unstable. Da'at would do exactly the same. Keter is your destination. The oars and the sides of the boat represent the side columns, and it is up to you to use the oars to steer you to where you want to go.

This analogy also works with a much larger, more sophisticated, vessel. Malkhut is again the ship, its condition, and its size. Yesod is the first officer, who carries out your commands—or not. You are Tiferet, the captain. Da'at is the radar or sonar system that alerts you to conditions ahead and Keter is the destination. Only if you take command as the captain and can filter and act on the information being given to you, will your ship take you where you want to go.

QUICK MEDITATION: THE ART OF CHANGE

Sit comfortably and cross your arms. Now cross them the other way. How does this feel? If just that little action feels odd, is it any wonder that it is hard to change an old habit? Even if it has been driving you crazy, it still feels uncomfortable to do anything else.

Consider which eyebrow you raise when you are puzzled. Which hand do you use to pick up a drink? With which leg do you take the first step? What part of your body do you wash first? In which order do you put on clothes or clean your teeth? You probably don't know the answer to most of these questions.

Your active meditation for the next week is to change these tiny habits; to do things in a different order and then watch your reaction and resistance to doing so. If you can do this, then you will find it easier to act consciously in all parts of your life.

ARE YOU BALANCED ON THE CENTRAL COLUMN?

If you are, your life is in perfect order; you are happy, confident, peaceful, and focused. You know when to make a conscious decision and when you can trust your reactions to take care of business for you. Keep practicing!

ASTROLOGICAL SIGNIFICANCE

Malkhut is the ascendant in astrology, the representation of your physical reality (*see page 73*). Yesod is the Moon, which we can see only because of the light of the Sun. Tiferet is the Sun, the source of life for our own personal solar system. Da'at is Pluto and its fellow planetoids—mysterious and incomprehensible, while Neptune is Keter, the place of our deepest dreams and inner desires. To live a life in balance is often likened to walking on a razor's edge or a tightrope; it needs us to be awake and consciously aware.

CHAPTER SIX

LEVELS OF THE TREE OF LIFE

VEGETABLE LEVEL

✳ THE TREE OF LIFE CONTAINS FIVE DISTINCT LEVELS: VEGETABLE, ANIMAL, HUMAN, SPIRITUAL, AND DIVINE. THE VEGETABLE SOUL OF A HUMAN BEING IS CONTAINED IN THE THREE TRIADS AROUND YESOD, THE EGO, OR FOUNDATION. IT IS THE PART OF US THAT EATS, DRINKS, SEEKS THE SUN, GROWS, HAS SEX, REPRODUCES, GROWS OLD, AND DIES.

Above: The vegetable soul of a person is concerned with physical needs, such as food, drink, sun, and sex.

These aspects are all vital parts in the makeup of every human being and, for most people, they are sufficient. There is much joy to be experienced at the vegetable level: a pleasant environment is sought and all appetites are satisfied. Vegetables always seek the sun—and so do most human beings, whenever we can! However, for the spiritual seeker there is an inner feeling that there must be a greater meaning to life.

The vegetable person is one who is primarily focused on the messages received from his or her body. There are three basic types:

1 Triad of Hod–Yesod–Malkhut

Dominated by the nervous system. These Thinkers are cerebral people, who may move jerkily and who always think things through logically before acting. Often this kind of person is a scientist, an analyst, a teacher, or an accountant. Since such people are primarily focused on the left-hand column of the Tree, they are respectful of tradition and law. They eat to survive.

2 Triad of Nezach–Yesod–Malkhut

Dominated by the muscular system. These Actors have great stamina. They make excellent soldiers, pioneers, sports people, engineers, dancers, and artists. They eat for strength. Actors are also strongly sexually motivated and will seek for physical stimulation and satisfaction.

VEGETABLE LEVEL

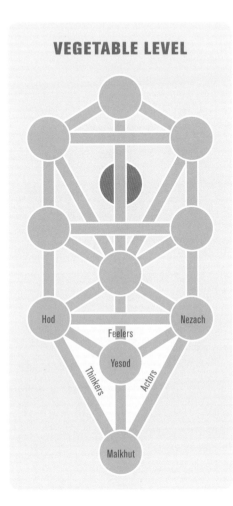

3 Triad of Hod–Yesod–Nezach

Dominated by the gut. These Feelers act on instinct; the link between the physical and psychological bodies helps them to assess what can be taken in safely and what needs to be rejected on both levels. They can also be teachers, artists, or dancers but are most likely to be impractical people—they have no direct link to Malkhut. They are the willing helpers of this level, backing up and supporting the other two triads. They eat for pleasure and tend to drown their sorrows in food or wine without realizing—or caring—how this will affect their physical body.

VEGETABLE SOUL MEDITATION: WHICH TYPE ARE YOU?

1 Close your eyes and relax. Imagine yourself in a great library: quiet and peaceful. You are here to research the life of a famous mystic. In front of you is a desk with a computer so you can search the Internet and locate the books that contain the information you need. You are going to be here for one full week, just doing this work. On the desk beside you is the food you will need for that time: packs of neatly wrapped sandwiches with healthy ingredients, some plain biscuits, and fruit. Does your heart rise or sink at the thought?

2 Now imagine yourself about to set off on a charity run across mountainous terrain. You have seven full days of walking, jogging, and running ahead. You get up early each day and set off with a group of others, some fitter than you and some less fit. It is not a competition but you want to get to the finish line in good time. You are provided with specific energy-giving foods and power drinks, and each day is harder than the last. Does your heart rise or sink at the thought?

3 Now imagine yourself in a meditation retreat by the sea. You are here for a week to listen to music, dance, meditate, and look at the view. For some of the time you will be silent, musing to yourself, and for some of the time you will be sharing your thoughts and feelings with a group of people. Each day you have a choice of succulent fresh foods, cheeses, wine, and desserts. You can eat as much or as little as you like. Does your heart rise or sink at the thought?

ANIMAL LEVEL

✳ THE TRIAD OF HOD–TIFERET–NEZACH IS KNOWN AS THE NEFESH, OR ANIMAL SOUL. WHILE THE VEGETABLE SOUL IS THE PART OF US THAT COPES WITH ROUTINE EVERYDAY MATTERS, THIS ANIMAL LEVEL IS ALERT AND CONSCIOUS OF ITSELF IN RELATION TO THE WORLD. THIS HIGHER LEVEL OF AWARENESS IS PRIMARILY FOCUSED ON ATTAINING A POSITION IN THE TRIBE.

Left: An engraving of an early astronomer. Both ambition and the desire for knowledge are pivotal to the awakening triad and the animal state. These can be used for personal power or the greater good.

The animal soul jostles for position, whether it is through leadership or some other area of status. It is the triad of clans, teams, clubs, competition, and sporting events, where there must be a winner and a loser. In its positive aspects, it is what pushes the human race to communicate; this is the triad of diplomacy, desire, and awareness. It is what makes us seek fame and fortune. In its negative state it is cunning, cruel, fearful, and willing to wage war.

In humans this triad is also the place where we become aware of being aware. Because it touches Tiferet, which has access to higher worlds, it is here that we begin the awakening process and the search for self-knowledge. However, once some personal growth has been achieved, we need the influence of Gevurah at the human level in order to maintain the discipline required for further growth.

ANIMAL LEVEL

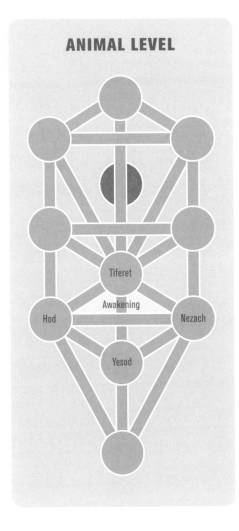

Tiferet

Awakening

Hod   Nezach

Yesod

ANIMAL LEVEL MEDITATION: WHAT'S YOUR PLACE IN THE TRIBE?

✡ Sit comfortably and close your eyes. Imagine that you are in a place or an era where you are part of a tribe of people who live off the land. Observe the people and their homes. Are they nomadic or settled? Are they warlike or peaceful?

✡ Approach the tribe's chief. Is it a man or a woman? What is his or her attitude toward you? Are you an outsider or a member? The chief tells you that you are welcome but that it is up to you to find your own place in the tribe.

✡ Wander among the villagers, observing their different tasks. There are people weaving; there are people making weapons; there are hunters, gatherers, and farmers; there is a medicine man or woman; a council of elders: and a shaman. Which group draws you? And what is their response to you?

✡ You settle into the group, taking the place that they offer you. What is your position? At dusk all the villagers gather for a meeting before a feast. Everyone walks to the fire; the highest ranking sit near the chief; the lowest ranking, farthest away. Where is your given place? Are you happy with this or do you feel yourself wanting to move higher?

✡ If you want to move, get up in your mind's eye and walk to the place where you want to be. What is the occupier's reaction? Does he or she accept or challenge you? And do you accept the challenge or return to your old place, either in peace or to bide your time?

In domesticated animals, this triad is where the animal learns to be a companion of humanity rather than a tribal beast. Pets will always find their place in the "human pack" but they can also demonstrate great character with both endearing and manipulative tendencies that would be of no use to them in the pack mentality of the wild.

Right: Wild horses always band together in herds around a leader who will fight to establish and maintain dominance. Politicians are nearly all animal people who wish to become head of a particular tribe and part of a system that is involved with power.

THE HUMAN LEVEL

✳ THE LEVEL OF TIFERET IS THE ESSENTIAL SELF OF A HUMAN BEING. IT IS ALSO KNOWN AS "THE WATCHER" BECAUSE FROM THIS LEVEL WE CAN OBSERVE OURSELVES AS WE THINK, FEEL, OR ACT. ONLY HUMANITY HAS THIS ABILITY TO BE SIMULTANEOUSLY CONNECTED AND DETACHED FROM ITS THOUGHTS AND ACTIONS. IT IS HERE THAT WE FEEL THE VIBRANCY OF BEING TRULY WIDE AWAKE AND AWARE.

HUMAN LEVEL

Soul

In the movie *Citizen Kane*, the one thing the successful businessman remembered on his death was his sled. The joy of racing downhill in the snow was the only time he had truly felt alive.

The Gevurah–Tiferet–Hesed triad is the soul triad or Neshamah, the place where we embrace our true humanity. In fairytales it is the point where Sleeping Beauty awakens with the kiss of Spirit. On Jacob's Ladder this triad stands alone between the physical and spiritual worlds. It is what makes each of us unique. Only at this level can we begin to face our destiny as opposed to being ruled by the fate of our family, tribe, or country. This is because of the ability of Tiferet to assess situations with judgment and compassion. People working at this level can observe the political and social climate around them and are strong enough to take evasive action if required. A person working at the soul level will be less concerned with physical possessions, job status or position, and the opinions of family and friends than someone working at a lower level. Mahatma Gandhi, Mother Teresa, and other people of destiny operate from this triad. However, this is also the place of human evil, where people act deliberately to cause harm in full knowledge that they are controlling and hurting others for their own aims. Hitler was working from the negative soul triad. If you wish to live your life from the human, soul level, you must understand the meaning of responsibility. This level carries great power and it can change the world.

MEDITATION ON THE SOUL TRIAD

✡ Taking this inner journey to the human level of our selves is a powerful way to work on inner discomforts and fears.

✡ Imagine yourself standing outside a house. This is the house of your psyche, the house that reflects your inner world. Take a good look at it. Is it in the kind of condition that you would like? Is it the kind of house that you want?

✡ Enter the front door, noting the hallway and the rooms to right and left and the condition that they are in. Climb the stairs. Are they wide, steep, safe, or dangerous? They represent the pathway from Yesod, your Ego to Tiferet, your Self. On the landing, look around you. There is a door right in front of you. Enter. This is your bedroom, the room of your secret self—your soul. Take a good look at this representation of the state of your soul.

✡ Now do whatever you need to do to make your soul chamber more comfortable and beautiful. Now leave the room. The rest of the house looks different. What are the changes?

✡ Leave the house and note the changes outside. Know that you can always return and that any time you do work on your soul level, it will filter through to the rest of your psyche and body.

THE SOUL TRIAD ON JACOB'S LADDER

In the soul triad we touch the worlds of Asiyyah and Beriah but are focused in Yezirah. Here we have free will.

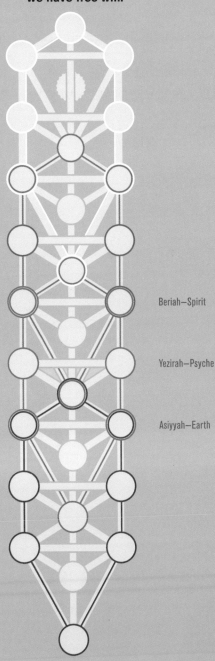

Beriah—Spirit

Yezirah—Psyche

Asiyyah—Earth

SPIRITUAL AND DIVINE LEVELS

✳ THE SPIRITUAL LEVEL OF THE TREE OF LIFE IS THE TRIAD OF TIFERET, BINAH, AND HOKHMAH. THE DIVINE LEVEL, OR SUPERNAL TRIAD, IS COMPOSED OF BINAH, KETER, AND HOKHMAH. THE SPIRITUAL LEVEL, KNOWN IN HEBREW AS THE RUAH, OR BREATH OF GOD, IS OUR DIRECT LINK TO HEAVEN.

SPIRITUAL AND DIVINE LEVELS

Divine

Spiritual

The spiritual triad is connected to the physical world by Tiferet, which is also the Keter of the Asiyyatic world, but mostly it is Spirit hovering over the psyche. Each person's perception of it is unique. The simplest way to describe the recognition of it is "awe." It is the deep inner knowledge of something that is much greater than us, almost inconceivable, but that also values us and our contribution to the world.

Something similar to this feeling can be felt by looking up at the star-filled night and understanding the vastness of space. Our place is integral to this incredible vista because at that moment of awe, God looks out through our eyes.

Right at the center of the spiritual triad is Da'at, the non-Sefira that is, in effect, an invisible door between worlds. It is through Da'at that you access the supernal triad in order to achieve union with the Divine.

These triads are the macrocosm of life, the larger picture or the transpersonal. They relate to things beyond the individual. They still have a profound effect on us; should one of the outer planets of the solar system explode, it would affect the whole balance of the system and the life of every single living thing.

THE SPIRITUAL AND DIVINE TRIADS

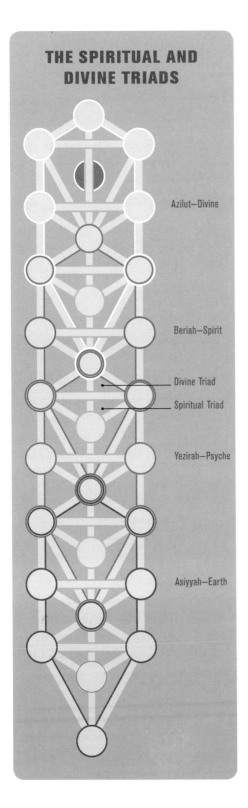

Azilut—Divine

Beriah—Spirit

Divine Triad

Spiritual Triad

Yezirah—Psyche

Asiyyah—Earth

MEDITATION: HOW TO TOUCH THE DIVINE

✡ You are in a garden, at the foot of some steps up to a small summerhouse surrounded by golden sunflowers. Climb the steps and you will see a lake on the other side. Moored nearby is a small boat, and you know that you must cross that lake. You climb into the boat, and it begins to move of its own accord, gliding onto the open water.

✡ It grows dark; you look up and see threatening rain clouds overhead. The heavens open. You are soaked. It is cold and miserable and you want to turn back.

✡ Gradually, the rain stops and you can see sunlight ahead. Even better, the boat is drawing ashore.

✡ You have reached moorland. You clamber out of the boat and feel bright sunlight drying you. Walk on, enjoying the feeling of the open air. Ahead of you is a white temple on a hill. Become aware of the scent of lilies. They cluster around the temple—great white flowers rising from a bed of tiny periwinkles, blue as the sky.

✡ Walk inside the temple; it is a place of soft, silvery light on white stone. This is the place where questions are answered. Close your eyes and form a question. Light streams around you and celestial voices whisper songs of glory in your ears. You are lifted upward, held by the lightest wings. Open your eyes to see the blue universe filled with stars. Up, up, up and there is only light. Light that is strength, love, understanding, and wisdom. You are before the throne of the Divine.

✡ You hear the voice: Be still and know that I am God.

✡ Ask your question.

✡ Hear the answer.

✡ Be still and know that I am God.

✡ The light lessens, the angelic touch draws you down into the great cosmic sky, through the universes and back down, down, down into the little temple on the moorland.

✡ Now it is time to go. You turn and, instead of the boat, you see a bridge over the lake and you walk over it easily. Soon you are back at the summerhouse surrounded by golden sunflowers and butterflies. You sit down in the house and contemplate what you have experienced.

THE LEVELS OF WILL

✳ THE FIVE TRIADS OF THE LOWER FACE OF THE TREE OF LIFE REPRESENT DIFFERENT LEVELS OF OUR WILLPOWER. AT THE SOUL LEVEL OF GEVURAH, TIFERET, AND HESED, WE HAVE FREE WILL AND A CHANCE TO CHANGE OUR DESTINY. ALL THE LOWER LEVELS OF WILL ARE CONSTRAINED IN SOME WAY. WE ARE NONE OF US ENTIRELY FOCUSED ON ONE OF THE TRIADS BUT WE CAN IDENTIFY WITH THE ONE THAT RULES US MOST FREQUENTLY.

Right: We learn that "I think therefore I am" but too much thinking can destroy us. Habitual thinking is a product of the lower triads.

WILL-LESSNESS

Hod–Yesod–Malkhut is the triad of will-lessness. People who identify with this triad may think a great deal but do very little about it. They will do anything for a quiet life and end up drifting through life, taking the path of least resistance—even to the extent of marrying their first boy or girlfriend because it is too much effort to look elsewhere. They may stay in a loveless relationship because it is too much effort to get divorced.

WILLFULNESS

Malkhut–Yesod–Nezach is the triad of will-fullness. The motto of people in this category is "me, me, me!" Willful people do what they want when they want, without caring what effect they have. They are not at the animal level because their wants are immediate and they have no higher goal than satisfaction in the now. Willful people often act before they think. They are often tactless and unwittingly selfish. We can be simultaneously will-less and willful in something such as dropping litter. We cannot be bothered to find a litter bin and we do not care that our action may inconvenience or upset others.

WILLINGNESS

Hod–Yesod–Nezach is the triad of willingness. This is the triad of the people who help to put the chairs away at the end of a meeting, wash up without being asked, and take out the garbage. However, as this triad is not connected to Malkhut, they are not very grounded. They may absorb every word of a book or workshop but they rarely act on it and soon they need another "fix" of inspiration. They often feel that they are in a kind of limbo without a direction of their own.

MY WILL

Hod–Tiferet–Nezach is the triad of "My Will." At first this appears very similar to Willfulness but it is more disciplined and has an aim rather than just immediate desires. It can be used in a purely animal manner to get to the top and be superior to others or it can be used for self-discovery. Positive "My Will" is the discovery of the Self. For most of us, the "My Will" stage of growth is the phase during which we find out who we really are and what we want from life as opposed to what we were always told we should want. This is also the level of real willpower where we are capable of making a decision and sticking with it.

CULTURAL EXPECTATIONS

Our levels of will are usually formed by the age of seven by the way we learn that we have to behave in order to win the love or attention we seek from our parents and peers. For a child, any attention is better than none.

THY WILL

The soul triad of Gevurah–Tiferet–Hesed represents "Thy Will" and it is the point where we are willing to hand over the power in our life to the Divine. This is not because we have to but because we finally understand that God knows the wider plan for our life and will direct us toward happiness and spiritual growth. The goal is to use our own willpower at Tiferet to simultaneously do what we judge to be "right" (Gevurah) and "merciful" (Hesed) but also to be open to spiritual influence and guidance through Da'at.

If you haven't developed your own willpower in the Hod–Tiferet–Nezach triad, then you cannot access this level, no matter how many workshops you attend or gurus you follow. You have to know who you really are before you can access the triad of the soul.

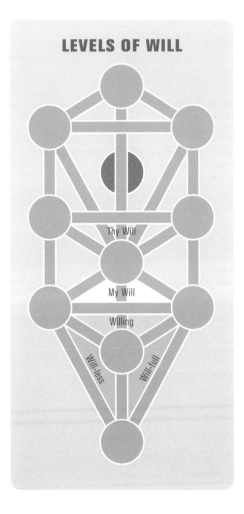

LEVELS OF WILL

Thy Will

My Will

Willing

Will-less   Will-full

TRIADS OF PAIN AND PLEASURE

✳ EITHER SIDE OF TIFERET THERE ARE TWO TRIADS THAT ARE UNIQUE TO EACH INDIVIDUAL. WE ARE ALL AFFECTED BY OUR GENETIC STRUCTURE AND LEARNED RESPONSES IN THE TRIADS BELOW TIFERET, BUT THESE SIDE TRIADS ARE WHERE WE HOLD OUR "HIDDEN" EMOTIONS OF PAIN AND PLEASURE. THESE HAVE A GREAT INFLUENCE ON OUR DECISION-MAKING PROCESSES.

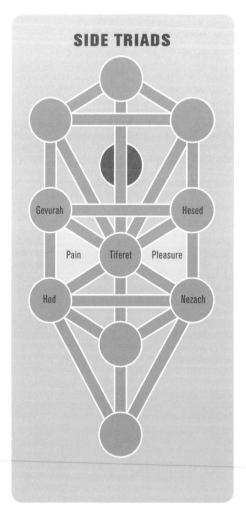

SIDE TRIADS

The triad of Gevurah–Tiferet–Hod is the place of fear and pain, while the triad of Tiferet–Hesed–Nezach is the place of pleasure and expansion. These, however, are not the passing emotions of the lower triad of feeling: Hod–Yesod–Nezach. Those are ruled by the reaction of the psyche and the body to internal and external physical stimuli. While those feelings are powerful, like the passion of falling in love, their intensity does not endure; it is the deeper connections that hold the relationship together.

Many first-time soldiers and pilots die swiftly in war situations because they react to the instant fear in the feeling triad without the depth of experience that comes from previous combat. However, good judgment (Gevurah) could hold them in position, despite that fear, until a time when it would be safe to run or attack. Those disciplined enough to be able to operate from the Gevuric level from the start generally survive.

SIDE TRIADS

The side triads operate from deep psychological programming, often caused by trauma. The left-hand triad is focused on the need to hold back

MEDITATION: HOW TO DISCERN THE STRENGTH OF THE SIDE TRIADS

In your mind, return to the house of your psyche (*see page 91*) and to the room of your soul. In the room is a desk, with a mirror and drawers on either side. Sit at the desk. Open the drawer to your left and take out an object. Place it on the desk in front of you. This object represents the emotional triad of pain. What is it? Do you recognize it? What emotions does it bring out? Now open the drawer to your right and remove another object. Place it on the desk in front of you. This object represents the emotional triad of pleasure. What is it? Do you recognize it? What emotions do you feel? Which of the two objects pulls you the most emotionally?

Replace the objects in the drawers and close them. Now focus strongly on your heart in the center of your body and repeat to yourself, "balance, balance." Smile—both in your mind and physically—and in your mind, open your eyes and look at the image in the mirror before you. What do you see? If it is a clear image of you, you are balanced. If it is a fierce image, you may be overbalanced toward pain; if it is a beautiful, angelic image, you may be overfocused toward pleasure. Leave the room, come back down the stairs, go out of the house, and open your eyes.

to limit suffering and the right-hand side on the urge to grow, improve, and perfect the Self. The left-hand triad keeps us safe in times of danger but can also cause paralysis that prevents us from developing. The right-hand triad is our wish to grow but can lead to carelessness over one's responsibilities.

These triads are programmed by our astrological blueprint together with any deep emotional experiences we have in life. Abuse or abandonment will program the Hod–Tiferet–Gevurah triad with fear of such situations and may impede commitment in any relationship. To be overloved and admired will program the Tiferet–Hesed–Nezach triad to seek constant approval and pleasure, even if it means jumping from one new relationship to the next instead of assessing what has gone wrong previously.

Above left: The tarot card of The Lovers reflects the possibilities of pain or pleasure in relationships and other areas of life. The couple are overlooked by the soul that can make conscious decisions.

Above: Religious teaching may program the triad of pain with the concept of "original sin," leading to guilt in the feminine and resentment in the masculine.

TRIADS OF RELIGION AND PHILOSOPHY

✳ OUR RELIGIOUS BELIEFS AND OUR PHILOSOPHY ARE REPRESENTED IN THE UPPER TRIADS OF TIFERET–GEVURAH–BINAH AND OF TIFERET–HOKHMAH–HESED. EVEN THOUGH WE MAY THINK THAT WE HAVE NO RELIGION OR THAT WE HAVE CHOSEN OUR OWN SYSTEM OF FAITH, THESE TRIADS CARRY AN UNCONSCIOUS IMPRINT.

Whatever spiritual beliefs that we may have experienced or learned about, the religion of our birth will be lodged in the right-hand triad and those strategies that we adopt on how life can best be lived will be lodged in the left-hand triad. Our religion is based on the teaching we have received on how we can best access God, whereas our philosophy is based on the ideas and principles that structure our life-path.

Of course, religion can be very restrictive and philosophy very freeing. For some people the triads may appear to be reversed but the basic principle is that the right-hand one is a source of revelation and the left-hand one is a source of structure.

An inspirational teacher can program the right-hand triad in a way that will cause us to seek spiritual joy throughout our life—although equally, the experience of a teacher

Left: Pythagoras (569–475 BCE) founded a philosophical and religious school in southern Italy called the Mathematikoi. They had no personal possessions, were vegetarians and believed that philosophy could be used for spiritual purification and that the soul could rise to union with the Divine.

TRIADS OF RELIGION AND PHILOSOPHY

MEDITATION: HOW TO DISCERN YOUR HIDDEN PREJUDICES

Imagine that you are seeking a teacher, a guru—someone who will help you to realize your inner truths and find enlightenment.

In your mind's eye, see a hillside with a path that leads up to a cottage. What kind of cottage is it? You know that there is a teacher there who may be able to help you. You open the gate and go up to the front door and knock. Someone opens it and you feel drawn to the person immediately. What does she (or he) look like? How is she dressed?

She invites you in and gives you a hot drink. You look around her home and like what you see. You talk and you feel comfortable with this person. She is certainly very wise. You tell her that you want to visit the higher realms and learn more about Spirit and she nods and smiles.

"Let's take a little trip," the teacher says. "I want to show you something."

You get up and go outside the house to the back. Your teacher turns toward a garage and opens it by remote control to reveal a sleek, brand new, Aston Martin.

"Come on!" says your teacher, opening the door and climbing into the driver's seat.

How do you feel? What is your reaction to this evidence of wealth in one so spiritual? You will have one of several possible reactions:

1 Outrage
2 Disappointment
3 Delight
4 Disbelief
5 Indifference

Each of these is caused by the belief system in your religion and philosophy triads about spirituality and wealth. Those of us raised in the Christian tradition have been taught that Jesus of Nazareth is poor, that it is virtuous to be like him, and that you have to work hard and suffer for money. Another belief is that money is evil, and that the Vatican is corrupt because of its wealth. Those raised in the Jewish and Islamic traditions generally have fewer issues about money as Islam has strong laws that forbid interest to be paid on loans, and Jewish people have been responsible for handling money for others for many centuries.

These deep-held philosophies were expressed around you all of your childhood and, unless you work consciously to release them, will color your entire life.

from eternal hell can influence the left-hand triad to make us live our lives in fear of damnation. We know by now that none of these triads are exclusively "good" or "bad" and it is equally true that a religion may cause great harm or great good and that a strong philosophy can lead to stoic lack of action or make sense of difficult times. The Spanish Inquisition and any kind of religious fundamentalism come from an imbalanced religious triad while the scientific view that only physical proof can be valid comes from an imbalanced philosophy triad.

PART FOUR

PRACTICAL
KABBALAH

PART FOUR

PRACTICAL KABBALAH

THE WORK OF THE KABBALIST IS TO PROVIDE BALANCE WHEREVER POSSIBLE;

KABBALISTS CAN WORK WITHIN ANY SPECIFIC RELIGION OR THOUGHT-SYSTEM

AND OFFER A BALANCING, UNDERSTANDING, DISCERNING, OR MERCIFUL

WORD WHEREVER ONE IS NEEDED. MOST KABBALISTS ARE "STEALTH PRIESTS,"

ATTEMPTING TO WORK FOR GOOD IN THE WORLD WITHOUT BEING VISIBLE.

THEY DO THE WORK FOR THE LOVE OF IT. YOU CAN EITHER BE A KABBALIST

WITH AN INTEREST IN HEALING, WRITING, MEDICINE, RESEARCH, OR ANY OTHER

PROFESSION, OR YOU CAN BE A HEALER, WRITER, DOCTOR, OR RESEARCHER

WITH AN INTEREST IN KABBALAH. AT SOME STAGE, A COMMITMENT IS CALLED

FOR, AND THIS IS OFTEN WHEN YOU FIND THAT UNDERSTANDING KABBALAH

HAS ENABLED YOU TO LIVE THE LIFE YOU ALWAYS WANTED TO LIVE. KABBALAH

CAN APPEAR TO BE COMPLICATED AND THEORETICAL AT FIRST BUT IF YOU ARE

DOING IT RIGHT, IT WORKS.

CHAPTER SEVEN
EXPERIENCING THE TREE OF LIFE

✳ THEORY IS AN IMPORTANT PART OF KABBALAH, BUT EXPERIENCE OF HOW IT WORKS AND HOW IT FEELS IS VITAL IN ORDER TO UNDERSTAND THE INFORMATION. BECAUSE THE TREE OF LIFE IS A UNIVERSAL MATRIX, IT CAN BE USED BOTH TO IDENTIFY AND CORRECT ISSUES WITHIN US.

Right: In this mystical interpretation of the Tree of Life, Z'ev ben Shimon Halevi shows the four elements existing in the physical world and a human being both invoking and experiencing the higher worlds while remaining grounded on Earth.

Meditation on the Tree of Life is surprisingly simple. First choose a picture of the Yeziratic Tree that you like (it is best to paint one yourself—see chapter 8). If possible, hang the picture on the wall in front of your chair or prop it up so that you can see it clearly.

Sit and make yourself comfortable. Look at the picture until you can see a negative image of it in your eyelids when you close your eyes. Then imagine that you are able to open a circular door that covers the whole of the Sefira of Malkhut, as if it were a cupboard.

What do you see in there? Is the cupboard neat and tidy or dirty and full of rubbish? This will tell you the state of your physical body. However, don't worry if the image is terrible. It doesn't mean that you are sick; it is simply your psyche giving you a gentle message that a little clearing up in life is a good idea. The psyche is not subtle in these matters!

If you are not happy with the contents of the cupboard, imagine yourself clearing it out (and imagine a special trash can where you can put the trash to be taken away). When you have finished, close the door, open your eyes, and look at Malkhut on the physical image in front of you.

Say to that Sefira, "Be cleansed, be whole, be healthy, be balanced." Now look at the whole Tree again until you can see the image on your closed eyes and repeat the process at Yesod.

Continue this process with Hod, Nezach, Tiferet, Gevurah, Hesed, Binah, Hokhmah, and Keter. Pass over Da'at because this non-Sefira is a passageway to other worlds and not a cupboard!

HOW TO USE THIS MEDITATION

This meditation works because it reveals to you any messages that your inner consciousness may want you to hear and it gives clear instructions, from your Tiferet, to these areas to sort themselves out. Strangely enough, consciousness is one of the greatest healing forces there is. If you repeatedly tell your body and psyche that they are to be well, your Yesod (foundation) subconsciously learns to look for methods of healing that will aid this process.

REAL-LIFE EXAMPLES

One Kabbalist, whose astrological chart and upbringing gave her a strong tendency toward paranoia in her psyche, often saw pictures of boilers hissing steam at Tiferet. In her case it was not a physical problem but a need to express some unresolved anger over feeling put down. However, another Kabbalist, who had no incipient paranoia and had clean, clear Sefirot, saw a similar image at Hod and went to his doctor for a checkup. The doctor was able to warn him that his blood pressure had gone up significantly since he changed jobs and it was time for him to slow down at work.

Here again, it is important not to become unduly concerned about any very negative images you may perceive. If you find that certain images persist over several mediations, it is certainly an issue that should be addressed, but it does not automatically mean that you are physically sick (see panel, below left). With practice and armed with the knowledge of the information that you carry in your side triads of pain and pleasure, you will be able to interpret what you see appropriately.

Below: Ezekiel's vision, which is the basis for Kabbalistic meditation, is a complex and confusing series of images for the beginner. In any visualization there will be a personal element that speaks only to the individual soul and not everyone can expect to see angels, thrones, chariots, or great beings in their attempts to rise up through the worlds.

FROM CONCEPTION TO THE BIRTH OF A BABY

✳ THE TREE OF THE PSYCHE IS A BLUEPRINT OF A PERFECT HUMAN BEING,

LINKED ABOVE TO THE SPIRITUAL AND DIVINE WORLDS AND BELOW TO THE

PHYSICAL BODY. WHEN IT COMES TO PHYSICAL CONCEPTION AND BIRTH, THE

TWO SIDES OF THE TREE HAVE TO WORK IN HARMONY IN BOTH THE YEZIRATIC

AND ASIYYATIC WORLDS IN ORDER TO PRODUCE A HEALTHY CHILD.

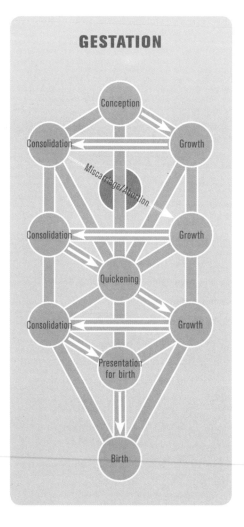

GESTATION

FIRST TRIMESTER

Da'at is the place of spontaneous abortion. If the balance of growth and consolidation between Hokhmah and Binah malfunctions during the first three months after conception, the fetus will either thrive or die. This does not hurt the soul, which at this time is only tentatively attached to its body. Should such a miscarriage (or abortion) occur, the soul will generally wait for a more suitable vessel to be formed or, if there is no further possibility of conception between that couple, move to another.

The potential for a baby begins in the supernal triad of the Yeziratic world. Here is where the masculine impulse (Hokhmah) embraces the feminine impulse (Binah). A spark from Keter then crosses the abyss of Da'at, down to the Keter of the Asiyyatic world where the physical sperm (Hokhmah) has met the egg (Binah). Conception occurs when the first link is made with the soul of the baby, which is still in the divine world of Azilut.

It is in the Keter of the physical world and also the Tiferet of the psychological world and the Malkhut of the divine world where the "I Am" of the human soul defines the growth of this particular child. Drawing on the energies of the Asiyyatic Hokhmah (also the Yeziratic Nezach), it imprints the egg with the essence and the genetic structure of this human being. At that point, Hokhmah's impulse begins to multiply cells in their millions, inspiring the first growth. Binah (also the Yeziratic Hod) then adds structure, defining sex, color, and build and formulating the cells.

THE GROWING FETUS

If the fetus survives, it begins to grow in earnest at Hesed, simultaneously balanced by Gevurah. This Sefira sees to the differentiation of the growing cells into three main categories: entoderm, mesoderm, and ectodermentoderm (digestion), mesoderm (muscles, tissues, connective tissue, and bone), and ectoderm (skin, brain, and spinal column). If this balance is incorrect, such results as Down's Syndrome or spina bifida may occur.

At Tiferet, where the spiritual, psychological, and physical worlds meet, the baby's lungs develop, making it capable of sustaining life should it be born early. The baby can be felt moving and kicking in the womb.

At Nezach, the baby's brain is growing rapidly, developing billions of new nerve cells; its bone marrow is producing its own red blood cells, and the baby will double and then triple its size. At Hod, muscle mass and fat stores consolidate, and the baby is sensitive to sound and light. Its eyes can now open and shut. At Yesod, the finishing touches are complete, including the process of storing iron in the baby's liver and waste products that will be excreted during the first bowel functions. The baby "drops" in the uterus to present itself ready for birth at Malkhut.

Above, left: Every soul is eternally linked to Azilut, the divine world. In this image, the Divine is depicted as the all-seeing eye of God watching over the physical world. It is only in the physical world that we are able to experience death.

Above: We are all familiar with the concept of a guardian angel who guides us throughout life. In this image of Tobias and the angel, the angelic figure is Raphael, the angel of communication and healing.

HUMAN GROWTH FROM BIRTH TO DEATH

✳ EVERY HUMAN SOUL IS ON A QUEST OF SELF-KNOWLEDGE THAT WILL
EVENTUALLY TAKE IT HOME TO THE DIVINE WORLD OF AZILUT. ONCE A BABY IS
BORN, THE RETURN JOURNEY BEGINS. THE BASIC FORMAT OF THIS CAN BE SEEN
IN THE LEVELS OF DEVELOPMENT OF A HUMAN BEING FROM BIRTH TO DEATH.

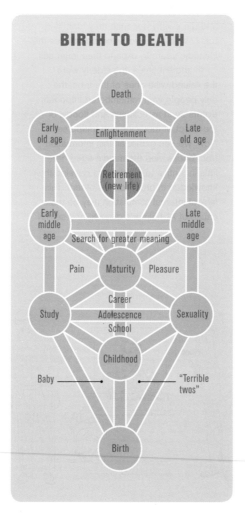

BIRTH TO DEATH

- Death
- Early old age
- Enlightenment
- Late old age
- Retirement (new life)
- Early middle age
- Search for greater meaning
- Late middle age
- Pain
- Maturity
- Pleasure
- Career
- Study
- Adolescence
- School
- Sexuality
- Childhood
- Baby
- "Terrible twos"
- Birth

The newborn baby's physical and psychological development begins at the point of birth, at Malkhut. From here it develops through the triads around Yesod, firstly the triad of will-lessness (Hod–Yesod–Malkhut), where it is completely helpless and only able to express its desires through crying and, later, smiling. From there it moves to the triad of willfulness (Malkhut–Yesod–Nezach), where it tries to take what it wants and explores the world around it with no thought of danger or the needs of others. Often this stage is known as "the terrible twos" because it is at its height at about age two to three.

CHILDHOOD

The third triad, willingness (Hod–Yesod–Nezach), is the desire of the young child to learn; at this point it is like a sponge taking in everything that it is taught, as well as the emotional patterns of its parents, teachers, and siblings. The Sefira of Hod is the age of approximately seven to puberty, when there is a refining of the information that is sought. During this period, children may become passionately attached to facts about dinosaurs or horses; there is a focus to their desire to learn.

Nezach is heralded by the flood of hormones that precede puberty, and from then on the desire to impress and be regarded as attractive becomes paramount. In ancient times, when we lived in hunting tribes, the Hod–Nezach times were used to teach youngsters the discipline of the hunt and how to feed the tribe. There were ceremonies to mark the onset of puberty, and a distinct purpose set out for each soul. The lack of recognition of status or training for life nowadays is often the reason for teenage depression and the self-created ceremonies of shoplifting and mischief.

ADULTHOOD

Maturity—the time of marriage and starting a family—is at Tiferet. Here the soul is capable of being balanced in the psyche and supervising the physical world below (both its own and the new life it creates).

Gevurah is the place of early middle age and a time for consolidation. Perhaps you become the boss or run your own company, and at home you may have your own teenagers to deal with. At this point a "mid-life crisis" can occur when an individual wishes to return to a more carefree time with fewer commitments.

Hesed is late middle age, a time for expanding one's own beliefs and hobbies.

Da'at is the experience of retirement, moving out of the routine. Ideally, Binah is the place of the wise and knowledgable mentor or grandparent who peacefully assesses his or her own life while advising others. Hokhmah is extreme old age, when the soul may even live between worlds, allowing the body to fall away in peaceful acceptance of death.

DEATH AND ILLNESS

Sometimes, people reach retirement and die swiftly because they identified totally with their work and do not use the Hesedic years to expand their inner self.

In ancient times, the elderly were the valued wise ones of the tribe, the only people who remembered important events such as eclipses and floods, or the effect of medicine and antidotes. Now, we can gather all this information from books, and the middle-aged have little incentive to continue to develop their knowledge in order to help others. This lack of internal stimulation may be the cause of Alzheimer's disease and senility.

A child is open to all knowledge but as we grow older we have to learn consciously or we become stuck in our ways.

PLANNING A PROJECT ON THE TREE OF LIFE

✳ PLANNING A PROJECT ON THE TREE OF LIFE IS A MOST EFFECTIVE BUSINESS STRATEGY. IT ENSURES THAT ALL ASPECTS OF THE PLAN ARE CONSIDERED AND IMPLEMENTED. OFTEN A PROJECT FAILS BECAUSE THE ATTRIBUTES OF ONE OR MORE OF THE SEFIROT HAS BEEN OMITTED—WHETHER OR NOT THE PERSON PLANNING THE PROJECT IS A KABBALIST.

TREE OF A BUSINESS

In fact, Kabbalists make excellent strategists for business because they have valuable insight into which areas of a company or its plans may be incomplete or overemphasized.

Where people sit at a board meeting in relation to the chairman or managing director tells you a lot about their attitude to the company, its products, and plans. Those who sit above

CORPORATE STRUCTURE

This is how the members of a company relate to the Tree of Life:

✡ The chairman is at Keter
✡ The creative team—Hokhmah
✡ The strategists—Binah
✡ The sales team—Hesed
✡ The analysts—Gevurah
✡ The managing director—Tiferet
✡ The marketing team—Nezach
✡ The accountants—Hod
✡ The receptionists—Yesod
✡ The product is Malkhut.

Tiferet are generally in tune with the company's goals and those below are either more involved with implementation or, in negative aspects, are not interested in the company.

This tree of a project is focused on setting up a one-day seminar but it can be adapted for anything from building a boat to writing a book.

Keter is the source of the idea or project. It is the sum total of the knowledge and experience of the project leader. Hokhmah is the inspiration itself—the idea to run a seminar on Feng Shui. Binah then assesses the thought. Do you have enough experience and confidence to do this? Are you living it and demonstrating it in your own life? At this stage, the idea either gets lost in the abyss of Da'at (often overnight) or it begins to grow.

Hesed provides the impulse and enthusiasm for the idea and gets you going, talking to other people about it, making preliminary plans for what you would do and how it might go, and considering a venue. Gevurah works in tandem with Hesed, reining it back when it thinks about expanding it into a three-day workshop instead of a one-day introduction, and making checks on your qualifications and insurance. It asks: what limits do you need to set on numbers, booking dates, and the range of participants? Are you really sure you can do it?

Tiferet is the point when the workshop becomes a viable event. You make the final decision on the title, date, and content and you book the venue. At Nezach you design and send out the brochures or flyers, talk to those who might be interested in coming, and make the seminar appear as attractive as you can.

At Hod, you assess the reaction. Are people interested? Do they want to learn from you?

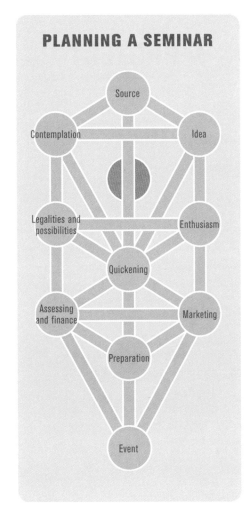

PLANNING A SEMINAR

Source

Contemplation — Idea

Legalities and possibilities — Enthusiasm

Quickening

Assessing and finance — Marketing

Preparation

Event

Are the numbers sufficient? When should you close the doors? Should you cancel? Yesod is the final stage of preparation and also a time to assess the plans according to feedback and how you feel about the seminar. Perhaps you need to re-present the workshop to attract different people? This is where you prepare the hand-outs, arrange for the chairs to be in place, and provide the participants with directions, instructions on what to bring, and where they can eat. Malkhut is the workshop itself taking place.

THE HOUSE OF THE PSYCHE

✳ YOU HAVE ALREADY VISITED YOUR HOUSE OF THE PSYCHE TO EXAMINE YOUR SOUL TRIAD AND THE TRIADS OF PAIN AND PLEASURE (*SEE PAGE 91*). HOWEVER, THIS CONCEPT ALSO HELPS YOU TO SEE HOW ALL THE LEVELS OF THE TREE OF LIFE OPERATE WITHIN YOU. YOUR HOUSE REPRESENTS HOW YOUR LIFE IS AT ALL LEVELS.

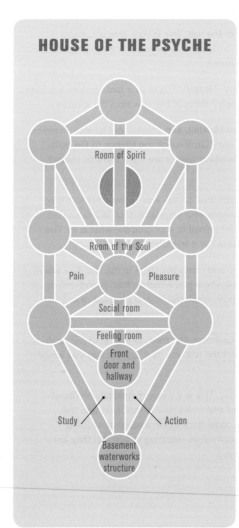

HOUSE OF THE PSYCHE

Room of Spirit

Room of the Soul

Pain   Pleasure

Social room

Feeling room

Front door and hallway

Study   Action

Basement waterworks structure

Right: The human mind is associated with the brain. However, it has many unacknowledged aspects that can only be revealed to us by internal journeys, where we can disconnect our circuits of logic and reasoning.

One word of warning: if your house is picture perfect from end to end you are not centered in Tiferet and your Yesod is hiding the truth from you. Try again.

When carrying out this practice, begin by viewing your house from a hillside and note whether it is in a town or city (you are socially oriented), in the country (you enjoy your own company or love the outdoors), by the ocean (you have strong emotions), or in a desert (you are strongly intellectual but overdetached from real life).

VISITING YOUR INTERIOR HOUSE

Close your eyes and imagine yourself approaching the house. Find out whether it is easy to get there or whether you isolate yourself. Once outside the house, walk around it in the following order.

✡ Malkhut is the outside of the house. Its design, sign, and state of repair indicates your physical self-image.

✡ Yesod is the door and the hallway. Is the door strong and sound (indicating solid boundaries) or flimsy and broken? Is the hallway (your persona) welcoming and representative of how you want the world to see you?

✡ Hod–Yesod–Malkhut is a room to the left of the hall. This is your study, the place of your thought processes where you read, contemplate, and write letters. Is it big or small, tidy or scruffy? Is there a library or a neglected empty space?

✡ Nezach–Yesod–Malkhut is a room to the right of the hall. This is your area of action, perhaps a studio. Here you dance or work out or do another physical activity. Is it well used and in good condition? What do you do here?

✡ At the end of the hall is a third room: Hod–Yesod–Nezach. This is your feeling room, a private sitting room. Is it furnished comfortably or sparsely? What is the view from the window?

✡ Go downstairs to the kitchen, another aspect of Malkhut, and check it out for size, facilities, and functionality. Is it clean? What is the food like? Go through the kitchen to the boiler room and look at all the equipment there. Is it working well or are there leaks or steam? Check the lavatory next to it too.

✡ Now go out to the garden, checking out the trash area on the way. Is this tidy? Is it filled with trash? Is it overflowing? The garden represents your vegetable soul. Is it cultivated or wild and neglected? Is it polluted? You see an animal in your garden—what is it? This represents your animal soul. Is it powerful or weak? Is it friendly or hostile?

✡ Go back into the house, go through the hallway and climb the stairs to the first floor where you find your social room (Hod–Tiferet–Nezach) where you entertain friends and colleagues. How many people can you fit in here? Is it friendly, comfortable, and pleasant or is it imposing, or much too small?

✡ From here, take another flight of steps to your bedroom, the room of your soul (Gevurah–Tiferet–Hesed). This is a room that should reflect the real you. Is it just the way you would like it to be?

✡ Now climb the final set of stairs to your sanctuary. This is a place of meditation (Tiferet–Binah–Hokhmah). Here you can sit in your mind and make your communion with the Divine. Once you have spent time in this room come back down through the rooms, making whatever changes you would like, and commit to returning to see that they are carried out. Leave your house and open your eyes.

EXERCISE: MAKING THE TREE OF LIFE WITH YOUR BODY

✳ MAKING THE TREE OF LIFE WITH YOUR BODY IS AN ACTIVE MEDITATION THAT RAISES YOUR CONSCIOUSNESS AND BALANCES YOUR BODY. THE MOVEMENTS REPRESENT CLIMBING THE TREE WHILE FOCUSING ON THE MIDDLE PILLAR.

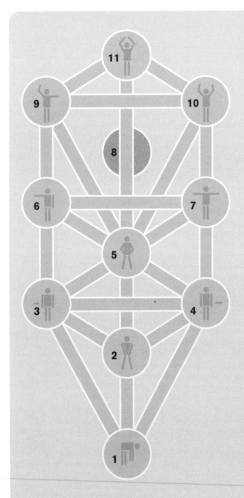

GOING UP THE TREE
Follow this exercise facing toward the Tree of Life.

1 **Malkhut:** Begin by standing and leaning down as if you are going to touch your toes. Relax and let your torso hang loosely.

2 **Yesod:** Stand up in a relaxed way with your hands clasped below your stomach.

3 **Hod:** Sway onto your left foot and maintain your weight there (the arrow indicates the direction).

4 **Nezach:** Sway onto your right foot and maintain your weight there (the arrow indicates the direction).

5 **Tiferet:** Stand up straight and tall with hands linked at your solar plexus.

6 **Gevurah:** Extend your left arm out at shoulder level, keeping your right hand on your solar plexus.

7 **Hesed:** Extend your right arm out at shoulder level, keeping the left arm at the Gevurah position.

8 **Da'at:** Raise your head to look upward.

9 **Binah:** Raise your left arm (at the angle shown in the diagram) keeping your right arm at Hesed.

10 **Hokhmah:** Raise your right arm, keeping your left arm at Binah.

11 **Keter:** Put your hands together in the prayer position above your head. When you are ready, draw your hands down to Tiferet, still in the prayer position and lower your head to face forward.

The exercise can be used to prepare you for prayer, meditation, or a particular event. It can help you to open up to seeing an answer to a problem or be used as a physical and psychological stretching exercise. It can also be used to ground you if you are feeling spaced out, overexcited, or overtired.

Follow the instructions, saying the name of the Sefira either to yourself or out loud at each stage. You can do this as slowly or as swiftly as you wish. Note which Sefirot are comfortable and which are uncomfortable; this will tell you much about your own inner balance. (The exercise should be done standing up, but if you have to sit down it can be performed symbolically through thought for the lower Sefirot.)

When you reach Da'at you may prefer to close your eyes and look inward for a moment, as a symbol of moving between worlds. If there is a particular problem that you are facing in your life, this would be a good time to offer up a prayer for resolution in the matter.

GOING DOWN THE TREE

1   **Keter:** Begin with your hands in the prayer position above your head, looking upward.

2   **Hokhmah:** Lower your right arm, keeping the left arm at Keter.

3   **Binah:** Lower your left arm, keeping the right arm at Hokhmah.

4   **Da'at:** Lower your head to face straight forward.

5   **Hesed:** Lower your right arm, keeping the left arm at Binah.

6   **Gevurah:** Lower your left arm, keeping your right arm at Hesed.

7   **Tiferet:** Draw both arms in to link at the solar plexus.

8   **Nezach:** Lean onto your right foot, keeping your hands at Tiferet (the arrow indicates the direction).

9   **Hod:** Lean onto your left foot, keeping your hands at Tiferet (the arrow indicates the direction).

10 **Yesod:** Lower your hands to below your stomach.

11 **Malkhut:** Bend down from the hips to relax your body and ground it.

CHAPTER EIGHT
DRAWING THE TREE OF LIFE

✳ SINCE THE TREE OF LIFE IS YOUR OWN PERSONAL BLUEPRINT, DRAWING IT BY HAND SHOWS THE STATE OF YOUR PSYCHE AT THAT TIME. BY REDRAWING THE TREE WITH COMPASSES AND RULERS, YOU SEND A DIRECT MESSAGE TO YOUR PSYCHE, BODY, AND SOUL TO AMEND ANY AREAS THAT ARE "OUT OF SYNC" OR IMBALANCED. THIS IS WONDERFULLY THERAPEUTIC.

It may seem oversimplistic to say that by drawing a specific diagram you can interpret your own state of mind, soul, and Spirit, but this practice has been used by therapists and advisors for centuries. They would ask a client or petitioner to copy an image of the Tree. From the lines that they missed out, the spacing between Sefirot, the relative sizes of the Sefirot, and any smudges or mistakes made, they would be able to tell what kinds of problems the person faced in life. Self-assessment is simple, as long as you are honest with yourself.

BASIC PRINCIPLES

An overlarge Sefira means overemphasis on that aspect of the psyche. If Hesed is larger than Gevurah, you may have problems saying "no" to other people. If Yesod is larger than Tiferet, your Ego tends to overrule you. If you forget Da'at then you tend to close your mind to spiritual impulses either through disbelief or fear of what you might hear, see, or sense.

A missed pathway means that there is no contact between those Sefirot so there is a level of your mind or soul that is not communicating successfully with another.

For example, no pathway between Hod and Nezach means that you find it difficult to find your place in society because your boundaries are blurred. You take everything that others say very personally and often feel put upon. You may also not be able to relate to either intellectual people or sexual people, according to whatever else is going on in your diagram.

Pathways that poke into Sefirot also mean an issue with boundaries; for example, perhaps you push yourself or others too far in certain areas. Pathways pushing into Binah mean that you are trying too hard and too soon to be the wise person, when more relaxation and time are needed.

PRACTICALITIES

It is important to remember, however, that none of us is perfect and that it is perfectly normal to have a slightly unbalanced Tree. The main principle is to ensure that all the links and Sefirot are in place. Also, remember that the Tree you draw reflects you at that exact moment so you may draw a very different one tomorrow.

Sefirot that are broken or unfinished point to issues in that aspect of your life. The way you can assess these is by drawing a mini-tree inside that Sefira and see where the boundary is incomplete. For example, a hole or overlap at the Gevurah of Nezach implies a lack of discrimination over sexual partners or a tendency to "shop till you drop." A break or overlap at the Hod of Hesed could mean that you cannot evaluate the effect of your kindness

TREE NO. 1

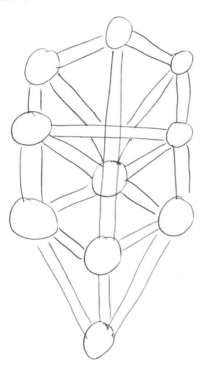 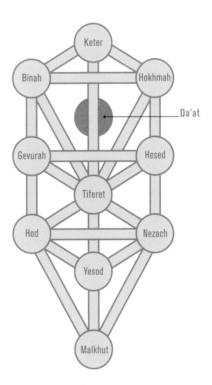

This person is a Thinker. The Sefira of Hod is larger than any of the others—but there is a gap in its linking path to Malkhut (where things become real), which means that theory is more important than practice.

They may be quite judgmental—Gevurah is about twice the size of Hesed and the left-hand pillar is far wider than the right-hand one.

The artist here has left out two horizontal paths and eliminated the non-Sefira Da'at entirely. At the top there is no linking path from Binah to Hokhmah so the person may find it hard to understand the concept of revelation or inspiration—or indeed any aspect of the higher worlds. Their spiritual triad is merged into the soul triad, demonstrating no consciousness of a difference between the two.

Tiferet, too, is overruled by the central column, indicating an impatience with the processes of life and with the Ego wishing to overrule the Self. This is exacerbated by that lack of a line between Hod and Nezach, implying that this person is not in touch with their feelings, even riding over them roughshod.

The thicker line between Malkhut and Nezach and the gap noticeable in the pathway between Nezach and Hesed imply strong sexual impulses but a reluctance to commit to love. There may be a love–hate relationship with sexuality.

on others and are secretly resentful. Perhaps you take no notice of information about how to carry out voluntary work but do it your own way.

If there is an area of your Tree that is broken or forgotten, the way to begin amending this is to fill it in, consciously. Do this either with a ruler or compass (though that may make the rest of the Tree look odd) or start again and make a more balanced Tree. It is hard to explain how profound an effect this will have internally.

TREE NO. 2

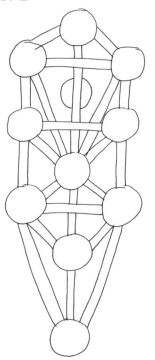
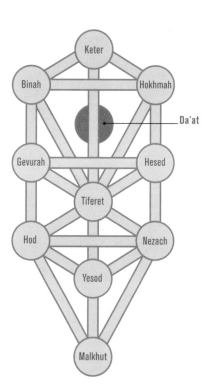

An introspective person who, nevertheless, is practical and who likes to see proof before they believe in anything (wide path between Hod and Malkhut). Possibly an artist or designer capable of strong feelings and emotions (lower three triads are large as are the side triads). Philosophy/science is more important than belief, which is seen as limiting or hard (the Tiferet–Hokhmah–Hesed triad is much smaller than its counterpart).

Da'at is left the same color as the other Sefirot indicating either a lack of willingness to embrace the idea of higher worlds or an innocence of anything real beyond reality.

Binah is broken into by the path from Keter, so there may be an inherent teaching, from a childhood faith/religion that you don't try to understand God/higher worlds or perhaps he or she was taught that God is not to be questioned.

The person may have been hurt in love— Hesed appears pulled in as in constricted by either pain or a difficult belief system.

The overall impression is that there has been emotional or physical pain here that is, on the surface, shrugged off.

TREE NO. 3

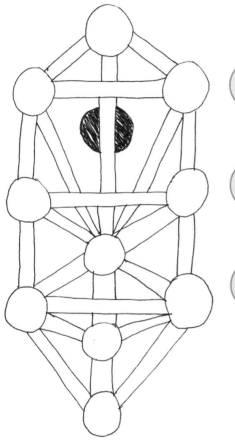

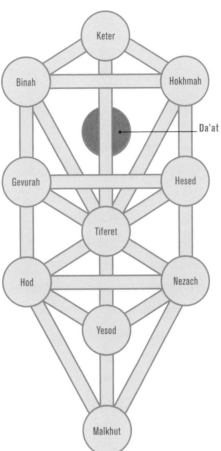

The bottom half of the Tree here is very compressed. This person appears exhausted (these areas depict physical energy), but they are also a "rock"—look at the strength and width of the paths from Malkhut to Yesod and from Yesod to Tiferet. The equivalent width of the path from Hod across Tiferet to Hesed as compared to a much thinner one from Gevurah through Tiferet to Nezach indicates that they take their sense of Self from how much help and guidance they can give to others. There may be ill-health from exhaustion and an insistence on being the rock for other people instead of taking good care of the true Self.

The strong emphasis on Da'at and the powerful supernal triad indicate a strong faith of some kind, but again it does not feed the Self as the paths become very narrow when they reach Tiferet: rather, the belief serves to make the person a pillar of the community.

More time needs to be taken for relaxation, and to allow perfectly natural feelings to surface. These are currently repressed (between Hod, Nezach, and Yesod) and may well have been repressed for a very long time. This is a good person—but they need to learn to be kinder to themselves.

TREE NO. 4

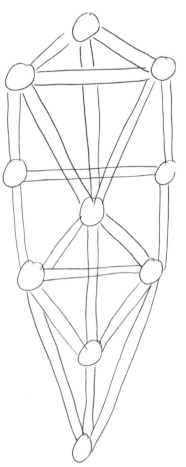

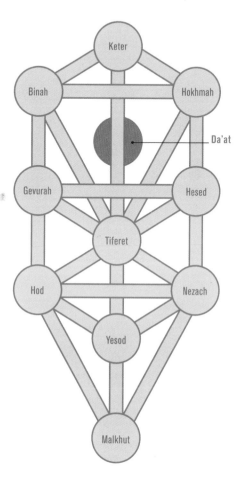

No soul triad and no Da'at. This person is most probably either an atheist or refers more to their religion than to the idea of God itself. There is a strong pathway from Keter to Hokhmah (revelation/inspiration) but the links between Hokhmah and Keter and Binah (understanding) have spaces—so there is no individual understanding of what is being taught or received from the higher worlds.

Religion and philosophy are strong—overruling the path between Hesed and Gevurah, implying that the person's individual development is not seen as being important. Similarly, the path between Tiferet and Yesod overrules the path between Hod and Nezach. This, in Jungian psychology, is known as the "liminal line" or the beginning of consciousness.

The Sefira of Tiferet is broken into by the paths from Hokhmah and Binah, neither of which path is complete. So a partially understood truth has been taken in but not examined in any depth; rather taken as gospel.

This person is capable of deep emotion—possibly sometimes overwhelmingly so. Both the side triads are open to the spiritual triad, which can lead to feelings of either almost unbearable pain or enormous ecstasy. Physical life is seen as less important than emotion.

TREE NO. 5

Someone who may be more interested in reaching their destination than the route along the way. All of the Sefirot are broken into by the paths that lead to them, indicating a restlessness and possibly an impatience of character. The lack of contact between Gevurah and Hod and the thinness of the path between Hod and Tiferet indicate flashes of temper or moodiness, and the size of the feeling triad indicates that either there is some deep-seated but unexpressed reason for inner pain or a deep dissatisfaction with life as it is on some level. This person is very rational and although there is a belief in a higher power they may wonder why they don't actually experience it. At heart there is a deep spiritual yearning and, if they can overcome their irritation of being pulled in all directions and focus down, they could be very clear and powerful.

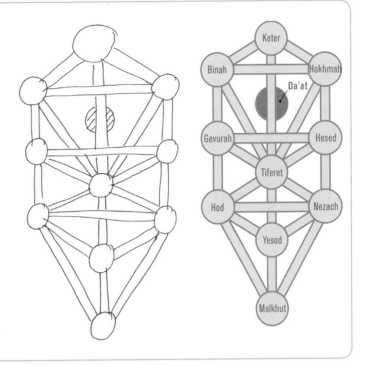

TREE NO. 6

The artist began the Tree at the top, ran out of space at the bottom, and forgot to add the side triads linking to Malkhut. He or she often has a great idea but it doesn't get carried through. This person may have a physical disability—if so, in the lower body—or it may be one who daydreams a lot but does not think their dreams through and fails to act on them.

The paths from Tiferet do not connect to the Self (apart from the path to Gevurah, which breaks through). This is a person with little sense of who they really are, someone disconnected from everyday life. The pain and pleasure triads have no strong boundaries, making them overemotional and unpredictable. They are impulsive, loving, but often confused when life does not fulfil what they are hoping for. A very introspective, probably highly intelligent individual; just with a need to connect and ground themselves in whatever way possible.

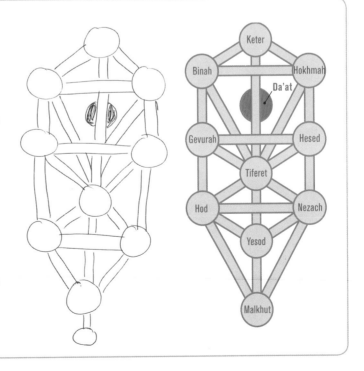

PAINTING THE TREE: A PROFESSIONAL JOB

✳ PAINTING A TREE OF LIFE WILL TAKE TWO DAYS IN ORDER TO ALLOW FOR
THE PAINT TO DRY. IT IS TIME-CONSUMING AND METICULOUS WORK, BUT ONCE
YOU HAVE FINISHED YOU WILL HAVE YOUR OWN MOBILE TABERNACLE FOR EVER.

Above: Remember to draw the basic structure very faintly with pencil so that it does not show through the completed image.

1 Find the center point of a piece of canvas, 3ft (1m) x 18in (48cm), which will be 18in (46cm) from the top and 9in (23cm) from the sides. Use a pencil to draw a very light vertical line right down the middle of the canvas.

2 Set the compass to 6in (15cm), which is the radius of the construction circles you are about to draw. Start by putting the compass needle at the center point of the canvas and lightly draw the central circle. Now put the needle at the upper intersection of the first circle with the center line and draw the second circle. The lower part should pass through the center point. Do the same at the lower intersection of the center circle with the center line of the canvas. Now you should have three overlapping circles.

3 Now set your compass to 1.5in (about 3.5cm), which will be the radius of each of the Sefirot. You have to draw five Sefirot down the middle and three on each side. You will find that the Sefirot are centered on the points where the circles intersect each other (at the sides) and/or the center line (down the middle). Draw the circles but do not draw Da'at too heavily because it will have a path straight through it.

4 Next are the paths, which are 0.5in (13mm) wide. Start with the horizontal paths. Line up the centers of the Sefirot (the holes where the compass needle went) and very lightly draw a pencil line between them. Then make a dot 0.3in (8mm) either side of this center line and draw in the paths as heavily as you like. Once you have drawn the three horizontal ones, draw the vertical ones. Note that the ones down the middle go "under" the horizontal paths and that the path between Keter and Tiferet goes through the Da'at Sefira.

5 Now put in the angled paths. There should be 22 in total; take care not to put in any extra ones or to leave any out!

6 When you are sure that you have everything right, place a black felt-tip pen in your compass and ink in the Sefirot. Then ink in the paths between the Sefirot.

PAINTING THE TREE

YOU WILL NEED:

✿ Canvas—3ft (1m) x 18in (46cm), taped to a piece of hardboard—about 5ft (1.5m) long and 2–3ft (0.75–1.5m) wide to stop it slipping

✿ Large compass, 6in (15cm) radius

✿ Pencil

✿ Ruler

✿ Black felt-tip pen

✿ Acrylic paint in white, black, red, orange, yellow, green, purple, and blue

✿ Paint brushes: one large, one small

COLORS

It doesn't really matter which colors you use but the traditional ones are as follows:

Sefirot and paths: White.

Triads:
Red in the bottom two (Malkhut–Yesod–Hod and Malkhut–Yesod–Nezach)
Orange for the two above (Yesod–Hod–Nezach)
Yellow for the two above those (Hod–Tiferet–Nezach)
Green for Hod–Tiferet–Gevurah and Nezach–Tiferet–Hesed
Purple for Tiferet–Gevurah–Binah and Tiferet–Hesed–Hokhmah
Blue for Tiferet–Binah–Hokhmah
White for Binah–Hokhmah–Keter.

7 Using the white paint, paint the paths and inside all the Sefirot. Then paint Da'at black (but not the path that runs through it) and paint all the canvas black around the Tree. Leave the canvas overnight for the black to dry.

8 Now go over the Sefirot and paths again with the pens to cover any little mistakes you may have made. Finally, write in the names of the Sefirot and any other attributes, such as astrological planets and angels.

PART FIVE

JACOB'S LADDER

JACOB'S LADDER IS A COSMIC MAP OF HOW GOD DESIGNED AND CREATED THE UNIVERSE. JACOB'S LADDER SHOWS THE "INVISIBLE LAWS" THAT MAKE LIFE WHAT IT IS. IT EXPLAINS THE PRINCIPLES BEHIND PLANETS; ANGELS AND ARCHANGELS; HUMANITY; ARCHETYPES; ANIMAL, VEGETABLE, AND MINERAL LEVELS; AND THE GREAT QUESTION OF GOOD AND EVIL. THE ORIGIN OF THE IDEA OF A LADDER FROM EARTH TO THE THRONE OF GOD COMES FROM THE BOOK OF GENESIS. THE BIBLICAL PATRIARCH JACOB DREAMED THAT HE SAW A LADDER TO THE HEAVENS, WITH ANGELS ASCENDING AND DESCENDING ON IT, AND THAT THE LORD GOD SPOKE TO HIM FROM ABOVE THE LADDER. LATER, IN THE SAME STORY, JACOB WRESTLED WITH AN ANGEL, AN ANALOGY OF HOW SPIRITUAL SEEKERS HAVE TO WRESTLE WITH THEMSELVES AND THE NEW AND CHALLENGING IDEAS ENCOUNTERED DURING THEIR SEARCH.

CHAPTER NINE

BODY AND SOUL

THE WORLD OF ASIYYAH

✳ SIMULTANEOUSLY THE DENSEST AND MOST FRAGILE OF THE FOUR WORLDS OF JACOB'S LADDER IS THE WORLD OF ASIYYAH. IT IS HERE ALONE THAT CREATION EXPERIENCES PHYSICAL LIFE AND DEATH. IN ALL THE OTHER WORLDS THERE IS ONLY TRANSFORMATION.

The Asiyyatic body and the Yeziratic psyche are linked by the interweaving of the upper and lower faces of their respective Trees. This makes a chain of connections until the time of death, when the Asiyyatic Tree falls away and the three upper Trees continue to exist and grow.

THE ASIYYATIC BODY

Humanity works on the standard mammalian model when it comes to bodily design, as indicated by the vestigial tail and appendix that humans still have even though they no longer have useful function. Although the skull of a dog, a horse, and a man may appear to be very different, it is only a question of elongation; the fundamental design is from the same root. Similarly, the mammalian skeleton is longer or shorter according to species. In a horse, the front knees are actually wrists and its hocks are its ankle bones.

All the elements of this standard design are focused on the left-hand side of the Asiyyatic Tree, the side of form. The pillar of action is associated with the life force, the processes of creating energy. Between these two, the body has a complex system of interlinking systems from circulation to molecular operations in individual cells.

In the Asiyyatic Tree, Keter represents nature itself. While nature is part of the Earth, it is also cosmic in scale, and our planet's existence is vital to the balance of the entire solar system. Everything that we do on Earth adds or detracts from that balance. The extinction of just one creature affects the entire balance of life. If it was a predator, then its prey multiplies, overgrazes land, and may even cause desert and famine. If it was a grazing creature, the whole biosystem of the area changes, with ongoing effects for all other creatures there.

THE TREE OF THE BODY

This interlinking system is exactly the same in the body; if one Sefira is out of balance, then the whole of the rest of the organism is soon affected.

In the Tree of the Body, Hokhmah is the life force; Binah the organic organization; Hesed the processes that create and expend all energy; Gevurah the processes that break down and transform energy; Tiferet the central nervous system; Nezach the motility systems; and Hod the body's communication systems. Yesod is the autonomic system that oversees the constancy of the gases, ions, and nutrients in bodily tissues. This Sefira is also responsible for the cardiovascular, digestive, and respiratory functions, as well as salivation, perspiration, alterations in the size of the pupils, and urination. Malkhut is the skin and special sense organs that enable us to experience the sensation of touch. This Sefira also forms the body's skeletal system and the muscles.

The levels of the Tree also reflect our bodily makeup with the electromagnetic system above the Da'at of the body, the metabolism in the body's soul triad, the tissue cellular systems in the awakening triad, and the organs of the body in the feeling triad.

If anything becomes out of balance in any of these processes, a message is sent to the Da'at of the Asiyyatic Tree, which is also the Yesod of the Yeziratic Tree. Because this forms the reticular activating system that filters information, consciousness of the problem may or may not be passed on to the Keter of the Asiyyatic body, which is also the Tiferet of Yezirah. Some individuals will disregard any messages that are sent, apart from severe pain—having been taught to endure discomfort in their childhood—while other individuals may overreact to every tiny stimulus, to the extent of hypochondria.

Above: In the modern world we are increasingly uncomfortable when encountering physical death. Our ancestors met it at all stages of life and learned that the process of grief is a natural part of life.

PHYSICAL HEALTH AND THE TREE OF ASIYYAH

✳ HOLISTIC HEALTH NOW TEACHES THAT EXACTLY WHERE WE EXPERIENCE DISCOMFORT IN OUR PHYSICAL BODY REFLECTS SOME DIS-EASE WITHIN THE PSYCHE. THERE MAY TRULY BE SOMEONE WHO IS A PAIN IN THE NECK OR A PAIN IN THE BACKSIDE OF YOUR LIFE!

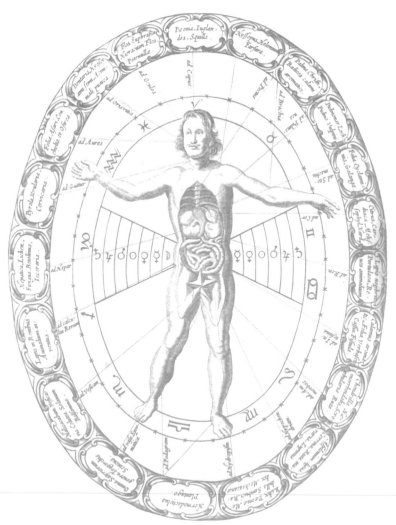

The cause of health problems may be understood through the links between the Yeziratic and Asiyyatic Trees. A problem in the digestive system could mean that you are taking in so much new information that you cannot process it, that you are emotionally "stuck," or that your life is cluttered in other areas apart from your physical self.

It is common knowledge that muscular strain comes from overexertion (Yesod–Nezach–Malkhut) and that intestinal troubles such as colitis are caused by worry and fear (Hod–Yesod–Nezach). What used to be called "nerves" (Hod–Yesod–Malkhut) is usually a paralysis of painful repetitive thoughts. Bipolar syndrome is a malfunction of the Sefira of Yesod; there is a lack of balance in the contemplative and active triads each side of it. Schizophrenia is frequently the result of a shattered or malfunctioning Yesod, which is confused about the strength or validity of the messages it is receiving from the physical and psychological worlds.

Left: Ancient physicians understood the links between mind, body and spirit, hope, rhythmical cycles, and levels of consciousness in promoting good health.

MEDITATION FOR SELF-HEALING

Since all four worlds of Jacob's Ladder interweave with each other, what happens in each world has an effect on the others. So visualization of health and happiness will find its way through from the psychological world to both the spiritual and physical worlds. In the spiritual world of Beriah, it invokes a command for health and in the physical world it soothes and heals. This simple meditation invokes all four worlds.

Sit comfortably and close your eyes. Imagine a cord from the base of your spine that goes down through the floor, through the earth and the rock and the magma right to the very center of the Earth. This is to ground you.

Now imagine that you are drawing up the strong energy of Asiyyah through the soles of your feet. This deep, vibrant energy flows up through your legs, up your back, down your arms, and into your head, cleansing and healing your physical body. Now feel it flowing down the cord at the base of your spine, taking all the tiredness and any physical pain with it to be dissolved and transformed by the magma at the center of the Earth.

Now focus on the crown of your head. Imagine the purple, watery energy of Yezirah flowing into you from above. This water flows down your shoulders and arms, down your back and your legs, washing and soothing you. Feel the water flow down the cord, taking with it all the worries and fears that you may have had.

Focus on your head again and feel the blue-tinted air of Beriah waft into your brain and down through your whole body, removing any cobwebs and mental blocks. Send this too down the cord, cleansing your spirit.

Then feel the clear, bright white light of Azilut shining down through your entire body. Bask in its heat and power. This light flows right through you, down to the center of the Earth, balancing, healing, and inspiring both you and the Earth together.

Now cut off the cord by clenching your buttocks and imagine the crown of your head closing so that you are still filled with light.

Open your eyes and make sure you are grounded by patting your feet on the floor three times.

ASTROLOGY

✳ KNOWING YOUR ASTROLOGICAL CHART IS VERY HELPFUL IN INTERPRETING THE TREE OF LIFE. IF YOU KNOW YOUR MOON SIGN THEN YOU CAN UNDERSTAND THE CHARACTER OF YOUR EGO (YESOD) AND HOW YOU REACT TO LIFE.

ZODIAC SIGNS AND TRIADS

 ✡ **Aries (fire):** Philosophy Triad (Binah–Tiferet–Gevurah)

 ✡ **Taurus (earth):** Action Triad (Yesod–Nezach–Malkhut)

 ✡ **Gemini (air):** Awakening/Feeling Triad (Hod–Tiferet–Yesod)

 ✡ **Cancer (water):** The Lower Face of the Tree—representing the mother

 ✡ **Leo (fire):** The Upper Face of the Tree—representing the father

 ✡ **Virgo (earth):** Thinking Triad (Hod–Yesod–Malkhut)

 ✡ **Libra (air):** Awakening/Feeling Triad (Tiferet–Nezach–Yesod)

 ✡ **Scorpio (water):** Passive Emotional Triad (Tiferet–Hod–Gevurah)

 ✡ **Sagittarius (fire):** Religious Triad (Tiferet–Hokhmah–Hesed)

 ✡ **Capricorn (earth):** Spiritual Triad (Binah–Keter–Tiferet)

≈≈ ✡ **Aquarius (air):** Spiritual Triad (Keter–Hokhmah–Hesed)

✡ **Pisces (water):** Active Emotional Triad (Tiferet–Hesed–Nezach).

Each Sefira of the Tree represents a planet and each triad of the Yeziratic Tree corresponds to a sign of the zodiac. Scorpio is placed in the pain and fear triad of Gevurah–Tiferet–Hod. This is a sign that has a tendency to paranoia but it is the most powerful of all the signs when it comes to cleansing. The opposite triad of pleasure is represented by the astrological sign of Pisces, which loves harmony and spirituality but has no boundaries.

Few non-astrologers are aware of how their signs affect their characteristics and characters. Even if you do not know any astrology except your sun sign, check out which triad it is placed in. This is the triad that has the greatest emphasis in your life. The fire signs are most associated with drive, power, and flair (Azilut); the air signs with thought, ideas, and impulses (Beriah); the water signs with emotions and empathy (Yezirah), and the earth signs with practicality (Asiyyah).

MOON SIGNS AND THEIR EFFECTS

An earth Moon can ensure that an air or fire Sun gets the job finished. A water Moon can make a fire, air, or earth sign more sensitive. A fire Moon can get an earth or water Sun

Ψ Neptune
♇ Uranus
♃ Jupiter
♀ Venus
⊕ Earth
☿ Mercury
♂ Mars
♄ Saturn
♇ Pluto
☉ Sun
☽ Moon

Above: This hand-drawn tree by Z'ev ben Shimon Halevi shows the astrological glyphs in the relevant triads.

MOON CHARACTERISTICS

✡ **Aries:** needs the stimulation of new projects; impatient.

✡ **Taurus:** anything for a quiet life. Very patient but when its patience runs out, watch out!

✡ **Gemini:** has the enthusiasm of a child but changes its mind in an instant and forgets that it ever thought anything different.

✡ **Cancer:** protective, nurturing, and a worrier.

✡ **Leo:** either the strong second-in-command or the usurper; problems with pride.

✡ **Virgo:** precise and accurate but too picky and dogmatic.

✡ **Libra:** likes life to be peaceful and pretty whatever the cost.

✡ **Scorpio:** passionate, loyal, paranoid, and fearful.

✡ **Sagittarius:** charming, philosophical, uncaring, and if pushed will make a fast getaway.

✡ **Capricorn:** cautious, restrictive, law-abiding, and totally fair.

✡ **Aquarius:** holistic, revolutionary, outrageous, and prone to sudden reactions.

✡ **Pisces:** emotional and offers little resistance; so very gentle that no one else can get their own way for fear of appearing unkind.

off its backside. An air Moon can make an earth or water sign lighten up.

This is how your Moon sign will affect your Self. Some combinations are naturally harmonious, which can be peaceful or lead to laziness. Others are very challenging. A Sun–Moon opposition can work well, with each sign stimulating the other, but will rarely lead to a quiet life. A Sun–Moon square means that there is almost always a fight between habit and free will.

ARCHANGELS, ANGELS, AND DEVAS

✳ ARCHANGELS, ANGELS, AND DEVAS (EARTH, TREE, AND PLANT SPIRITS) ALL HAVE THEIR PLACE ON JACOB'S LADDER. ARCHANGELS CORRESPOND TO THE WORLD OF BERIAH, ANGELS TO YEZIRAH, AND DEVAS TO ASIYYAH.

Above: The Bible story of Jacob seeing angels ascending and descending steps to the higher realms is the origin of the name "Jacob's Ladder."

Angels are not human; they have no sex and they never incarnate on Earth. With the advent of the "New Age," many people assume that angels are discarnate human spirits who watch over us. The word "angel" is Greek for messenger, so the discarnate humans who act as guides for humanity could conceivably be called angels, but a true angelic being is a focus of force that is a non-human form of energy.

As children of God, humans can operate in all four worlds and we possess the gift—and challenge—of free will. Angels are the servants of God, the beings that ensure that the process of life continues in good order. They have no free will, cannot act of their own accord, and obey orders implicitly.

HOW ANGELS OPERATE

When we pray, give thanks, or cry out for help, it is an angel of prayer that carries that message to the Divine and a different angel that brings the answer, whatever it may be. If it includes the manifestation of a miracle, we often think it was an angel that responded to us, but Kabbalah teaches that it is God who responds and sends a perfect, specific angel to perform the miracle. This is essential because we humans cannot see the wider picture; we might pray for a

GUARDIANS

We become confused because of the term "guardian angel," which leads us to believe that we have a personal guide who has free will. Our guardian is an angelic being that has been given the task of protecting us and helping us on our life's path. If you are destined to be a ballet dancer but refuse to practice or attend auditions, it can do nothing; it does not have the power to deny your free will.

An angel can offer us a warning of potential danger and even place an obstacle in front of us to prevent us from running out into the road in front of a car. But if we choose to jump that object and keep running then that is our decision; it has to allow us that choice. It can, however, operate outside of time as we understand it and will be able to contact the guardian angel of the car driver. It is then up to that angel to alert the driver to the danger if he or she is conscious enough to heed the warning.

Often we have a small inner thought alerting us to a possibility and it is only later that we realize it would have been wise to have paid attention to the thought. That is the work of a guardian; it cannot tell us what to do, only hint at what possibilities lie ahead.

particular angelic influence when a very different one is required. For example, calling on the Archangel Michael to protect you from a hostile person is like calling for the level of energy of a sun when the level of energy of a gas cooker is required. The appropriate response from within the protective sphere of the appropriate archangel will be sent, but not the whole of the archangel—or the whole of planet Earth would explode!

THE SPIRITS ON THE LADDER

Humanity, as the child of God, is the only being that can exist in all four worlds.

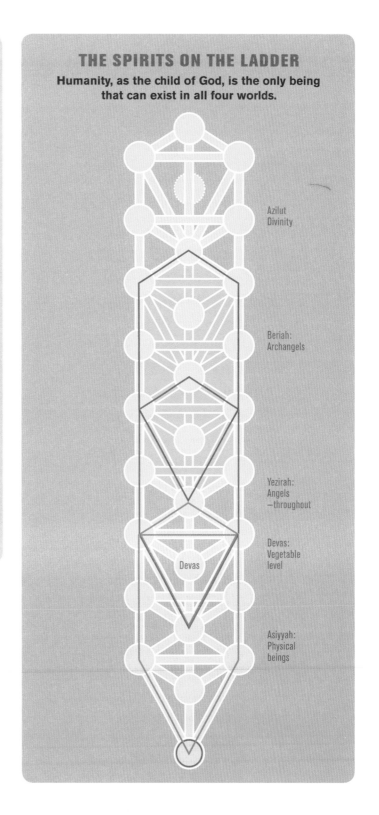

Azilut
Divinity

Beriah:
Archangels

Yezirah:
Angels
—throughout

Devas:
Vegetable
level

Devas

Asiyyah:
Physical
beings

POSITIVE AND NEGATIVE ANGELS

✳ THE EARTH HAS ITS OWN ANGEL, COUNTRIES HAVE THEIR OWN ANGELS, AND SO DO CITIES AND TOWNS. TREES AND PLANTS ALSO HAVE ANGELS. THESE "ELEMENTALS," AS THEY ARE CALLED, ARE THE NATURE SPIRITS THAT WE CALL FAIRIES OR ELVES.

Fairies and elves are concerned with the cycles of nature and their influence can tug at a human being's vegetable level, usually through Hod and Nezach. In the world of radio waves, television, and cellphones, most humans are "tuned out" of their level, consciously at least, though unconsciously most of us have intuition and instinct. Whether we choose to ignore or acknowledge them is up to the individual.

FAIRIES AND ELVES

Angel of Reason
Angel of God
Angel of Prayer
Angel of Understanding
Angel of Revelation
Gabriel
Negative Angels
Angel of Justice
Angel of Mercy
Positive Angels
Angel of Compassion
Angel of Work
Salamanders (Djinn)
Angel of Play
Dryads
Satyrs
Elves
Naiads (Mermaids)
Fairies
Devas
Sylphs
Gnomes
Elementals

ANGELS

Angels all have their place on the Tree of Life; those on the right-hand pillar are responsible for "positive" aspects such as growth; those on the central column are the guardians or concerned with issues of balance or Grace, and those on the left-hand pillar are focused on "negative" aspects such as destruction or death. People often have problems with the idea of negative angels—demons—but these are as necessary as the positive ones. It is their task to recycle life so that it can grow again. Both negative and positive angels are involved in a process such as making a cake in which flour must have been milled, eggs must be broken, and ingredients bound together before they can rise to make the finished food.

DEMONS

As well as God's angels (always named with the word "el"—"of God"—as in Micha-el or Rapha-el), there are mischievous or hostile energetic beings called demons. There are two ancient Kabbalistic schools of thought that explain why demons exist; the first is that they are remnants of previous incomplete universes before the creation of this one and the second, that they are parts of shattered vessels from the creation of this universe (*see pages 16–17*).

Most modern esoteric thinkers believe that demonic forces are the result of human thought. As we are children of God we do have the power to create angelic beings, although of a less pure order than those created by God. Repetitive thought creates vibration, and energy forms can take a Yeziratic shape. Poltergeists are one example. These often occur in a house where there are adolescents experiencing forces of new and uncontrolled energy. Such energetic beings are often powerful enough to move objects, but since they exist only in the lower levels of Yezirah, they can be dissolved (or exorcised) by the conscious drawing down of a higher level of energy.

Some buildings have an atmosphere created by the energetic forces drawn to them by humanity. Places of worship attract angels of prayer, while places of torment attract angels of destruction and demonic energies.

WORKING WITH ANGELIC ENERGIES

When beginning work with spiritual energies it is vitally important to understand both the power of the human in creating vibrations and the nature of the angelics. Many an aspiring angel worker will call in positive energies. Yet if they do not know how to protect themselves through appropriate prayer—or if they do not realize that when an energy without free will is summoned, it must be instructed to depart when it is no longer required—they can find themselves in very uncomfortable circumstances.

The Christian Mass, for example, carries a specific ritual for calling for the "presence" of the angelics and another for dismissing them.

If angelic energy is not dismissed, it will eventually dissolve or return to God, but it will leave a space behind it. This space has to be filled by something, and often this will be any vibrational energy that is seeking a home. A house where angel work is often carried out without this knowledge may well become filled with uncontrolled energies, generally not harmful but still very uncomfortable.

Left: The angels and devas are all focused on a particular job of work that only they can do. It is these beings that keep the planet Earth abundant.

CHAPTER TEN
SPIRIT AND DIVINITY

✳ ABOVE YEZIRAH ARE THE WORLDS WHERE FORM DOES NOT EXIST. AS HUMAN BEINGS WE FIND IT HARD TO IMAGINE SOMETHING THAT DOES NOT HAVE SOME KIND OF SHAPE, SO WE CREATE IMAGES IN ORDER TO UNDERSTAND IT.

THE SEVEN HEAVENS IN BERIAH

✡ **The seventh heaven**, called Arabot ("heaven of heavens") is the supernal triad of Beriah where every created being cries out the Name "I AM" as it emerges from Keter to begin the process of life. This is also the storehouse of peace and blessings.

✡ **The sixth heaven** (Binah–Hokhmah–Tiferet) is called Makom ("place"). It is where the trials and rewards of creation are ordained long before they become manifest and the place from where the Holy Spirit emerges. Both these heavens are directly linked with Azilut, the divine world.

✡ **The fifth heaven** (Gevurah–Tiferet–Hesed) is Maon ("dwelling"), the place where color and sound are created.

✡ **The fourth heaven** (Tiferet–Nezach–Hod) is Zebul ("habitation") the source of the Sun, Moon, stars, and planets.

✡ **The third heaven** (Nezach–Hod–Yesod) is Shehakim ("Skies"), the place of the rhythms of birth, growth, decay, death.

✡ **The second heaven** (Yesod) is Rakiyah ("firmament"), the veil that prevents humanity from seeing the higher worlds before being ready for that knowledge.

✡ **The first heaven**, or Vilon ("veil of heaven"), is Malkhut, or the Kingdom of Heaven, the first level of spiritual experience possible to natural man and the highest manifestation of our individual Self.

Within Beriah are the Seven Heavens referred to in the Book of Revelation. Beriah is the world of cosmic good and cosmic evil, a realm of pure spirit and pure thought. It is also outside of time as we understand it. It is in Beriah that the ideas of God exist—the concept of a human being or a cat or a tree. Lower down, in Yezirah, they become a specific human being; for example, African, Oriental, tall, or red-headed; or a specific cat, such as a lion, tiger, lynx, or Siamese; or a specific tree, for instance, an oak, elm, or laburnum.

We humans can contact this realm of thought when we are balanced in our Yeziratic Tiferet, at the place where three worlds meet—Asiyyah, Yezirah, and Beriah. But even so, in order to describe an experience of this higher world, we have to draw it down into Yezirah in order to be able to give it a form that we can comprehend.

To experience Beriah is to feel awe; it is a knowledge that you are both infinite and tiny; powerful and fragile. It is not easy to ascend mentally into the heavens because they reveal our individual place in the universe and our cosmic destiny. Such knowledge is too great for most of us to bear. This is because the truth in Beriah is stark and uncompromising. It is the place of cosmic good and cosmic evil—these are totally dispassionate and transpersonal compared with the human ability to be good and evil; at the human level there is consciousness of the effect of one's actions. In Beriah, good can be defined as constant expansion and evil can be defined as constant destruction. Each, unleashed without the equilibrium of the other, would destroy the universe. The archangels in charge of the Beriatic Sefirot of Gevurah and Hesed are in charge of the birth and destruction of nebulae. They hold the whole of creation in balance.

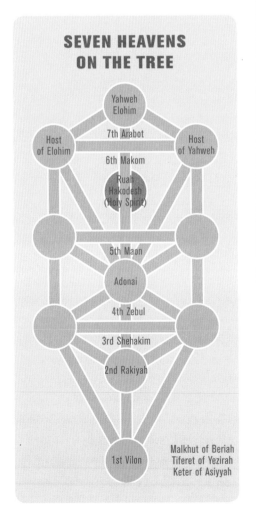

SEVEN HEAVENS ON THE TREE

Yahweh Elohim

Host of Elohim

7th Arabot

Host of Yahweh

6th Makom

Ruah Hakodesh (Holy Spirit)

5th Maon

Adonai

4th Zebul

3rd Shehakim

2nd Rakiyah

1st Vilon

Malkhut of Beriah
Tiferet of Yezirah
Keter of Asiyyah

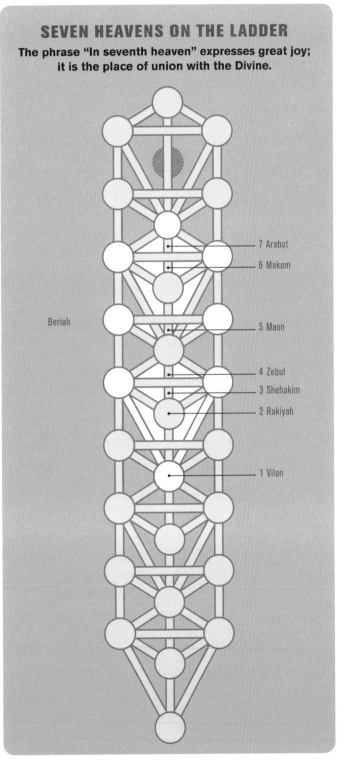

SEVEN HEAVENS ON THE LADDER

The phrase "In seventh heaven" expresses great joy; it is the place of union with the Divine.

Beriah

7 Arabot
6 Makom

5 Maon

4 Zebul
3 Shehakim
2 Rakiyah

1 Vilon

ARCHANGELS: THEIR PURPOSE AND HIERARCHY

✳ THERE ARE NINE RANKS OF ANGELIC BEINGS ACCORDING TO JEWISH AND CHRISTIAN THEOLOGY: CHERUBIM, SERAPHIM, THRONES, DOMINATIONS, VIRTUES, POWERS, PRINCIPALITIES, ARCHANGELS, AND ANGELS.

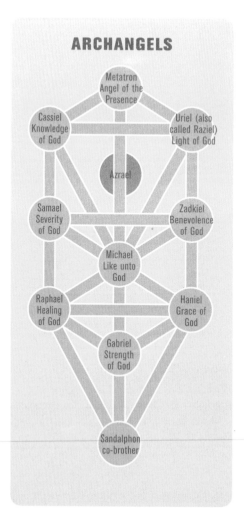

ARCHANGELS

Metatron
Angel of the
Presence

Cassiel
Knowledge
of God

Uriel (also
called Raziel)
Light of God

Azrael

Samael
Severity
of God

Zadkiel
Benevolence
of God

Michael
Like unto
God

Raphael
Healing
of God

Haniel
Grace of
God

Gabriel
Strength
of God

Sandalphon
co-brother

This listing dates back to the fifth century BCE and was first cataloged by the theologian Dionysus. The best-known ranks are angels and archangels. Archangels live in the world of Beriah and include Michael, Raphael, and Gabriel. Only Gabriel is mentioned in both Old and New Testaments and in the Qur'an. It was Gabriel who told Mary that she was to give birth to Christ. Michael and Satan are also mentioned in the Old and New Testaments but two other angels are named in the Apocrypha: Raphael (Book of Tobit) and Uriel (2 Esdras).

Angelologists have long discussed the number of archangels. Traditionally, there are seven, though their names and duties vary according to sources. Islam recognizes four; Christianity, Judaism, New Age, Occult, and Wicca all say twelve. Kabbalists place nine on the Beriatic Tree of Life but also acknowledge other archangelic beings.

Traditionally, Satan was once an archangel. He was Lucifer, greatest of the angelic beings, but when humanity was created his task was to test those who would approach the divine realms. So Satan also serves God in halting those whose egos or lack of training in discipline led them to attempt to get higher than their natural level.

CALLING ON ARCHANGELS

New Age teachers and healers who call on the archangels at the slightest provocation forget that these great beings consist of the energy level of a star and that their role in creation is far greater than aiding a human. However, if the Archangel Michael is called on for protection, then his angelic helpers will take that prayer to God, who will assign one of them, with a fraction of the appropriate archangelic energy, to answer the prayer.

The most knowledgable practitioners of the Sacred Magic of Angels work with archangelic energies on the Sefirot of the Tree of Life within the range of human self-awareness: Tiferet and below. Above it they work with angelic energies. This is less confusing than it seems since angels are members of the hosts controlled by archangels. So angel Samael is of the legion of the Seraphim and represents the Gevuric energy of Archangel Samael at the lower level of Yezirah so that we can understand. The level of light emitted by the archangel is so truly awesome that it cannot communicate with us effectively. Angels Sachiel (or Zadkiel) and Cassiel (or Zaphkiel) are the equivalent of archangels of Hesed and Binah.

ARCHANGEL URIEL

Those who call on Archangel Uriel (Hokhmah) must be of a sufficiently developed consciousness to work at such a high level or be in such need of a miracle that they are prepared to have their life transformed and re-created. Any angel-lore teacher who encourages a student to invoke Uriel's energy without due knowledge and experience is acting irresponsibly and could cause great harm.

ARCHANGELS

Archangels have no form but are represented winged because they live in the world of air.

- Metatron
- Cassiel
- Uriel/ Raziel
- Azrael
- Samael
- Zadkiel
- Michael
- Raphael
- Haniel
- Gabriel
- Sandalphon

ARCHANGELS: PLACEMENT ON THE TREE OF BERIAH

✱ EACH ARCHANGEL IS RESPONSIBLE FOR ONE ASPECT OF THIS SPIRITUAL WORLD. METATRON, PLACED AT KETER, OVERSEES THIS WORLD FROM THE HEART OF THE DIVINE WORLD OF AZILUT.

Asariel ("Beatitude of God"), Lord of Neptune, is placed at Keter.

Azreal ("Whom God Helps"), Lord of Pluto, is placed at Da'at. He is the one who orchestrated the death of the firstborn in Egypt before the Exodus and is generally associated with death, although his role is actually transformation.

Uriel ("Light of God"), Lord of Uranus, is placed at Hokhmah.

Cassiel, also known as Zaphkiel ("Knowledge of God"), Lord of Saturn, is placed at Binah.

Zadkiel, or Sachiel ("Benevolence of God"), Lord of Jupiter, is at Hesed.

Samael ("Severity of God"), Lord of Mars, is at Gevurah. Zadkiel and Samael keep equilibrium. If Samael ruled, creation would implode, while if Zadkiel ruled, creation would explode.

Michael ("Like unto God"), Lord of the Sun, is placed at the Tiferet of the Beriatic world, which is also the Malkhut of Azilut and the Keter of Yezirah. He is therefore guardian of heaven, gatekeeper of the divine world, and watcher over humanity. Michael is also traditionally the patron angel of the Jewish people, often shown fighting the dragon of Satan in a cosmic war between the forces of order and chaos.

Raphael ("Healing of God"), Lord of Mercury, is at Hod. Other systems place Raphael at Tiferet and Michael at Hod. This is because in the ancient Greek metaphysical system, Raphael the healer was equated with Apollo who is often referred to as the Sun God. In fact, Helios was the Sun God and Apollo the God of the Light of the Sun. Michael is also associated with Re, the Egyptian God of the Sun.

Haniel ("Grace of God"), Lord of Venus, is placed at Nezach.

Gabriel ("Strength of God"), Lord of the Moon, is placed at the Yesod of Beriah, the Da'at of Yezirah. He is the archangel who brings messages from the foundation of the upper world into the consciousness of humanity.

Left: This image by 12th-century nun and mystic, Hildegard of Bingen, shows nine ranks of angels in three rows of three.

Sandalphon is at Malkhut. He is the only being at that level not to have a name ending in el ("of God"). Sandalphon means "co-brother," and he is the manifestation on Earth of archangelic energy from the Crown of Beriah—Metatron. It is through Sandalphon that Enoch, Elijah, or other great souls can manifest on the Earth.

APPEARANCE OF ARCHANGELS

Since the beginning of time, angels and archangels have been spoken of as "winged beings" and we see very few images of them without great, feathered wings. Symbolically, this image comes from ancient observations of the speed and height attained by an eagle, one of the four beasts depicted in the vision of Ezekiel (*see page 103*). Each of these is allotted

its own world on Jacob's Ladder: the bull is Asiyyah; the lion, Yezirah; the Eagle, Beriah; and the man, Azilut.

However, non-biblical teachings refer to the energy of angelics as being surrounded by "aura-wings." The aura is the electromagnetic energy field around and within a living entity. It is usually observed as a fan-like series of energy lines radiating out from the being, like the filaments from the quill of a feather. All angelic beings, which include all planets and stars, have auric fields that extend around them, often for miles. The Sun is an archangelic being and its outer layers—the photosphere, chromosphere, and transition region—are approximately 8,000 miles (13,000 km) wide, the diameter of the Earth.

INVOKING THE ARCHANGELS SAFELY: GABRIEL, RAPHAEL, AND HANIEL

✳ HUMAN BEINGS HAVE EVOKED THE HELP OF GOD THROUGH THE ANGELS SINCE THE BEGINNING OF TIME. HOWEVER, BEFORE LEARNING HOW THIS IS DONE IT IS IMPORTANT TO KNOW THAT THE ANSWER TO A PETITION CAN OFTEN BE "NO."

Angels and archangels send all petitions to God for instruction. Sometimes the request is contrary to the greater good of the applicant, such as wanting the love of a particular person when their soul mate is just around the corner, or asking for a career move that would damage them at a soul level. Also, the timing may not be right: do not ask for your perfect home in the next six months if it has not yet been built. Here is a basic guide to petitioning.

GABRIEL

For issues concerning a happy home, petition Gabriel on Monday or at a new or full moon in the Theban script using blue ink on white paper. If he consents, you will receive or experience one of the following within 28 days: shellfish, melons, lychees, pears, spiders, moths, white flowers, or silver; being bathed in moonbeams; the news of a birth; or, a dog persistently barking outside your home.

RAPHAEL

For all issues concerning the health of young children and pets, communication, or completion of contracts, petition Raphael on Wednesday in either of the scripts using black ink on yellow paper. If Raphael consents, you will receive one of the following signs within seven days: a bird entering your home, yellow flowers, monkeys, a plague of flies, aspens, silver birch trees, the gift of a mirror or the accidental breaking of one, a surprise short journey, or an increase in mail.

HANIEL

For all issues concerning love, petition Haniel on Friday in the Passing of the River Script (though your name should be written in Theban script) in blue or red ink on pink or blue paper. If Haniel consents, you will receive or experience one of the following within 28 days: apples, doves, blue tits or any blue birds, roses, delphiniums, a gift of pink or blue clothing, or any kind of ring.

PETITIONING THE ARCHANGELS

British Kabbalist, Dr. David Goddard, an expert in alchemy and angelology, and author of *The Sacred Magic of the Angels* (Samuel Weiser, 1996), gives a full account of how to petition the archangels. He stresses that no archangel is to be invoked lightly. There are specific rituals that should be observed if a life-changing or life-enhancing petition is to be made. Time should be set aside, discipline followed, and deep consideration must be given. However, in times of emergency, a verbal call for help will always be answered.

THE LANGUAGES OF PETITION

From the beginning of the written word, there have been two specific languages used to petition the archangels: the Theban Script and the Passing of the River Script. The first has equivalent letters to the majority of those of our alphabet and is named after Honorius of Thebes, a mythical character from ancient Egypt. The second script is a primitive form of liturgical Hebrew; like all ancient languages, its power is evoked by being spoken at the same time as it is written. Both scripts were widely documented in the 16th century but have been used in sacred magic for millennia.

Above: All archangels are associated with signs. Those of Archangel Gabriel are the zodiac sign of Cancer (the crab), the waxing moon, and the stellar–lunar corona.

THEBAN SCRIPT

A		N	
B		O	
C		P	
D		Q	
E		R	
F		S	
G		T	
H		U	
I		V	
J		W	
K		X	
L		Y	
M		Z	

PASSING OF THE RIVER SCRIPT

A		N	
B		SH	
G		O	
D		P	
E		J	
V		Q	
Z		R	
H		K	
TH		L	
I		S	
M		T	

INVOKING THE ARCHANGELS SAFELY: MICHAEL, SAMAEL, SACHIEL, AND CASSIEL

✳ MICHAEL, SAMAEL, AND SACHIEL ARE THE ANGELS CORRESPONDING TO THE SOUL TRIAD OF BERIAH. THEIR WORK FOR HUMANITY IS FOCUSED ON THE DEVELOPMENT OF THE HUMAN SPIRIT AND THEY ARE NOT TO BE INVOKED LIGHTLY. CASSIEL REPRESENTS BINAH—HIGHER UNDERSTANDING.

MICHAEL

For issues concerning achievement and legitimate ambition from promotion to running a business, marriage, or priesthood, petition Michael on Sunday using orange ink on white paper. His name and your own should be written in the Passing of the River Script but the petition itself should be in the Theban Script.

If Michael consents, you will be given or experience one of the following signs within seven days: gold or orange flowers, a gold or orange butterfly, sunflowers, pomegranates, oranges, any gift with a crown on it, being adopted or visited by a passing cat, hearing a stringed instrument, being invited to a wedding, being bathed suddenly in sunlight, or having a crane fly enter your home.

Left: Great Michael is known as the "captain of the host" and is probably the best-known of all the archangels. He is associated with the Sun and the color gold.

Right: The symbols of Sachiel, clockwise from top left: the arrow of Sagittarius; the symbol of Pisces; Sachiel's call sign, the "Part of Fortune"; the glyph of planet Jupiter.

SAMAEL

For matters concerning courage, the overcoming of problems, protection from hatred, hostility, or fearful situations, petition Samael on Tuesday in the Passing of the River Script in red ink on white paper.

Samael is the great protective angel but is not invoked as much as Michael because some people associate him, incorrectly, with Satan. Samael will not harm your enemies; his energy will help the situation to be resolved, even if it means moving the disliked person to a better position or place. The angels have no sympathy with human resentments or issues and a petition to Samael may make you see the light about a difficult situation so that you change your own views. Samael is ruler of Mars, the armed forces, and of surgery and protecting the human body.

If Samael consents, you will receive one of the following signs within seven days: the gift of a knife or sword, a knife, salt or spices falling to the ground, sparks from a fire, being stung by an insect, being given horse chestnuts or a sheepskin (or any gift to do with sheep), or seeing a monkey-puzzle tree (*Araucaria araucana*). If you have asked for help overcoming surgery or injury, a feeling of heat in that part of the body is a sign of consent.

SACHIEL

In matters concerning finance, earnings, recovery of debt, legal matters, authority, and pay rises, petition Sachiel on Thursday in the Passing of the River Script in blue ink on white paper. Sachiel will not bring you windfalls of money or help you to prosper by doing nothing yourself, but will help you to earn.

If Sachiel consents, you will receive one of the following signs within seven days: a foreign coin in your change, finding a coin on the street, taking an unexpected trip at sea, seeing golden motes dancing in the air, being given purple grapes or flowers, seeing or noticing a particular oak tree for the first time, hearing or being given a gift concerning the sea, whales, fishing, elephants, seeing a member of a Royal Family, or having a bee enter your house.

CASSIEL

For matters of home ownership, land, or agriculture, for the elderly (human or animal), for long-standing illness, or for the relief of poverty, petition Cassiel on Saturday in the Passing of the River Script in black ink on white paper. Cassiel is ruler of Saturn and often thought of as a harsh teacher. He does not make things easy but he does give the strength to endure. If Cassiel consents, you will receive one of the following signs within three months: encounters with tortoises or parrots, gifts of evergreens, a worm on your path, a gift of coal or lead, going to a funeral or memorial, tasting something unexpectedly bitter, receiving dried flowers, or an unexpected visit from an elderly person.

AZILUT: UNDERSTANDING THE DIVINE WORLD

✳ AT THE CROWN OF BERIAH AND AT THE CENTER OF THE DIVINE WORLD OF AZILUT IS THE GREATEST ANGELIC BEING OF ALL: METATRON. THIS IS THE ONLY BEING IN GOD'S CREATION THAT IS BOTH ANGEL AND HUMAN.

METATRON

Metatron acts as God's agent over all evolving creatures. He is said to be Enoch, the first fully realized man, and is known as the Archangel of the Presence of God in Creation. Even those who rise to the level of the Christhood are not as evolved as Metatron. At this level, the human soul passes from the lower worlds to direct communion with God. Those who rise to the level of Metatron have fulfilled their role in creation and pass through to take their place within the divine body of Adam Kadmon.

Below: Legend says that Metatron, the only being which is both human and angel, can manifest on Earth through his co-brother Sandalphon.

AZILUT

Even though Azilut is the divine world, so bright and filled with glory that we cannot even imagine it, it is still not God. The Absolute is beyond even Azilut, way beyond comprehension. The root of the Hebrew word *Azilut* means "to stand near." Azilut is the "buffer zone" between the unknowable Ayin Sof and the three lower worlds of Beriah, Yezirah, and Asiyyah. Azilut was in existence before the story of creation as told in the Book of Genesis. It is said to have begun with the ten utterances of God. These ten words correspond to the ten Names of God, which came out of the "no-thing-ness" of unmanifest existence, into the "white fire" of Azilut. This world is associated with the aspect of fire and the color white, symbolizing divine radiance.

Azilut is an eternal, unchanging world untouched by time, emotion, or decay. Here, according to the most ancient Kabbalistic tradition, the Sefirot are at their most beautiful and pure. However, according to the Lurianic tradition, the vessels are not perfect but shattered. This is despite the fact that Azilut is known as the "World of Unity" and as the "Glory of God" that shines through all four worlds. As time and space do not exist in Azilut, there is never any type of motion, therefore this world

ADAM KADMON

The nearest thing we are able to perceive to God is Adam Kadmon (*see page 15*), the primordial being and the divine image in Azilut. This being is androgynous—neither male nor female—but is often depicted in esoteric literature as a bearded old man. This is actually a depiction of the Hokhmah of Yezirah, the highest inspiration that humanity can experience in the world of Form (where we can understand things through images). The masculine head, the beard, even the divine body and its dimensions are only symbols in an attempt to illustrate the nature of the World of Azilut.

This issue over the image of God—and the idea of humanity in God's image—is why the Tree of Life became the most acceptable symbol in Kabbalah. Not only does it include all the information that is needed to study and practice mystical knowledge, but it also contains no literal images— nothing that can actually be seen in the heavens or on Earth.

is always in perfect balance. Evil and error do not exist at this level; they can only begin to exist one world further down in Beriah.

Duality begins in Beriah with the creation of cosmic good and cosmic evil, so it is hard for Kabbalists who don't follow Isaac Luria's teachings to understand how any shattering of the vessels could have occurred in Azilut—which is sheer perfection. In the personal, emotional world of individual men, the Sefirot can appear as shattered; particularly in the case of mental disturbance. However, higher than Yezirah, any room for error or imbalance would mean the immediate destruction of the universe.

PLACE OF METATRON ON THE LADDER

Metatron is at the Tiferet of Azilut, higher even than the Messiah who is placed at the Malkhut of Azilut.

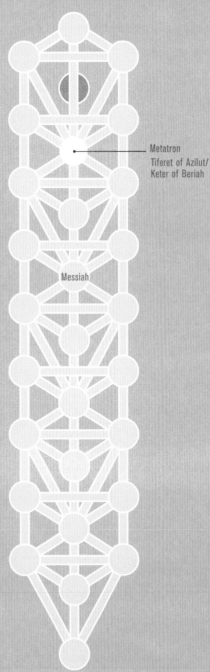

Metatron
Tiferet of Azilut/
Keter of Beriah

Messiah

REINCARNATION

✳ KABBALAH TEACHES THAT THE HUMAN SOUL ORIGINATES IN THE SOUL TRIAD OF GEVURAH–TIFERET–HESED IN THE DIVINE WORLD OF AZILUT. IN THIS PLACE, KNOWN AS "THE TREASURE HOUSE OF SOULS," EVERY SPARK IS PERFECT.

Right: the *Sigillum dei Ameth*, a pantacle or teaching story by Dr. John Dee. "Ameth" is Hebrew for truth and this circular symbol is the Seal of the Truth of God. It has the names of God and his angels inscribed on it.

THE FOUR JOURNEYS

✡ **The first**, from Azilut to the Malkhut of Malkhuts in Asiyyah, is to learn how to live in the physical world with all its challenges.

✡ **The second**, from Asiyyah back to the Malkhut of Azilut, is to learn how to develop the soul and spirit.

✡ **The third**, from the Malkhut of Azilut to Asiyyah again, is to teach what has been learned by others.

✡ **The fourth** is the final return to take your place within the heart of Adam Kadmon.

Journeys two and three are usually taken almost simultaneously; what has been learned in one life is passed on either in that life or in the next.

If there is perfection in Azilut, how can imperfection exist on earth? Such questions have been asked for millennia and have two levels of answers. The first is that we should not associate the varying strengths and weaknesses of the worlds of Yezirah and Asiyyah with any imperfection of the soul. The second is reincarnation.

In relation to the first answer, every human is divine but there are a thousand reasons why a physical body may not perfect in the uterus or a psyche may not develop in Yezirah. We know about genetic diseases in the physical body but the founder of homeopathy, Samuel Hahnemann

(1755–1843), discovered that certain genetic issues or chronic miasms (from the Greek for "pollution") affect the psychological makeup of a human. The most common come from ancestral diseases such as syphilis and tuberculosis, which can lead to emotional tendencies, including alcoholism and depression, in those people's descendants.

HELPER SOULS

It is sometimes said that a child murdered in one life might be a soul that killed someone else in a previous life. This is possible, but Kabbalah teaches that some souls taking the third or fourth journeys volunteer to come and assist less-developed souls who are finding the first and second journeys difficult. If those other souls cannot overcome difficult situations and hurt or kill the more experienced, helping soul, then that is a chance that the developed soul has chosen to take and is willing to forgive. This does not lessen the pain of those around that soul, but very often, experience of such a tragedy changes lives for the good, giving them a purpose in helping to ensure the event does not happen again.

It is Kabbalistic teaching that all human life is inherently good and will recognize that fact. The choices that we make that lead to disillusionment, pain, and even death are not the permanent choices; there is always an opportunity in a new life to learn happiness.

REINCARNATION

The concept of reincarnation and Karma are often resisted in spiritual teaching as they are seen to be judgmental and unfair. However, it would truly be unfair if the human soul had only one chance to live a fulfilling life. It is not possible for every soul to be born into a life of happiness, prosperity, and health and this is because of the human choices that have been made for centuries. Therefore, it is a much fairer system for the soul to have a succession of lives, each with its own points of learning. For this reason, Kabbalah says there are four journeys, each of which is made over many lives.

THE TREASURE HOUSE OF SOULS

These four journeys may mean myriads of different lives for each individual.

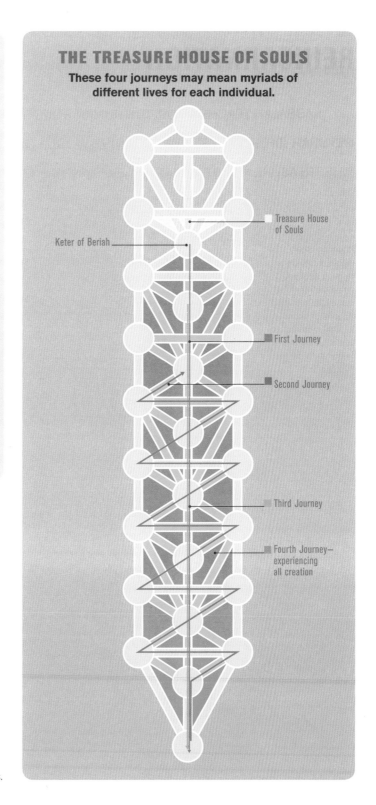

Keter of Beriah

Treasure House of Souls

First Journey

Second Journey

Third Journey

Fourth Journey— experiencing all creation

SHEKHINAH, THE DAUGHTER OF THE VOICE

✳ MUCH HAS BEEN WRITTEN IN MODERN POPULAR CULTURE ABOUT THE NEED FOR A BALANCING FEMININE ASPECT TO THE PERCEIVED MASCULINITY OF GOD. KABBALAH TEACHES THAT GOD HAS NEITHER MALE NOR FEMALE BUT IT IS ONLY HUMAN TO SEEK THIS BALANCE IN A WORLD OF DUALITY.

In Azilut, the Divine is One, and Adam Kadmon is androgynous. In Beriah, Adam Kadmon is One with masculine and feminine aspects. The Bible describes this Beriatic Adam in Genesis 2:18 when it says, "So God created man in his image, in the image of God created he him; male and female created he them both."

In Yezirah, the male and female aspects separated into two beings (Genesis 2:18: "the Lord God said, 'It is not good that the man should be alone; I will make him an help meet'"). Misinterpretations of these two phrases led to the legend of Adam's first wife, Lilith, who refused to be his subordinate. Incidentally, the phrase "Adam's rib" ("tsela") is better translated as "Adam's side," meaning that he was divided in half.

THE SHEKHINAH

In Kabbalah, the feminine aspect of Divinity itself is seen as the Malkhut or Kingdom of Azilut. This is the dwelling place of the Shekhinah ("the Divine Presence"), also known as "the Daughter of the Voice." This Sefira consists of the most elemental levels of the divine world of Azilut and is the last stage in the calling forth, creating, forming, and making of Adam Kadmon. In more accessible terms, this is the aspect of Divinity that gives birth to human souls from Azilut and receives them back at death. For women in biblical times, this was entirely appropriate as they were the people concerned with the birth and death of humanity; men as doctors came later, although the carpenter of a town was generally also its surgeon.

The Malkhut of Azilut may be situated at the bottom of the Great Tree of the divine world but it is by no means the least important of the Sefirot. All are equally important because as the symbol of Adam Kadmon demonstrates, they are all part of one unified being.

The place of Shekhinah is also the place of the Messiah—the Anointed One of a particular age and the highest point to which an incarnated human being can aspire.

Feminine power and priesthood was an acknowledged fact in ancient times before the all-conquering Greeks brought centuries of imperial control. Despite the low social position of women in Greek culture (with the dramatic exception of the city of Sparta), feminine deities were still common. In the Jewish tradition, the feminine was equated with Shekhinah.

In the *Zohar* (*see page 30*) it was said that a man was incomplete without a wife because only on marriage could he be united with Shekhinah, which was present within the woman. In fact, when a married man was apart from his wife, God would have to descend in the form of Shekhinah in order for the man to be whole.

THE SHEKHINAH IN CHRISTIANITY

In Christianity, the role of Shekhinah was taken by the Virgin Mary, who Catholics believe was bodily assumed into heaven when she died. The Regina Coeli (Queen of Heaven) is an anthem used in Catholic churches at Eastertime. Mary was declared to be the Mother of God by the Christian Church in the 5th century CE at Ephesus, Turkey. It is interesting that Ephesus was a center of worship of the pagan mother-goddess, Artemis, one of whose titles was also Queen of Heaven. In the 16th-century Reformation, which gave birth to the Protestant faith, Mary's role was seen as much less important than in Catholicism.

ADAM THROUGH THE WORLDS

Adam and Eve only became physical humans when they "put on coats of skin."

Adam Kadmon
Perfected being with Treasure House of Souls

"Male and female created he them both"
Beriatic Adam containing concept of feminine and masculine

"It was not good for the man to be alone."
One soul split into two psyches, wholly masculine and wholly feminine

"They put on coats of skin"
Man and woman incarnate on Earth as separate entities

PART SIX

THE WORK OF THE KABBALIST

THE KABBALIST'S WORK IS TO BRING THE DIVINE DOWN TO EARTH AND TO NURTURE THE HUMAN SOUL. IT CAN BE SUMMED UP BY THE IMPORTANCE OF THE ORDER THAT THE BIBLE GIVES US FOR LIVING A GOOD LIFE. THIS IS DEMONSTRATED IN THE TITHING SYSTEM. A TITHE IS A VOLUNTARY OFFERING OF TEN PERCENT OF ANYTHING THAT YOU HAVE GAINED. IT COULD BE MONEY, TIME, INSPIRATION, OR KINDNESS. THE BIBLE DESCRIBES THE SPIRITUAL TITHE (LEVITICUS 27:30); THE FESTIVAL TITHE (DEUTERONOMY 12:6, 17–18; 14:22–27), AND THE CHARITY TITHE (DEUTERONOMY 14:28; 26:12). THIS SYSTEM IS FREQUENTLY MISUNDERSTOOD TO MEAN THAT TITHES SHOULD BE GIVEN TO CHARITY. YET KABBALAH TEACHES THAT TO LIVE AN INSPIRATIONAL AND COMPASSIONATE LIFE, YOU SHOULD PUT GOD FIRST, THEN JOY, THEN HELPING OTHERS. IN ANY OTHER ORDER, WE WORK AGAINST GOD'S PLAN. A TREE CANNOT BEAR FRUIT AND FEED OTHERS BEFORE IT HAS BLOSSOMED.

CHAPTER ELEVEN

CHOOSING A TRADITION

✳ KABBALAH IS NOW TAUGHT THROUGHOUT THE WORLD IN SIX DISTINCT TRADITIONS. THESE ARE: THE ORTHODOX JEWISH TRADITION; THE MAGICAL SYSTEM, INCLUDING THE TEACHINGS OF THE FAMOUS "GOLDEN DAWN"; CHRISTIAN KABBALAH; THE LURIANIC TRADITION; THE TOLEDANO TRADITION; AND THE TEACHINGS OF THE KABBALAH CENTER. THE TEACHINGS OF THE LOS ANGELES-BASED KABBALAH CENTER ARE CURRENTLY THE MOST COMMONLY KNOWN THROUGHOUT THE WORLD.

There is an ancient saying that goes, "Two Jews, three opinions." Differing interpretations of spiritual law are a natural outcome when a faith based on the importance of discussion and interpretation is disseminated throughout the world. Because Kabbalistic knowledge is seen as sacred, it has been subjected to the common regulations that beset so many religions: that it is only for men, for those of a certain social standing, and only for members of the religion that has taught it for centuries. However, except for within Orthodox Judaism, Kabbalah is now being taught to women and non-Jews by both Jewish and non-Jewish teachers.

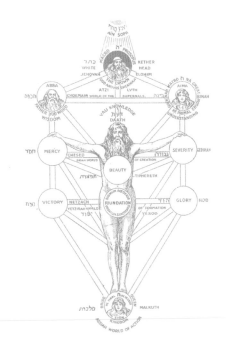

ANCIENT SPIRITUAL SYSTEMS

Between the 17th and 20th centuries, many ancient spiritual systems were brought to light such as Hermeticism, based on the writings of the mythical Hermes Trismegistus, an amalgam of the Egyptian god Thoth and the Greek god Hermes. Rosicrucianism developed from the 15th-century writings of the mythical Christian Rosenkreutz, while Tarot (*see page 162*) can be traced back to 14th-century Italy, although it was influenced by far more ancient Chinese and Indian systems. All of these were influenced by Kabbalistic teaching and now include aspects of Kabbalah.

Above: Interpretations of Kabbalah are so varied that some traditions even reverse the Tree of Life, putting feminine on the right-hand column and masculine on the left.

SELECTING A TRADITION

In choosing a tradition, there are two criteria which must be considered.

1 Does this teaching work? That is, can you apply it to your life in order to understand yourself and your relationship to the universe and to God better?

2 Are you free to choose? Studying Kabbalah requires commitment and at some stage it is important to select your group or tradition—but when and how you do that is up to you. Kabbalah should never tie you to a certain center, group, or tradition. While Christian Kabbalah exists, there are very few other groups that can be attended. This is because at the root of Kabbalah is the belief that an ultimate Messiah has not yet come. Outside of Orthodox Judaism, Jesus of Nazareth is seen as *a* Messiah—the Axis of his Age—but not *the* Messiah.

For traditional Christians this is not a viable belief. However, it is very helpful in all interfaith studies because the Kabbalah tradition can acknowledge that great souls such as Moses, Buddha, Krishnamurti, and Zoroaster were Messiahs of their day and that their teachings are as important (but not more so) than those of Jesus.

For most people, the Kabbalah Center is the most accessible way to study Kabbalah, although it does not use the Tree of Life or Jacob's Ladder. The center follows the Lurianic belief that God's universe was not strong enough to hold the light.

Magical Kabbalah is also Lurianic in basis but less so in practice. Practitioners in the past

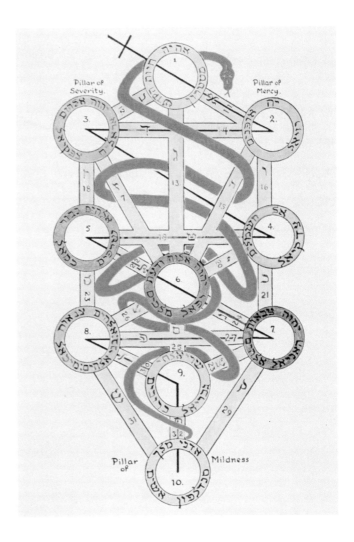

have been known for summoning angelic and demonic energies and believing that achieving power over these areas of Yezirah would bring spiritual enlightenment. Many modern-day witches use strands of magical Kabbalah but generally do not have a deep knowledge of either the Tree or the Ladder.

The 20th-century Toledano tradition, which returns to the original, pre-Lurianic system that was followed in biblical times, is becoming steadily more popular because of its emphasis on how to understand and live Kabbalah in daily life.

Above: It is believed that the Tree of Life is one source of inspiration for the game of "snakes and ladders" where players aspire to climb a ladder but often slide down the snake back to where they started.

LURIANIC KABBALAH

✱ UNTIL THE 16TH CENTURY, KABBALAH, LIKE MODERN-DAY NEW AGE TEACHINGS, WORKED ON THE PREMISE THAT THE WORLD WAS PREDOMINANTLY A PLACE OF WELL-BEING AND ABUNDANCE. SINCE KABBALAH HAD FOR MANY CENTURIES BEEN STRONGLY CONNECTED WITH THE JEWISH RELIGION, IT HELD TO THE BELIEF THAT GOD CREATED THE WORLD PERFECTLY.

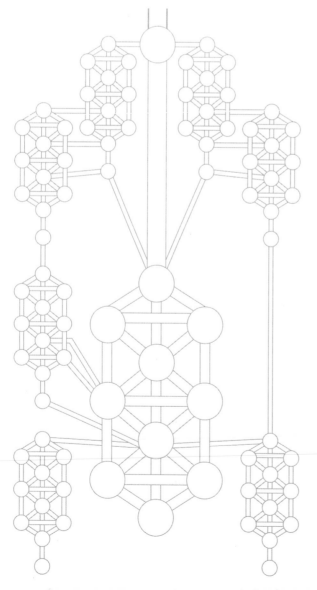

This belief was based on the first chapter of the Biblical book of Genesis (1:31): "God saw every thing that he had made, and, behold, it was very good." Mystics from the beginning of time have taught the principles of responsibility; that we are stewards of the Earth and that every action has a consequence. Therefore any tragedies and misfortunes that fell on humanity were seen as being caused by the misuse of human free will.

In the 16th century, for the Jewish people who were persecuted during the Inquisition and expelled from their Spanish and Portuguese homelands, this teaching was both unhelpful and possibly even cruel. They had done nothing to deserve such ill-treatment and it was too hard to expect them to believe that they had, themselves, persecuted others in a previous life. Therefore, a new impulse was needed in the Kabbalistic mystical tradition, which was attempting to keep the Jewish faith together as its people were scattered around the world.

Left: An illustration based on a 19th-century representation of Isaac Luria's teachings through complex new interpretations of the Tree of Life.

ISAAC LURIA

This impulse was provided by a charismatic young man from Palestine called Isaac Luria (1534–72). Luria was a mystic who spent years in seclusion communing with the higher worlds. He believed that he was guided by the prophet Elijah. Luria joined the school of a respected rabbi and author, Moses Cordovero in Safed in Syria (now Israel). On Cordovero's death, he took over the group and began to teach a new line of Kabbalah that helped to explain the tragedy of what had happened to the Jewish nation. He taught that when God created the universe, He made a mistake: the great divine vessels created to hold the light of emanation were not strong enough and broke. This sent shards of matter throughout the universe, which became evil impulses. They are the cause of bad things that happen to good people—an external evil that strikes at random.

THE GROWTH OF LURIANIC KABBALAH

Later Lurianic Kabbalists explained the apparent dichotomy of an omnipotent God who was capable of error by saying that the Holy One intended the mistake to happen in order to test humanity. Lurianic Kabbalah spread like wildfire, not only because it brought comfort but because it emerged at a time when the printing press had been established and people could spread the word via literature.

However, a curious thing happened with the dissemination of Isaac Luria's teachings by his followers: Jacob's Ladder was not taught and it disappeared from conventional Kabbalistic study for the following 400 years. No one is certain why this happened or whether the Ladder was

ANI MA'AMIN (I BELIEVE)

✡ I believe in the sun even when it's not shining.

✡ I believe in love even when I cannot feel it.

✡ I believe in God, even when He is silent.

Translation from Hebrew poem found in 1945. It was written during the Holocaust on a wall in a cellar in Cologne, Germany.

suppressed because it was thought that it could not support Luria's theory. Instead, Luria's own diagrams were taught. These were very complicated, and the links between levels and worlds were easily misunderstood. Therefore students of Kabbalah began to study the tradition in alternative ways. The Tree of Life was still seen as relevant, but the diagrammatic part of Kabbalah was reduced in importance in favor of the study of the significance and power of the Hebrew alphabet.

Below: An illustration representing an early Lurianic interpretation of the way the four worlds link together on different Trees of Life.

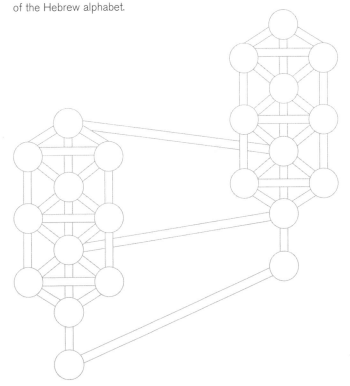

MAGICAL KABBALAH AND THE GOLDEN DAWN

✳ ONCE THE PRINTING PRESS HAD BEEN DEVELOPED, THE GREAT KABBALISTIC BOOKS, PARTICULARLY THE *ZOHAR*, COULD BE READ AND INTERPRETED BY PEOPLE OF ALL FAITHS. BETWEEN THE 17TH AND 20TH CENTURIES, MANY SPIRITUAL SEEKERS SAW AND UNDERSTOOD THAT ALL THE DIFFERENT MYSTICAL TRADITIONS CAME FROM ONE TRUTH AND THAT THEY COULD ALL BE USED TOGETHER.

The best-known Kabbalistic group that formed on the basis of this realization was the Hermetic Order of the Golden Dawn, founded in London in 1888. Its followers studied what they called "high magic" —visualization and ritual, and calling forth spirits, angels, or demons. They carried out these practices in order to learn about their own psyches and in hope of controlling the external world.

Two of the most famous members of this group were Dion Fortune (1890–1946) and Aleister Crowley (1875–1947). Dion Fortune was an occultist who later formed her own order known as the Fraternity of the Inner Light, based upon esoteric and Kabbalistic Christianity and Jungian psychology. Aleister Crowley was a charismatic magician famed equally for his dissolute lifestyle as for his work.

The Golden Dawn developed a complex system of interpretation of the paths of the Tree of Life, based largely on the ancient Sefer Yezirah. Its work is best known through the writings of Israel Regardie, a student of Aleister Crowley and the author of various books, including *The Tree of Life, A Study in Magic,* and *A Garden of Pomegranates.*

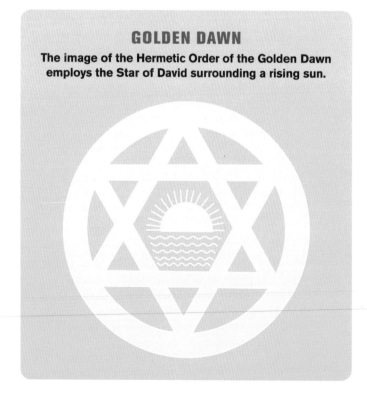

GOLDEN DAWN
The image of the Hermetic Order of the Golden Dawn employs the Star of David surrounding a rising sun.

THE DANGERS OF MAGIC

For many centuries orthodox religions have condemned magic as dangerous heresy. While much of what they interpreted as magic was actually helpful folklore and the inner sacred worship of women, who were not, at that time, permitted to take part in conventional worship as priestesses, there was a reason behind the anti-magic stance.

Magic, like astrology, is Yeziratic. The easiest way to see it in operation in the modern world is through advertising, where it makes people believe that they cannot be lovable or happy without a product that, five minutes beforehand, they did not know existed.

MANIPULATION THROUGH MAGIC

Magic is defined as bending the Yeziratic world for someone's own will, whether it be for good or for bad. Hitler used a form of magic to make his people believe that Germany had a right to rule the world. Magic, as explained by Kabbalah, is the manipulation of the world of Yezirah by any invocation or prayer that demands a specific result—for example, to help you pass an exam or make someone fall in love with you.

INTERFERENCE IN THE YEZIRATIC WORLD

Even good or "white magic" is an intention to bend the "matrix" of the Yeziratic world. A prayer for someone to recover from sickness is not magic; it is a request to the higher worlds. Healing is not magic; it is a focus on clearing the existing link between the sick person and Spirit, with the intention of creating the best outcome—even if that outcome is death. To cast a spell for someone to recover from sickness is to specify what should happen and could represent interference in a person's greater spiritual, emotional, or physical development.

UNBALANCING THE UNIVERSE

It is perfectly possible for a human being to impose his or her will on another person or situation through magical means, but this pushes the universe out of balance. It takes a continuous effort of will to keep the magic working against the natural flow of creation, which will rebound to its correct structure. This will cause the magic to catapult back to its creator and also to the person under his or her enchantment.

TOLEDANO KABBALAH

✳ IN THE 1970S THE ORIGINAL KABBALISTIC TRADITION THAT GOD CREATED THE WORLD PERFECTLY BEGAN TO BE TAUGHT AGAIN IN PUBLIC. THE KABBALISTIC SCHOOL THAT BROUGHT IT BACK TO LIGHT IS KNOWN AS THE TOLEDANO TRADITION.

This line of the teaching is named for the Spanish city of Toledo, where Jewish, Christian, and Muslim mystics and intellectuals studied together in the 11th century. It is also known as "The Work of Unification" or the "Toledano School of the Soul," and its followers feel that the tradition has increasing importance in supporting religious tolerance. Its founder is an English Sephardi Jew, Z'ev ben Shimon Halevi, (b. January 8th, 1933) who is the author of about a dozen books on the subject. Toledano Kabbalah is now taught all over the world by men and women of all faiths. Halevi's work has spread into the public domain through the Internet making much of what was previously impenetrable more understandable for those investigating Kabbalah. There is no cult of celebrity in the school although its followers come from a wide range of professions. They are encouraged to revere the work itself, not the teachers.

THE CAUSES OF EVIL

Since the 1970s, spiritual seekers of all traditions have begun to adhere to the belief that it is human thoughts and actions that cause evil, not an external force. This has come with a revitalized interest in understanding the ancient law of Karma (or "Law of Attraction" as it is now often called). During the 20th century, when spiritual seekers began to focus on self-responsibility and accept the ancient beliefs of reincarnation and the law of Karma, there was a great need to understand how the four worlds could influence each other. Without Jacob's Ladder it was hard to see how either inspiration or a negative belief (Beriah) could create an emotion (Yezirah) which could then have a direct effect for good or bad on the physical body (Asiyyah). With that understanding, we

EVERYDAY LIFE FOR MEMBERS

Members of the Toledano School meet in people's own homes rather than in official buildings; the school has no corporate structure and teaches theory through discussion and meditation. Followers are encouraged to live the work in their daily lives and to understand the workings of the Sefirot and triads in their own bodies. They are also taught to attempt to integrate the vegetable, animal, and human levels within themselves so they can become detached from the everyday pressures of society while still living full family, work, and social lives. This is done by focusing on the conscious use of free will to see the world from Tiferet rather than from Yesod and to observe the patterns and cycles of history, politics, and public opinion. The school runs an annual summer school in Gloucestershire, UK, and Kabbalistic pilgrimages all over the world. Its members include traditional Jews, ordained Christian ministers, Muslims, Buddhists, Hindus, Shintos, and Baha'is.

JACOB'S LADDER REINSTATED

It was through the Toledano Tradition that Jacob's Ladder returned to the public domain. Knowledge of it had been kept secret since Lurianic times, and many 20th-century Kabbalists had speculated, with varying degrees of accuracy, on how the four Trees of the four worlds fitted together. During the 20th century, when spiritual seekers began to focus on self-responsibility and accept the ancient beliefs of reincarnation and the Law of Karma, there was a great need for the restoration of this diagram, which could demonstrate the workings of the four worlds in harmony.

no longer view Karma as something evil that happens to the innocent. A Toledano Kabbalistic interpretation of the cause of the Holocaust of the 1940s would be that the evil was caused by the will of human beings and the lack of action by humanity as a whole when the views of the Nazi regime became increasingly obvious.

When such evil is perpetrated, it comes from a distorted soul triad and affects those living and working at the animal and vegetable levels below. Even today, dictators and warlords can destroy the lives of those they rule, but the world is changing. In some countries at least, people are able to have a say through free speech and the world media. Another Holocaust would, it is hoped, never be permitted to happen. However, this leads to other moral and ethical issues such as whether it is right to invade a country to try to prevent such cruelty.

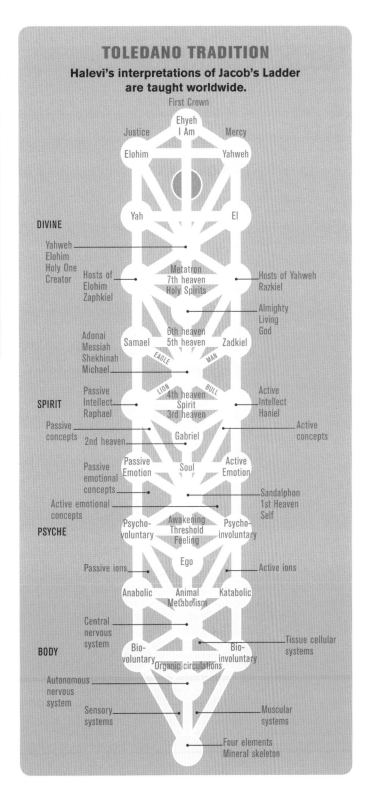

TOLEDANO TRADITION
Halevi's interpretations of Jacob's Ladder are taught worldwide.

THE KABBALAH CENTER

✳ THE KABBALAH CENTER WAS FOUNDED IN 1969 BY AN AMERICAN RABBI, PHILIP BERG. IT IS NOW A HIGHLY SUCCESSFUL ORGANIZATION, WITH A MULTI-MILLION DOLLAR HEADQUARTERS IN LOS ANGELES AND BRANCHES IN TEL AVIV, LONDON, NEW YORK, AND TORONTO.

The Kabbalah Center is now run by Rabbi Berg's wife Karen, along with his sons Michael and Yehuda. Karen, Yehuda, and Michael Berg have written many books about Kabbalah, including *The Kabbalah Book of Sex, God Wears Lipstick,* and *Secrets of the Zohar,* making the tradition very accessible to people of all religions.

The Kabbalah Center has a strong presence on the Internet and its teaching has evoked strong reaction from Orthodox Jews. Members of the Center are expected to tithe to it on a

Above: Red string bracelets are worn on the left wrist as a talisman to protect against the "evil eye."

regular basis. This is very similar to the annual charge made for membership to a Synagogue and is in line with the Old Testament tithing system and many Christian churches.

WORK OF THE KABBALAH CENTER

The Center, which is a charitable foundation, and runs courses and a children's education program. Its interpretation of Lurianic Kabbalah teaches that when God created the Sefirot to receive the light of creation, the Sefirot did not want only to receive but also to give, and resisted the light that was being poured into them. The Creator then stopped the flow of Light and, when the Sefirot felt its loss, flowed it back to the Sefirot again. The Sefirot were unable to handle the Light and shattered.

The Kabbalah Center also teaches that the task of humanity is to learn to receive the Light for the sole purpose of passing it on to others. This is said to be the way to repair the vessels that shattered. The principle that the vessels should receive for the sole purpose of fulfilling God's will and not pass on the Light until they are filled is mooted to be appropriate only on the Sabbath. This belief is in line with the traditional Christian principle of the virtue of self-sacrifice and giving. The Kabbalah Center focuses much of its work on the *Zohar* and meditation on Hebrew letters that spell the 72 names of God. Members of the Center believe that reading or speaking the names creates a deep resonance within the reader and that it is not necessary to understand them. The Center does not teach about the Tree of Life or Jacob's Ladder.

The Center has many famous followers, including the international rock star Madonna. In popular culture it is probably best known for the sale of red string bracelets said to protect the wearer from the "evil eye" or the envy of others. This is string that is regarded as sacred, having been wrapped around the tomb of the Jewish matriarch Rachel, located on the southern West Bank outside Jerusalem and considered the third holiest site in Judaism

The Kabbalah Center's website states:
Long ago, the ancient Kabbalists revealed a powerful technology of protection. Its purpose is twofold: to protect us from the envious looks of others, and to help us eliminate feelings of jealousy and resentment in ourselves. The technology is the Red String: a strand of red wool worn around the left wrist. This technology is an indispensable tool for spiritual and physical protection.

In addition to the bracelets, the Center also sells candles, incense, books, posters, meditation cards, and "Kabbalah Water" about which www.kabbalahwater.com states:
Years ago, Rav Berg and the great Kabbalists who were his teachers made an astonishing discovery: a truly sharing consciousness, channeled through certain Kabbalistic blessings and meditations, has the power to return water to its primordial state of completely positive, healing energy. Through the power of these meditations and the consciousness of sharing that is their foundation, Kabbalah Water came into being—and its miraculous powers of restoration and healing became available to the world. Infused with sharing consciousness, Kabbalah Water manifests water's primordial capacity to heal and protect.

Left: The 72 names of God are an important part of the teaching of the Kabbalah Center with students learning to meditate on appropriate names for their situation.

TAROT AND KABBALAH

✴ IN A TAROT READING, SEVERAL CARDS ARE DRAWN AT RANDOM FROM A DECK. THE CARDS ARE USED TO PREDICT THE FUTURE AND FORETELL HOW THE PERSON CONCERNED IS EMOTIONALLY EQUIPPED TO DEAL WITH THE POSSIBILITIES AHEAD.

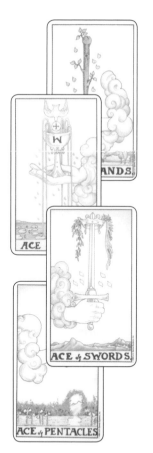

Above: Each of the four suits of the Tarot pack corresponds to one of the four worlds—a part of a universal matrix discovered by humanity in many forms.

The forebears of Tarot date back several thousand years to ancient China and India, but the practice became widely known in Europe during the 14th and 15th centuries. By then, the cards had symbolic and sacred emblems on them, although it is also possible to use a normal deck of cards as a Tarot pack.

THE TAROT DECK

Nowadays there are dozens of different designs of Tarot but every deck contains 78 cards, 22 of which are known as trump cards or the major arcana. Each of these is associated with a letter from the Hebrew alphabet, which is one of the two main reasons that Tarot is associated with Kabbalah. The other 56 cards consist of the four suits of cards, each numbered from one (Ace) to ten. These are known as the minor arcana and correspond to the Four Worlds of Jacob's Ladder: wands (or clubs in a conventional pack of cards) for Azilut; swords (spades) for Beriah; cups (hearts) for Yezirah; and pentangles (diamonds) for Asiyyah.

Each court card also represents a level in the four worlds: the kings correspond to Azilut; the queens to Beriah; the knights to Yezirah; and the pages to Asiyyah. Therefore the knight of wands represents the Yeziratic level of Azilut, and the queen of pentangles represents the Beriatic level in Asiyyah. The ten numbered cards are assigned to the ten Sefirot with the Ace as Keter, the two as Hokhmah, the three as Binah, and so on. So the five of swords corresponds to the Gevurah of the Beriatic world, and the seven of cups represents the Nezach of the Yeziratic world.

The Kabbalistic correspondences were first written down by a 19th-century French teacher of occult magic called Eliphas Levi, and his work was developed by two founders of the Golden Dawn, S. L. MacGregor Mathers and A. E. Waite. Even now the Rider-Waite Tarot pack is the most popular one used.

TAROT READING

Tarot readers use the major arcana to describe our journey through life together with the important events that we may expect along the way, such as love, marriage, divorce, career changes, and crises. The minor arcana describe daily life and how we cope with it. The major and minor arcana together can act as a spiritual guidebook, providing helpful pointers and directions as we go through life.

UNDERSTANDING THE CARDS

Here are some of the attributions of the cards according to two different systems
(ways of linking the Sefirot in the Yeziratic world; *see pages 164–5*).

The fool
Rulership: Air
Hebrew Letter: Alef
Numerical Value: 3
Path: Keter–Hokhmah or Yesod–Hod

UPRIGHT
✡ The start of some kind of journey whether emotional, physical, or spiritual
✡ Overturning of the status quo through unexpected events
✡ Innocence—the beginning of a new stage of life
✡ Important decisions to be made

REVERSED
✡ Taking risks without due consideration
✡ Foolishness, gambling at all levels
✡ Difficulty with commitment

Justice
Rulership: Libra
Hebrew Letter: Lamed
Numerical Value: 12
Path: Keter–Tiferet or Gevurah–Tiferet

UPRIGHT
✡ Clear resolution of conflicts ranging from court cases to family disagreements
✡ Clarity and fairness

REVERSED
✡ Injustice, delay, and prejudice
✡ Complications in legal matters

The tower
Rulership: Mars
Hebrew Letter: Peh
Numerical Value: 9
Path: Hod–Tiferet or Hod–Nezach

UPRIGHT
✡ Conflict and disruption
✡ Dramatic upheavals and sudden, maybe violent losses, but leading to breakthroughs and enlightenment

REVERSED
✡ Negativity and drastic change, which may lead to less fortunate outcomes such as a feeling of being trapped or, outwardly, financial problems

TAROT PATHWORK AND KABBALAH

✳ MANY STUDENTS OF KABBALAH LIKE TO FOCUS ON *PATHWORK*, WHICH IS THE STUDY OF THE PATHS THAT LINK THE SEFIROT IN THE YEZIRATIC WORLD AND WHICH, LIKE THE TAROT CARDS, CAN ALL BE SEEN TO CORRESPOND TO A PARTICULAR LETTER OF THE HEBREW ALPHABET. UNLIKE THE SEFIROT, WHICH ARE OBJECTIVE, THE PATHS ARE SUBJECTIVE.

ON THE TREE

There is no definitive ruling on which letter represents which path because it could be different for every single human being. Interpretation of the attributes of the pathway between two particular Sefirot is dependent on each individual's astrological makeup. For example, a Kabbalist with Mercury in Taurus and Venus in Cancer would experience a very different quality to the pathway between Hod and Nezach than would a Kabbalist with Mercury in Gemini and Venus in Leo.

THE PATHWORKING SYSTEM

According to the Tarot system most commonly used by modern Kabbalists, the paths are numbered 1–32 rather than 1–22. In this system, the Hebrew alphabet is not used and the first ten numbers are designated to the Sefirot so that the pathworking begins with the path between Keter and Hokhmah at number eleven. Twelve is the path from Keter to Binah and thirteen

Left: The 22 paths on the Tree of Life correspond to the 22 cards of the Major Arcana. The best-known interpretations of tarot cards on the Tree of Life come from the teachings of the Golden Dawn, but more than one system can be used.

Above: Hebrew, like Chinese, is a language of pictures and so open to wide interpretation.

the path from Keter to Tiferet. This creates a pattern of energy from Keter to Malkhut.

The oldest known pathworking system does use the Hebrew letters, together with the numerical values attributed to them. However, Hebrew letters have more than just an alphabetical meaning: each one is imbued with cosmic symbolism. Alef, the first letter (Keter–Hokhmah) means both "to create thousands" or "to domesticate and civilize." Bet, the second letter (Hokhmah-Binah), has the varying meanings of "house," "tribe," or "instrument." This system follows the lightning flash of creation but appears to be more complex as it fills in the triads along the way.

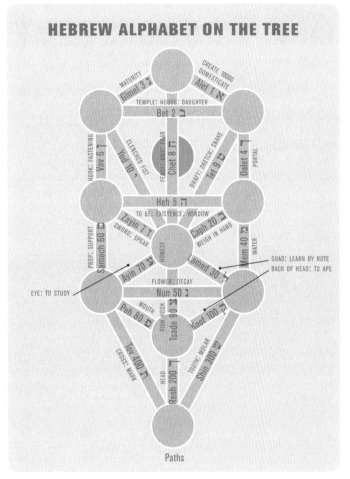

HEBREW ALPHABET ON THE TREE

Paths

FINDING MEANING FROM THE HEBREW LETTERS

While much of the pathworking system is very complex, it does provide insights. In Hebrew most words are formed from three-letter roots. Groups of words, which are generally related, are based on the roots (*see pages 17 and 18*). In this system (according to unverifiable Hebrew interpretations by the hermetic Order of the Golden Dawn), the letters corresponding to the Nezach–Malkhut–Hod triad (Shin, Nun, and Tov) form the ancient Hebrew root for cycles, day, year, and sleep—very appropriate for the vegetable triad that they represent. The letters corresponding to the triad of Hod–Nezach–Yesod (Nun, Kuf, and Peh) form the Hebrew root "to go around in a circle," and the path letters from Hod to Gevurah, Gevurah to Binah, and Binah to Keter spell out Samech Vav Gimel meaning "return to the source."

Such complex wordplay requires a deep understanding of Hebrew, which most modern Kabbalists do not have. Though fascinating, it can lead to an over-theoretical study of the Tree without practical application.

NUMEROLOGY AND GEMATRIA

✳ FOR THOUSANDS OF YEARS, KABBALISTS HAVE USED GEMATRIA, A SYSTEM OF MATHEMATICS THAT WORKS ON CORRESPONDENCES BETWEEN THE 22 PATHS OF THE TREE OF LIFE, THE TEN SEFIROT, AND THE 22 LETTERS IN THE HEBREW ALPHABET. EVEN TODAY SOME KABBALISTS BELIEVE THAT THE *TORAH* WAS WRITTEN IN A SECRET CODE BASED ON NUMBERS. THE STUDY OF THIS SYSTEM OF NUMBERS IS KNOWN AS NUMEROLOGY.

Gematria follows the idea that each letter of an alphabet corresponds to a number. Numerical values of words are added together and these words are believed to have a special relevance to other words that have the same numerical value.

Gematria is one reason why many different names are attributed to aspects of God as well as Ayin, Ayin Sof, Ayin Sof Or, and the ten names of God on the Sefirot of the Azilutic Tree of Life.

Probably the best-known form of gematria is "the 72 Names of God," which is derived from a sequence of 72 specially arranged letters found in the biblical Book of Exodus (14:19–21). This sequence is also made up from three verses of 72 letters each. To be strictly accurate it is a 72-syllable name of God, which is part of a 216-letter name of God. This was calculated by the idea of putting together the first letter of verse 14:19, the last letter of verse 14:20 and the first letter of 14:21 to create what is called a triad (this is a different kind of triad from the ones on the Tree of Life). The next triad is created from the second letter of 14:19, the second to last of 14:20 and the second letter of 14:21. This form of gematria continues until all the letters are used up. There is even a 304,805-letter name of God revealed by reciting all the letters of the *Torah* in a series.

כהת	אכא	ללה	מהש	עלם	סיט	ילי	והו
הקם	הרי	מבה	יזל	ההע	לאו	אלד	הזי
ההו	מלה	ייי	נלכ	פהל	לוו	כלי	לאו
רשר	לכב	אום	ריי	שאה	ירת	האא	נתה
ייז	רהע	חעם	אני	מנד	כוק	להה	יחו
מיה	עשל	ערי	סאל	ילה	וול	סיכ	ההה
פוי	מבה	נית	ננא	עמם	החש	דני	והו
מחי	ענו	יהה	ומב	סצר	הרח	ייל	נמם
מום	היי	יבם	ראה	חבו	איע	מנק	דמב

Left: The 72-lettered name is based on three verses in Exodus (14:19–21) beginning with "Vayyissa," "Vayyabo," and "Vayyet," respectively. Each verse contains 72 letters, and when combined they form 72 names, which are known collectively as the "Shemhamphorasch."

The calculation of the value of the Hebrew letters is a very Hodian process involving the intellect. Although many Kabbalists see great significance in it for purposes of meditation, it takes years of study to acquire the knowledge to use this system to explore hidden meanings in sacred texts. It is also worth noting that there are many different translations of the Bible, which produce different calculations.

What we know as Bible Codes, or Torah Codes, are similar but they interpret the Bible through the number of spaces between particular letters rather than the numerical values of the letters themselves.

WAYS TO CALCULATE THE VALUE OF THE HEBREW LETTERS

✡ **Absolute Value** is the system that gives the first ten letters of the alphabet numbers from one to ten, with specific values from 20 to 400 given to all the letters after that.

✡ **Ordinal Value** is the system that gives each of the 22 letters a number from 1 to 22.

✡ **Reduced Value** is the system that begins in the same way as Absolute Value but then reduces each letter to the total of their numbers, i.e., it adds the individual numbers together. For example, 31 is counted as three and one, which adds up to four. Both 20 and 200 are reduced to two and both 400 and 40 are reduced to four.

✡ **Integral Reduced Value** adds up the numerical value of the letters in a word and adds them together to reduce them to one digit for the whole word. If when the number is reduced it is 10 or more, then the digits are added together again. For example, a word that totalled 39 letters would be reduced to 12, which would then be reduced to three. This last system is the most used by modern numerologists.

Above: Orthodox Jews consider the Hebrew Bible (known in the Christian tradition as the Old Testament) to be the dictated word of God. Therefore every word—or arrangement of words—is deeply significant.

CHAPTER TWELVE
WORKING ALONE

✳ THE BEST WAY TO STUDY KABBALAH IS IN A GROUP OF PEOPLE WHO MEET TO DISCUSS HOW THE SYSTEM WORKS FOR THEM IN EVERYDAY LIFE. JUST READING ABOUT KABBALAH WITHOUT LIVING IT THROUGH DISCUSSION, EXERCISES, AND MEDITATION IS JUST A THEORETICAL EXERCISE AND WILL NOT CHANGE YOUR LIFE.

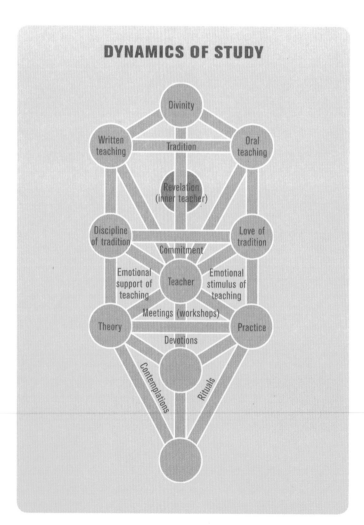

DYNAMICS OF STUDY

If you meet with others, you can discuss the difference between Tiferet (Self) and Yesod (Ego) by looking at your own life and astrology and comparing how you react to events with others. This interaction will give you a strong understanding of who you are and how your Ego can support you.

PITFALLS FOR THE LONE KABBALIST

Not everyone can find a Kabbalah group. For the lone Kabbalist, it is hard to maintain a level of study and practical application but it can be done. For most spiritual seekers, it is easy to climb from the vegetable triad around Yesod to the awakening triad of Hod–Tiferet–Nezach. However, the next stage on the spiritual journey is to lift yourself to the soul triad. That means practicing Gevurah-discipline. A dislike of discipline is understandable in those who have had bad experiences of it in childhood, at school, or at work but this is self-discipline and it is vital for any Kabbalist.

Left: All spiritual groups, not just a Kabbalistic one, will use all these attributes of study to form a successful "school of the soul."

SOLO OR TEAM PLAYER?

An Astrological table of group workings

✡ **Happier working alone:**

Aries—short attention span. Gets impatient with others.

Taurus—prefers to work at own pace

Capricorn—dedicated to structure and discipline

Aquarius—has a unique viewpoint about life

Scorpio—interested in hidden elements.

✡ **Happier working in groups:**

Gemini—gregarious and chatty

Cancer—likes to take care of others

Leo—wants to lead or challenge leaders

Virgo—keen to discuss details

Libra—likes to create harmony

Sagittarius—life and soul of the party

Pisces—dreamy and unstructured.

---

*Everyone is a house with four rooms, a physical, a mental, an emotional, and a spiritual. Most of us tend to live in one room most of the time but, unless we go into every room every day, even if only to keep it aired, we are not a complete person. (*Indian proverb. Source: Rumer Godden).

The spiritual seeker must enter each of the four rooms to create a balance in life and draw down the Divine to the mundane.

LIVING A KABBALISTIC DAY

Since the work of the Kabbalist is concerned with the four levels of existence—divine, spirit, psyche, and body—it is a good idea to start each day with this focus in mind.

The four levels can be accessed very swiftly in this simple exercise, which is best done on waking.

1 Give thanks for the day and for any other good things you can think of. If you are of a naturally negative tendency, it is a good idea to practice gratitudes as often as you can. In this way, you turn your attention to the beauty and abundance of the world rather than to its perceived disharmonies. This equates to the world of Azilut because it is acknowledging the divine hand in the constant re-creation of the world every day.
A good list might be:
Thank you for this new day; for this comfortable bed; for this good night's sleep; for my healthy body; for my loving partner; for miracles that will come this day; for my pets, and for my work.

2 Set your intention. As Beriah is a world of pure thought without emotion, an idea or a strong intent is very powerful—capable of being a driving force behind the day. You will have experienced days where everything went wrong from the start; this helps to ensure that everything goes right from the start.
Intents could be: Today I am happy, healthy, prosperous, and awake to every trick. Today I sail through my work with efficiency and enjoyment, get to and from work easily, and have a lovely evening to round off a perfect day.

3 Clothe yourself carefully. As Yezirah is the world of forms and images, how you present yourself for the day has a psychological effect on you for the whole of the day. You may find that having already touched Azilut and Beriah you have a different idea of what you want to wear from what you had previously intended. Go with that instinct.

4 Feed yourself carefully. We all know the dictum to eat five portions of fruit or vegetables a day and the importance of a good breakfast. However, your body needs you to start the day in a way that serves you. Some people need protein in the morning while others need fruit. Some have undetected allergies to wheat or dairy products, and their cornflakes and milk do more harm than good. You can find out what serves you best through trial and error or through visiting an iridologist or naturopath.

WHEN IS IT EGO AND WHEN IS IT SELF?

✳ IN A KABBALISTIC GROUP, PEOPLE GET TO KNOW EACH OTHER'S ATTRIBUTES SO WELL THAT IT IS EASY TO SPOT WHEN SOMEONE IS COMING FROM YESOD (THEIR EGO) AND WHEN FROM TIFERET (THEIR SELF). IT IS NOT MADE "WRONG," JUST OBSERVED. SUCH INSIGHTS FROM OTHERS CAN BE VERY VALUABLE IN A SAFE, MUTUALLY SUPPORTIVE ENVIRONMENT.

Above: Jacob wrestling with the angel. This biblical story tells of how both the Ego and the Self battle with the idea of spiritual development and the will of God.

Yesod reacts in the same way to the same experience. To change our life in any way, it is important to use Tiferet—to "think again" and to check out whether our reaction is good or just habit. If we do not change our responses, our lives will remain the same as they always were.

The Ego can be hard to understand. A good way to check out how yours is getting in the way of your Self is to go through this checklist. You know your Ego is getting in the way when:

1 You still have exactly the same relationship with your parents as you have had ever since you left home. They're still just as exasperating, intrusive, or unhelpful as they were, and they still annoy you with criticisms or assumptions. If this is the case, it means that your way of reacting to them has not changed or grown. If it had, their attitudes would have changed too.

2 You have to reply to an unpleasant email or accusing letter immediately. The idea of sleeping on a response or the realization that it is not a personal attack does not occur to you. This is Yesod making sure that you come from reaction

PHASES OF THE MOON AND THE EGO

The Moon's orbit affects tides and all water on the planet in regular phases. It also affects the Yeziratic watery world of the human psyche, especially the Ego, which can become very inflamed through passion or anger at the time of a full Moon.

rather than thinking over the situation logically and finding an alternative answer. How many times have you reacted and then realized the following day that you did not even read the offending missive properly in the first place?

3 You go shopping whenever you feel miserable. Yesod appears to crave new experiences and new purchases but really it seeks a quick high that can only work temporarily. Have you ever been shopping and then just left your purchases in the bag when you got home—or worn new clothes once and then decided you did not like them? Yesod (working with Nezach) wanted the quick hit of the purchase so it could mask its woes, rather than the goods themselves.

4 You do not realize that the very last thing the "News" ever is, is new.

5 You would rather be right than happy.

6 You turn down the offer of something you have always secretly wanted because it is scary and you might fail.

7 You use money in a way that does not strengthen or nurture you, such as missing or making late payments, buying things you do not need, or going into debt without a definite plan for getting out again. The subject of money is one that the Ego often uses to make people feel unworthy or threatened.

8 You prefer to go for the same old holiday with the same old crowd rather than trying something different. The main purpose of a holiday is to wake us up and present new experiences so that Yesod cannot rule our lives 365 days a year. When we have a new experience, Yesod has to hand over control to Tiferet, so it cannot run the old "worry patterns" any more. That is why we feel so alive and happy on holiday.

9 You say, "you can't tell me that," or "it's just the way I am," or "I don't want to talk about it."

10 You say, "yes, but…" and argue for your limitations. Doing this reinforces your existing negative beliefs.

WHAT IS YOUR SOUL'S PURPOSE?

✳ MUCH UNHAPPINESS COMES FROM A FEELING THAT YOU DO NOT HAVE A

PURPOSE. EVERY HUMAN BEING HAS A SOUL'S PURPOSE AND IT IS NOT ONLY

TO MARRY AND HAVE CHILDREN. THAT IS THE PURPOSE OF THE LOWER TRIADS

OF NATURE. ALTHOUGH IT CAN GIVE MUCH JOY AT THE TIME, ONCE THE JOB IS

DONE, IT CAN LEAVE YOU FEELING EMPTY.

Right: Robert Fludd's 17th-century engraving of the relation of man, the microcosm with the universe, the macrocosm encapsulates waking up from the Ego and discovering the soul's purpose.

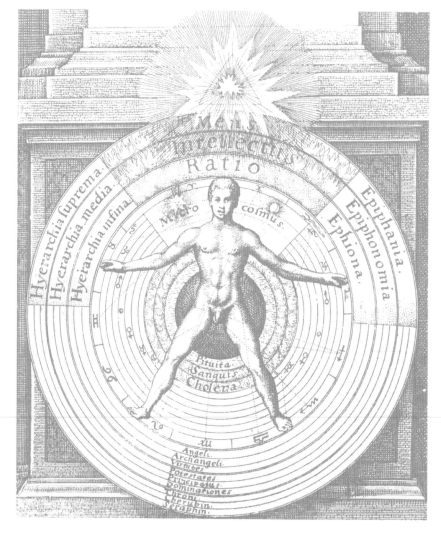

Above: To realize that we are spiritual beings with divine origins is vital in understanding how the world works.

EXERCISE: THE SHIP OF THE SOUL
Try this simple exercise to see the state of your soul.

✡ Imagine that you are standing by a ship-filled harbor. One ship is yours. Which one is it? Take a good look at its size, color and shape, and its condition. Does it have a crew?

✡ Go on board this ship. Can you see a captain and a first officer? Do they recognize you? Who runs this ship? Who gives the orders? What are the current orders? Is there a plan for sailing or is the ship in dry dock for repairs?

✡ Take a good look around your ship. Does it need repairs or a coat of paint? How is it stocked?

✡ Now take the ship out into the open water. Who does the work? How does it sail? Is it seaworthy?

The ship represents your soul as it is today. Is it the kind of ship you would like? If not, then there is work to do on moving toward your destiny. Who is in charge of it? The answer is that it should be you. If anyone else is running your ship it is either Yesod or external circumstances. If it is Yesod, it needs to be demoted to first officer. This can be done kindly, and Yesod may be relieved. Yesod is there to carry out the captain's or owner's orders, not to make its own decisions. If it is external circumstances, then you need to take charge even more.

Your soul should know where it is going even if your consciousness does not, so there should be a plan for sailing. If not, create one—to an island where you can learn healing, to a country of Kabbalists, or to a land where you learn to manifest prosperity. It is up to you. If your ship is damaged or unseaworthy, ask the first officer why, and instruct him or her to get it repaired. It will be done. However, any damage or repairs are a good indication of an imbalance within you. Look at the ship of the Tree of Life (*see page 84*) and see where on your ship the damage is. That Sefira or triad needs to be examined.

Our soul work springs from a deep inner need that must be balanced with the rest of our lives. Those who discover their soul's purpose and act on it are always happy even if they may lead challenging lives. One way to find out is to discover the astrological signs corresponding to Mars and Jupiter in your natal chart. These, together with your Sun sign, can give important clues.

Usually the soul triad is made up from three different signs. Your authentic Self is represented by your sun and your soul's strengths and weaknesses by your Mars and Jupiter. A sun in Virgo with Mars in Scorpio and Jupiter in Libra indicates someone focused on service, accuracy, and health (Virgo). This person can see right to the root of a problem through any illusion and is willing to act to destroy or save where appropriate (Scorpio); he or she has the ability to balance all points of view and find the most harmonious outcome (Libra). This soul triad would indicate a person whose soul's purpose was to discover and heal inner problems—whether as a psychiatrist, healer, or surgeon.

OBSERVING KABBALAH IN THE WORLD

✳ FROM THE POINT OF TIFERET, WE CAN ALL OBSERVE THE HAPPENINGS IN THE WORLD DISPASSIONATELY. WHILE THAT DOES NOT STOP US FROM ACTING TO RIGHT WRONGS OR GIVING WHAT HELP IS NEEDED, IT DOES MEAN THAT WE ARE DETACHED FROM THE DAILY PASSING SHOW OF EVENTS.

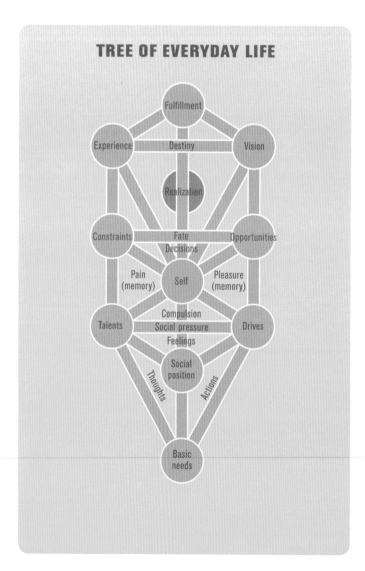

TREE OF EVERYDAY LIFE

Any news reporter quickly learns that events in the world are cyclical. Even great triumphs or disasters are a mirror image of previous events. An important exercise for the student Kabbalist is to wean him- or herself off the idea that the passing show is important. This will activate strong resistance from Yesod, and often also from friends, family, and colleagues. It is not Tiferet that becomes addicted to soap operas, reality shows, and celebrity magazines, it is the triad of Hod–Nezach–Malkhut. Often Tiferet is called in to make a decision based on the animal desires of Hod–Tiferet–Nezach as to which film star is the most powerful, good at their job, or sexy, but the authentic Self knows that such an opinion is essentially unimportant.

In the 21st century we have access to more information than ever before. It is said that the 17th-century poet John Milton, although blind toward the end of his life, was the last person to know everything because he had read virtually every book ever written at that time. Nowadays it would be impossible to know and understand all that is going on in the world, but we are still encouraged to jump to conclusions and follow the opinions of commentators, politicians, and celebrities. Anyone who has had a news story

USEFUL EXERCISES FOR THE KABBALIST WORKING ALONE

1 Operate a complete news blackout for a full month. Do not listen to, watch, or read the news (obviously this is only possible if your work does not require you to do any of the above).

2 From then on, strictly limit your intake of news. If you do see or hear the news, ask yourself the following questions:

a) Can I be of any help in this situation? If yes, then act on it. If not, turn your attention away.

b) Is my observation of this situation adding positive or negative energy to it? If the former, keep observing; if the latter, turn away.

3 For a full month, only watch television programs that make you laugh, entertain you, or add to your level of knowledge.

Yesod will challenge all these exercises strongly because it has probably been trained to empathize with people in distress. In fact, quantum physics demonstrates that attention given to negative situations only draws more negative energy to them.

When you have done the above exercises, you will have a far stronger sense of which outside influences are of value to you and which are not. You are likely to find that levels of residual fear within you are lower and you sleep better.

written about them knows that there is nearly always some level of unintended inaccuracy, even if there has been no deliberate effort to make a story more exciting.

The majority of the world's events are a nine-day wonder with no one but the participants even remembering the names of those involved within a month.

For the lone Kabbalist, assessing what is useful and helpful information is harder than as a member of a group that can address all sides of the issue and come to a common consensus. A group dynamic can discover what is really important in a particular event—what will have ramifications for years to come and what is a passing show.

Above: Many pilgrims go to the cathedral of Chartres to walk the labyrinth. This is placed at Yesod in the great cathedral's design but the exercise of walking it can raise consciousness to Tiferet.

WAKING UP FROM EGO

✳ THE FIRST AND SIMPLEST WAY OF TELLING WHETHER YOU ARE ACTING FROM
YESOD, THE EGO, IS WHETHER SOMETHING HAS TO BE DONE NOW. THE EGO THRIVES
ON DEADLINES AND THE IDEA OF FEELING IMPORTANT. IT IS YESOD THAT INSISTS THAT WE
CHECK EMAILS BEFORE HAVING BREAKFAST OR MEDITATING!

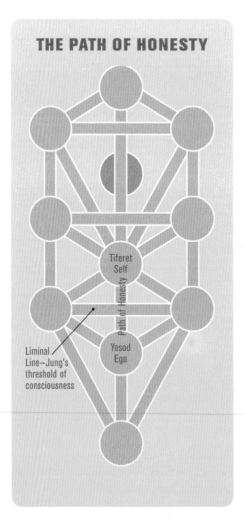

THE PATH OF HONESTY

Tiferet
Self

Path of Honesty

Liminal
Line—Jung's
threshold of
consciousness

Yesod
Ego

ACTING FROM YESOD

To wake up from Yesod, all you have to do is
to look at yourself as if from outside. If you can
actually step back from any situation and ask
that question, you are immediately conscious.
Tiferet is known as "the watcher," and it is from this
balanced state that we can observe our reactions.

Take the following everyday scenario, for
example. You are busy at work and receive a
personal phone call that is time-consuming and
demands your attention when you are short of
time. Being swept up in that situation may mean
that you give scant attention to the caller and
feel deeply irritated and rushed.

If you can think "I am feeling irritated" as
opposed to being in the irritation, you have
moved away from Yesod. Hold that comment
about yourself and you will stay conscious. It is
sometimes helpful to talk to yourself by name,
actually saying, "Watch out, Sarah/John, can you
see yourself being irritated? Can you observe

Left: Within the human psyche there are many levels
of consciousness but all are filtered through the brain's
reticular activating system—the ego. If we cannot
consciously wake we never see our full potential..

this for a minute? Can you step out and watch yourself being worried about a deadline and not being happy about taking this telephone call?

Is there any solution to this? Perhaps if you stop resisting the situation by being angry then it will sort itself out."

THE BLUE FAIRY

It is useful to have a token or a talisman that reminds you to "wake up" when you see it. This needs to be something that works on a deep level. One woman who loved the blue fairy who made dreams come true in the children's story *The Adventures of Pinocchio*—and who appears again later in the Steven Spielberg movie *Artificial Intelligence: A.I.*—found that keeping a little blue angel on her work desk could always remind her of the blue fairy and spark a move in consciousness to Tiferet.

Above: The blue fairy has the power to grant your heart's desire. But it is important to know that the wish does come from the heart and not the ego.

EXERCISES TO FOCUS YOUR CONSCIOUSNESS IN TIFERET

1 Set the alarm on your watch or cellphone to go off three times a day at 10 a.m., noon, and 3 p.m. When it rings, stop whatever you are doing and focus on that exact moment in time. If you have a spiritual group, think of the group members for a minute.

Yesod will resist this and tell you that you should do something else first before you take the time to be conscious. If you let it win, the time will never arise. Once you have done this exercise for a week, turn off the alarm and attempt to remember the three moments in the day without a reminder. Again, Yesod will resist this but it is worth persevering. If you can do this with fellow companions in the workplace, the energy field created by perhaps a dozen people stopping and thinking consciously will be helpful—and you will find it inspirational.

2 Follow the system of tithing in your consciousness (*see page 151*). Place something that will remind you of this exercise by your bed. As soon as you are awake, think first of Spirit or Divinity; this could be a greeting, such as, "Good morning, God!"—as opposed to Yesod's "Good God, Morning!"—or a moment's gratitude for the night's sleep and the new day ahead. Then think of something fun that you can do this day and plan it before you allow yourself to think of work, perhaps a favorite lunch or a visit to a favorite shop? Only then should you allow yourself to focus on the tasks of the day.

3 Get up every morning at 5 a.m. for a full month and go for a walk, preferably in the countryside. This will challenge your Ego hugely—it will tell you that it is cold, tired, afraid of the dark and that this is a stupid idea. But if you control it through your will power and make it obey, then such an active meditation can become an inspirational experience.

4 Fast for a day. The Ego will fight any attempt to starve the body. But, as long as you drink water and have no form of illness, a fast will not harm your body. The resistance to the bodily comfort of regular food will show just how strong the Ego's control of you is. Do take medical advice first if you have any physical weaknesses.

5 Sit still in a room and do nothing for 20 minutes a day for two weeks. The ego will tell you in no uncertain terms how you are wasting your time and may scream with frustration or boredom. Note how many automatic and protesting thoughts you have and how long it takes you to become calm and accepting of the situation.

VISITING HOLY SITES

✳ TRUE HOLY SITES HAVE AN ATMOSPHERE OF PEACE AND REVERENCE THAT SPEAKS TO THE SOUL. MOST CATHEDRALS OR SACRED SITES REGULARLY VISITED BY TOURISTS LOSE MUCH OF THIS FORCE OF SPIRIT BECAUSE THE FOCUS OF HUMAN ATTENTION IS NOT GIVEN TO PRAYER OR WORSHIP.

Nowadays, the most sacred places are those where worshippers alone are permitted. Some of the prayer halls of the enormous mosques of Islam (one is the Great Mosque of Kairouan in Tunisia), where no one enters except to pray or clean, have atmospheres so powerful that they will make you fall to the ground in awe.

VISITING PLACES OF WORSHIP

The idea of a holy building is for people to gather and simultaneously lift their consciousness to Tiferet and beyond. For Christians, this was easier to attain in the days before Christian priests faced the congregation. With both priest and congregation facing the High Altar, they formed a lens to focus on the divine revelation, with all energies channeled in one direction. Now many churches have an altar in the center with the priest celebrating communion behind it. This stops the flow of energy at the lower altar, with the priest being a barrier rather than part of the lens holding the host up to God. This has led to many great churches losing spiritual focus at all levels.

If you can find a church that was built earlier than the 16th century, you will almost certainly be able to spot the work of a Kabbalist. Many old churches were built by master masons who understood the concept of sacred geometry— how to design a building on the universal matrix that drew spiritual energy.

In fact, many churches were built on the design of the Tree of Life, among them the cathedral at Chartres, France. St. Paul's Cathedral in London, UK, is a blueprint for Jacob's Ladder. Walking through these great spiritual places is a good exercise for focusing in Tiferet.

The labyrinth at Chartres is a very popular "walk" for the spiritual seeker. This formation is placed at Yesod in the great cathedral. If walked with perception, it can lift the consciousness, but it is a deceptive device that can also lock people's awareness in Yesod by holding their attention to a favorite area of unconsciousness, such as pleasure in achievement.

Some places in nature have great spiritual presence. This is either because they form part of a sacred landscape—being located, perhaps, on an earthly energy center or chakra where the ancients sensed a particular power source—or because they have been used for spiritual purposes by humanity.

SACRED GEOMETRY

Design of a great cathedral in medieval times was the responsibility of a master mason. This man would have decades of knowledge of material selection, geometrical proportioning, load distribution, architectural design, and a firm sense of liturgy and Christian tradition. Today freemasonry is viewed as a secret society and the roots of this come from the sacred practices of ancient masons, many of whom understood sacred geometry and Kabbalah. They saw no distinction between things material and things spiritual. Many—if not most—medieval churches parallel the design of the Tree of Life. Prof. Keith Critchlow's placing of the Tree on the design of Chartres is very clear, but the rudimentary Tree is visible in the design of another cathedral, Lichfield.

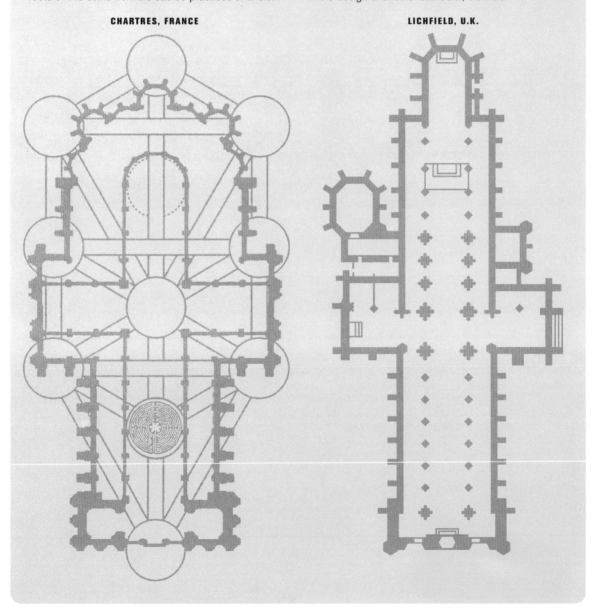

CHARTRES, FRANCE

LICHFIELD, U.K.

CREATING HOLY SPACE

✳ HOLY SPACE IS CREATED THROUGH PRAYER AND RITUAL. IF YOU HAVE A ROOM THAT CAN BE SET ASIDE AS A SANCTUARY, DO SO. IF NOT, A CORNER OF A ROOM WILL DO. BEST OF ALL, MAKE ALL OF YOUR HOME A SACRED SPACE.

Whether it is a house or a room that you choose, you need to begin with a space cleansing. This involves clearing the atmosphere of a house so that its etheric energy becomes neutral and can then be imbued with positive, healing, and life-enhancing energy. The house's residual Feng Shui is overruled by spiritual energy. Energy in houses rises and drops according to the energies of those who live in them. Walls retain memory and there can be residual energy from the after-effects of illness, death, divorce, or a relationship breakup. It is also important to cleanse a new home when you move into it or if you are preparing to get pregnant.

CLEANSING A SPACE

Cleansing should be done four times a year for full effect but once you know what to do, it is quick, easy, and fun.

1 Bring yourself to Tiferet by making the Tree of Life with your body. Then sit quietly and peacefully and ask for protection and guidance. Light two candles (the fire represents Azilut and the two pillars represent the Tree of Life), saying an appropriate prayer such as: "Blessed art thou O Lord our God who has sanctified us by thy commandments and enabled us to reach this season."

2 Light the smudge stick over a saucer or pot that will catch any ash. The fire in the smudge

TREE OF SACRED SPACE

Source

Divinity

Candle understanding

Candle inspiration

Spirit

Grace

Philosophy

Faith

Holy image (female)

Holy image (male)

Altar

Forgiveness

Self

Joy

Awakening

Thoughts

Feelings

Meditation

Contemplation

Prayer

Aspirant

Room

stick represents Azilut and the smoke Beriah. Blow on the smudge stick to make it smolder. Then, using the feather to waft the smoke, walk around the room—or the entire house—from the entrance door, ensuring that smoke goes to every corner of the room.

3 While smudging, say a prayer as feels appropriate such as: "By the Grace of God, this room is cleansed and healed and filled with light." Once the house has been smudged, extinguish the smudge stick by wetting it or by putting it out in earth or sand.

4 Using an atomizer, spray the room/house with a mixture of air (Beriah) and water (Yezirah) containing aromatherapy oils while saying a prayer such as: "This room/house is anointed with the sweetness of God's Grace."

5 When you have finished, sit quietly for a while, focusing on what you want to bring into your life. Then make yourself an altar—a small table is ideal. Place on it a cloth; two candles; whatever spiritual symbols move you; some personal possessions that represent happiness; some crystals or rock, and flowers.

If you go to that place first thing every morning and bless yourself and the day, you will create a small area of sacred space within a week. Make sure that the altar is never cluttered; keep the flowers fresh and renew the sacred objects when you feel moved to do so. Very soon, you will find yourself drawn there whenever you need some peace, time to think, or whenever there is an issue that needs to be resolved.

For work, prepare a small box with sacred and special objects and open it whenever you wish to lift your energy. This will become your moving tabernacle.

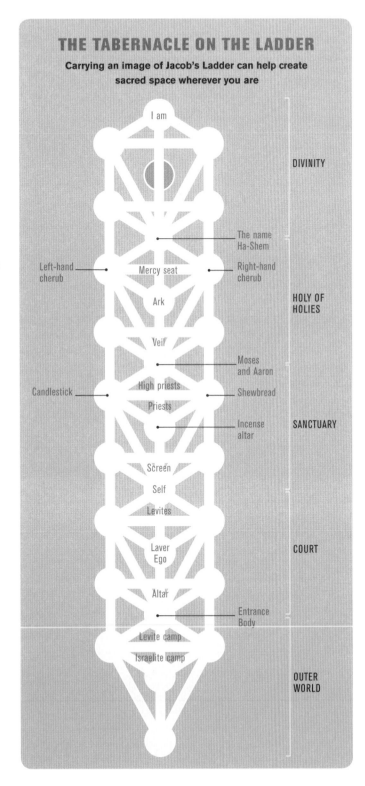

THE TABERNACLE ON THE LADDER

Carrying an image of Jacob's Ladder can help create sacred space wherever you are

I am

DIVINITY

The name Ha-Shem

Left-hand cherub

Mercy seat

Right-hand cherub

Ark

HOLY OF HOLIES

Veil

Moses and Aaron

Candlestick

High priests

Shewbread

Priests

Incense altar

SANCTUARY

Screen

Self

Levites

Laver
Ego

COURT

Altar

Entrance
Body

Levite camp

Israelite camp

OUTER WORLD

CHAPTER THIRTEEN
GROUP WORK

✳ FOR MANY PEOPLE, JOINING A KABBALAH GROUP IS THE OBVIOUS WAY TO BEGIN STUDYING KABBALAH. HOWEVER, IF YOU HAVE NO ACCESS TO OTHER KABBALISTS, YOU ARE LEFT WITH THE OPTION OF STARTING YOUR OWN GROUP.

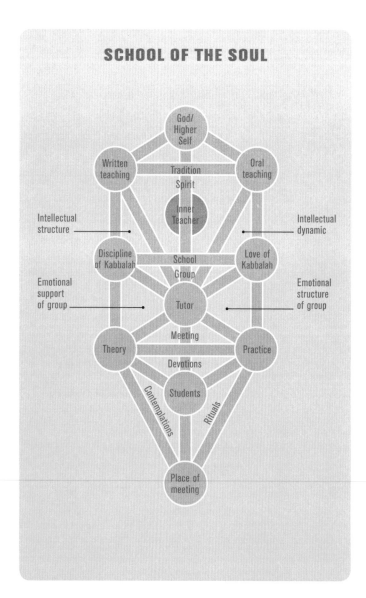

SCHOOL OF THE SOUL

Starting a Kabbalah group is not difficult, but maintaining one is. Many people may be interested in the idea of studying Kabbalah at first, but fall by the wayside when they find that it requires discipline and that it will reveal their Ego to themselves and to others. Traditionally, a group should have ten people, one for each of the Sefirot, but in reality it usually takes time to build up to that number.

The ideal starting point for a group is seven people, one for each of the Sefirot below the supernal triad. If the group is any smaller—and especially if it is not run by an experienced Kabbalist—it may become too personal and be unable to examine a wide range of views and take a detached view of world affairs. A group is best run by one person rather than by a committee. This is because only one person can take the place of Tiferet. The lead person can change between meetings; this is often a good idea because some people are better at leading discussions and others at leading meditations. It may be that the group takes place in different people's homes by rotation and it may be a good idea for the host to act as Tiferet—but that decision is up to you as the founder. Whoever initiates the group is required to take responsibility for it.

Left: All great spiritual teachers have a group of very diverse followers. The Bible clearly states that Jesus' disciples frequently did not understand him and that he found their lack of faith frustrating.

RUNNING THE GROUP

To run a group, you need only be half a step ahead of the others who are participating. If you have a copy of the Tree of Life and a book about the tradition, then you have all you need to start off.

Participants should be encouraged to draw their own diagrams; just doing this is a very good basis for discussion. They can also be taught how to make the Tree with their bodies and discuss the uses of the Tree in planning projects or demonstrating life stages. If you have a good book on Kabbalah, you can set homework for the group to read a chapter and then discuss it at the next meeting.

ACTING AS TIFERET

If you take the place of Tiferet, you will find that the others in the group may project on to you issues they may have with religion, spirituality, or authority. Some people may love you while others may resent you; as long as you are aware of the pitfalls and do not indulge in pride, the issues will mostly resolve themselves.

You will find that a core group develops that is deeply interested in Kabbalah and strongly supportive of you, the teacher. Generally, this is good and offers much-needed support, but you should guard against it becoming an "inner sect" of intimates, which may intimidate or cause resentment in others. Acting as a guru—or believing that your teacher is a guru—is a Lucific temptation. The best teacher is one who acts with authority, but who firmly and courteously disabuses students of any illusion that they are more than one step ahead of the others.

GROUP STUDY AND DISCIPLINE

✳ KABBALAH IS A SPIRITUAL DISCIPLINE. THOSE WHO STUDY IT MUST LOVE IT IF THEY ARE TO BE WILLING TO COMMIT TO THE WORK. A GOOD SPIRITUAL GROUP IS ONE WHERE THE PARTICIPANTS SUPPORT AND HELP EACH OTHER BOTH INSIDE AND OUTSIDE OF THE MEETINGS. THIS IS THE MEANING OF THE PHRASE "COMPANIONS IN THE WORK."

Above: Students of Kabbalah are encouraged to debate and challenge the work so they can fully understand it. However, they must do so with discipline and a genuine desire to learn.

It is the job of the person holding Tiferet to set a discussion subject for the others and to hold them to it. He or she must also maintain the balance in the group, ensuring that no one individual takes all the attention or is allowed to alter the focus of the meeting without the consent of all.

The first discipline required is to understand that people need to take turns to speak. In a large group, it is good to ask the participants to hold up their hand to be selected to speak by the leader. If there are those who object to this, it should be explained that the ability to work under the discipline of a group leader is the beginning of training of the human will so that it can be handed over to God.

People should arrive punctually for the meetings. While it is understandable that people are sometimes late, persistent latecomers are a distraction and they should either be asked to act with more politeness to the others or, in extreme circumstances, be denied attendance if they continue to arrive late.

Many Kabbalah groups have a set time for exercises or discussion, followed by some

GROUP DISCIPLINE

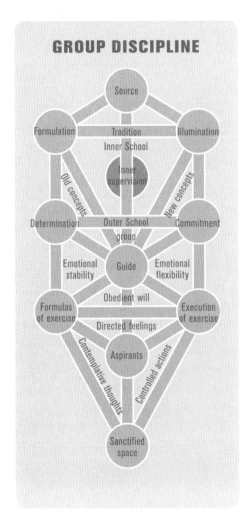

GROUP RITUAL

Any Kabbalistic group should begin with a short period of silence to gather the participants' thoughts and focus on the proceedings. Then the person acting as Tiferet should take his or her place at the Hokhmah of the room (this would be to the right-hand side of any altar or focus place with candles), facing the rest of the group. Kabbalistic groups may sit in a circle but even if they do, the Tiferet should be at the right-hand side of the altar place.

A short prayer is said, which should include the principle of rising up the Tree (*see page 203*) and the lighting of two candles with the words, "from Thee comes all Grace." The discussion, meditation, or ritual then begins. The leader may start with a short talk, but the essence of the group is full participation from all those attending, especially if it is a contemplative group that is learning the tradition through the study of books or images.

KEEPING THE FOCUS

The leader should hold the energy of the group, guiding it away from personal reminiscences and unrelated subjects and bringing it back to the topic at hand. If some new impulse or inspiration comes through, either via the teacher, at Hokhmah, or from one of the group itself, this can be allowed to develop— at the discretion of the person at Tiferet. Holding this level of discipline is vital.

Themes for discussion will often emerge and it will be productive to examine the same subject, such as free will, levels of perception, or aims and goals for several meetings with participants encouraged to observe the subject in their life between meetings.

At the end of the discussion, the leader calls for silence, closes with a prayer that comes down the Tree of Life, and extinguishes the candles.

refreshment and perhaps even a shared meal. The person holding Tiferet should designate certain tasks to members of the group, such as making tea, clearing away, and washing up. In this way, the participants can repay the time and knowledge that they have received. Any group leader will soon discover who is willing to help and who is not, and it is one of the leader's responsibilities to encourage people to change roles and not to accept the constant "willing" person's help when others have not volunteered at all.

GROUP DYNAMICS AND ASTROLOGY

✳ MOST KABBALAH GROUPS WORK BEST WHEN FOCUSED ON ONE OF THE THREE TRIADS AROUND YESOD. GROUPS WILL BE CONTEMPLATIVE (FOCUSED ON DISCUSSION OR READING), DEVOTIONAL (MEDITATION AND RITUAL), OR ACTIVE (PAINTING, DANCING, OR BUILDING TEMPLES).

Right: Placing your own astrological chart on the Tree shows how your views on each Sefira might differ from that of others and how you are likely to relate to a group. This person has what is known as a "grand cross" in fixed signs in his or her chart. This means he or she could be very inflexible. However, the moon and ascendant are both water so he or she may also be highly emotional at the Yesodic level. Such a student can be a challenge but will benefit greatly from understanding his or her own psychological tree.

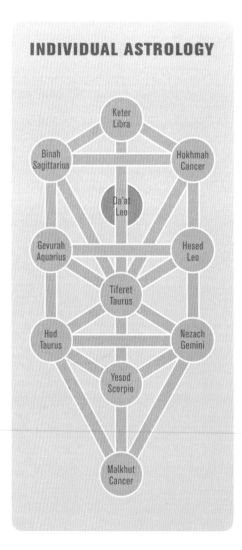

INDIVIDUAL ASTROLOGY

Keter
Libra

Binah
Sagittarius

Hokhmah
Cancer

Da'at
Leo

Gevurah
Aquarius

Hesed
Leo

Tiferet
Taurus

Hod
Taurus

Nezach
Gemini

Yesod
Scorpio

Malkhut
Cancer

The level of spiritual development, personality, and astrology of the founder affects how the group develops and who is attracted to it. Groups most often work on the four elements of astrology: a Taurean founder will draw fellow earth signs such as Virgo and Capricorn; a Leo founder will draw Sagittarius and Aries, and a Cancerian founder will draw Scorpio and Pisces. This may not be immediately obvious through the Sun signs of the participants but their Moons will almost certainly be associated.

A group with a predominance of Scorpio Moons will often work with the dynamics around death and the soul; a group of Leo Moons will often work with the lives of famous Kabbalists and the historical significance of a tradition. A group of Cancerian Moons will work with how to raise Kabbalistic children or work within the caring professions.

THE GROUP'S ASTROLOGY

It is good both to work with the strengths of the group's astrology and also to challenge it at times. Each participant should be encouraged to discover his or her own astrological chart and to draw it on a diagram of the Tree of Life.

Right: This astrological clock by Z'ev ben Shimon Halevi shows the positive and negative aspects between each of the Zodiacal signs.

Discovering how each star sign and planet feels in its placement on the Tree can provide discussion for an entire semester. A person with an Aquarian Mars (Gevurah) will have a very different attitude to discipline to a person with a Capricornian Mars. A simple discussion of how all members of the group perceive discipline and judgment will widen the knowledge and understanding of all.

Even more important is an examination of the respective Suns and Moons of the group members and how they see their Yesod as supporting or opposing their Tiferet. In general, Kabbalistic work in a group is contemplative or devotional, with the participants expected to perform Kabbalistic action every day, such as observing the structure of the Tree of Life in themselves, and in their family and work life through the vegetable, animal, and human levels.

USING KABBALISTIC MEDITATION

An enduring Kabbalah group will include Kabbalistic meditation in its work on a regular basis. This involves the leader inviting the participants to follow him or her in visualizing a story set on Kabbalistic principles (such as a visit to the House of the Psyche—*see page 110*—or a journey taken on the Ship of the Soul—*see page 173*).

An active meditation can also be performed by placing the chairs in the room in the form of the Tree of Life as demonstrated on page 202 (you can do this in a private space outside if there is no room in the house).

Even if there is insufficient space to carry out such an exercise, it is still worthwhile to ask people to move the chairs in the room and to sit in an area where they are not so comfortable. Since all areas of the room correspond to the Tree (with the candles as Keter and the leader at Hokhmah), it is still possible to realize which areas of the matrix are comfortable and which are not.

IDEAS FOR EXERCISES AND GROUP STUDY

✳ ONE OF THE MOST BEAUTIFUL, LASTING, AND FASCINATING KABBALISTIC EXERCISES THAT CAN BE CARRIED OUT ALONE OR IN A GROUP IS BUILDING A KABBALISTIC GARDEN ON THE STRUCTURE OF THE TREE OF LIFE.

The garden can be as big or small as the available space. If possible, there should be an area of water for Da'at. If not, a mirror is a good substitute.

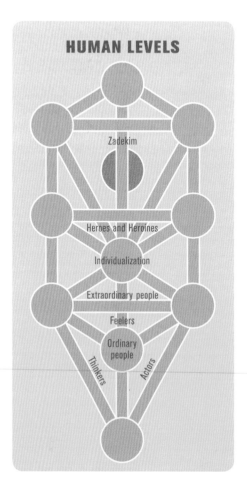

HUMAN LEVELS

Zadekim

Heroes and Heroines

Individualization

Extraordinary people

Feelers

Ordinary people

Thinkers

Actors

SUGGESTED SUBJECTS FOR GROUP DISCUSSION

Jacob's Ladder The four levels of Jacob's Ladder and how they interweave in the human body, the landscape of the Earth, and in the psyche.

People Ordinary people (vegetable level); extra-ordinary people (animal level); heroes and heroines (soul level); Zadekim—holy people (spiritual level). A discussion of people in the news and characters from favorite books and from history can illustrate the different levels on which people operate and their effect on the world around them.

Aims in life Short-term, medium-term, and long-term aims can be discussed at different levels, including work aims, personal aims, and soul aims. For example, a long-term soul aim might be to become a knowledgeable and respected teacher in a spiritual discipline. The medium-term goal would be to write a book on the subject and the short-term goal to find and/or lead a study group. A long-term personal aim might be to find a life partner. The medium-term goal would be to overcome a fear of intimacy and the short-term goal to join more groups in order to meet people.

BUILDING A GARDEN

Silver clematis

Evergreens (laurel, bay tree)

Violets

Stargazer lilies

Pool

Holly

Water lilies

Morning glory

Roses

Nasturtium   Sunflowers   Rhododendron

Larkspur

Bamboo

Orchids

Lilies of the valley

Convolvulus

Lobelia

Ivy

Snowdrops

Observation The group can also be set an observational and contemplative exercise. Subjects for discussion such as "watching the passing show" can be instructive in the attempt to observe news and local events dispassionately and to work out what is really going on, not what appears to be happening.

Another excellent exercise is to look for the faces of people who are at Tiferet in the street and on public transport. They will look and act awake, and to exchange glances with someone when you are both fully conscious is a life-changing experience.

FLOWERS FOR A KABBALISTIC GARDEN

Keter
A bower of soft, silvery clematis surrounded by violets
Astrological rulings: *(Neptune)*
Traditional flower: lupin
Colors: soft, silvery blues and grays *(foggy colors)*

Hokhmah
Sweet peas, Aquilegia, lilies, ceanothus
Astrological rulings: *(Uranus)*
Traditional flower: pansy
Colors: electric blue, bright pink, pale green

Binah
Hardy shrubs, bracken, evergreens
Astrological rulings: *(Saturn)*
Traditional flower: fuchsia
Colors: brown, black, and gray

Da'at
Water lilies, bulrushes
Astrological rulings: *(Pluto)*
Traditional flower: anemone
Colors: dark red, brown, and black
(Around Da'at, plant aromatic herbs to give a sense of Beriah in Yezirah)

Hesed
Iris, morning glory, rhododendron
Astrological rulings: *(Jupiter)*
Traditional flower: hydrangea
Color: imperial purple

Gevurah
Red-hot pokers, holly and yew with berries, salvia
Astrological rulings: *(Mars)*
Traditional flower: nasturtium
Color: bright red

Tiferet
Sunflowers, Chinese lanterns, fruit trees
Astrological rulings: *(Sun)*
Traditional flower: marigold
Colors: orange, warm yellow, and gold
New Testament character: Jesus (**soul triad:** roses of all colors—beauty, scent, and thorns)

Nezach
Dahlias, carnations, orchids
Astrological rulings: *(Venus)*
Traditional flowers: carnation, orchid
Colors: green, cream, Madonna blue, pale green, pink

Hod
Rose of Sharon, Hosta, mallow, bamboo
Astrological rulings: *(Mercury)*
Traditional flower: larkspur, clover
Colors: sharp yellow, black and white combinations, soft browns and greens, dusky hues

Yesod
Climbers, ramblers, ivy, lobelia, lilies of the valley
Astrological rulings: *(Moon)*
Traditional flower: convolvulus
Colors: silver and pastel colors

Malkhut
Fragile rockery plants and baby daffodils, snowdrops, aconite, and annuals—because life is fragile and is continually replanted by God and the seasons
Astrological rulings: *(Earth-Ascendant)*
Traditional flower: according to rising sign

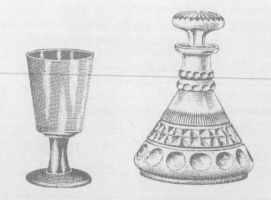

PART SEVEN

RITUALS AND PRAYERS

MANY GREAT RELIGIOUS RITUALS WITHIN BOTH THE JEWISH AND CHRISTIAN FAITHS ARE BASED ON EITHER THE STRUCTURE OF THE TREE OF LIFE OR JACOB'S LADDER. SINCE THE TREE OF AZILUT REPRESENTS THE TEN ASPECTS OF THE HOLY ONE, INCLUDING ALL TEN SEFIROT, THERE IS A RITUAL TO HONOR ALL LEVELS OF CREATION. USING THE TREE ALSO GIVES A SUBCONSCIOUS SENSE OF SATISFACTION TO THE PEOPLE CARRYING OUT THE RITUAL. AT A DEEP INNER LEVEL THEY KNOW THE INHERENT "RIGHTNESS" OF THE SERVICE. IT IS ALSO QUITE SIMPLE TO USE EITHER THE TREE OR THE LADDER TO DEVELOP YOUR OWN RITUALS AT HOME. THE LIGHTING OF TWO CANDLES IS A SYMBOLIC ACTION RECOGNIZED AT ALL LEVELS AS THE PREFACE TO A DIVINELY INSPIRED SERVICE. THE CANDLES REPRESENT THE TWO COLUMNS OF THE TREE OF LIFE, WHILE THE PERSON BRINGING THE FLAME TO LIFE ACTS AS THE CENTRAL COLUMN.

CHAPTER FOURTEEN

USING RITUALS

✳ THE BEST-KNOWN WORDS OF JESUS OF NAZARETH ARE WHAT WE NOW CALL THE LORD'S PRAYER. THIS FITS ONTO THE YEZIRATIC TREE OF LIFE BUT WAS MOST LIKELY INTENDED TO BE A REFLECTION OF THE CENTRAL COLUMN OF JACOB'S LADDER OR THE FIFTH TREE, AS IT IS ALSO KNOWN.

THE LORD'S PRAYER ON THE TREE

Keter: Our Father. God the source. This Sefira touches Azilut, the divine world.

Hokhmah: Who art in heaven. This Sefira is not connected to Azilut but is within Beriah, the heavenly world. This corresponds with "no graven image." It is teaching us that God has no form.

Binah: Hallowed be thy name. The Sefira of understanding and corresponds to "Do not take the name of the Lord thy God in vain."

Hesed: Thy Kingdom come.

Gevurah: Thy will be done.

Tiferet: On earth as it is in heaven. These three lines encompass the soul. This is the kingdom of the soul—compassion and love in doing the will of God. "On earth as it is in heaven" demonstrates how Tiferet is the link point between worlds—the Malkhut of Beriah/Keter of Asiyyah.

Nezach: Give us this day our daily bread. The active Sefira of the everyday world: the line refers to physical food and psychological support.

Hod: Forgive us our debts as we forgive our debtors. Hod is the Sefira of thought and of remembered and perceived wrongs.

Yesod: Lead us not into temptation. The Ego is often led by social convention and habit. This is a plea not to be allowed to lose our way.

Malkhut: Deliver us from evil. Malkhut is the farthest Sefira from Keter and it is here that our thoughts and actions are made manifest.

THE LORD'S PRAYER ON JACOB'S LADDER

Our Father. Keter of Keters. God the source. This Sefira is the crown of Azilut.

Who art in heaven. Tiferet of Azilut/Keter of Beriah. This Sefira is both connected to Azilut and Beriah, the point of transmission between worlds.

Hallowed be thy name. Yesod of Azilut/Da'at of Beriah. This is a Sefira of communication between worlds. Beriah hears and understands the word of God here.

Thy kingdom come. Malkut of Azilut/Tiferet of Beriah/Keter of Yezirah. The Kingdom of Azilut is the Kingdom of God to which Jesus refers. It is a state of communion with the Divine.

Thy will be done. Yesod of Beriah/Da'at of Yezirah. Where we hear the word of God or receive Grace.

On earth as it is in heaven. Malkhut of Beriah, which Jesus called the Kingdom of Heaven. It is the Tiferet of Yezirah and the Keter of Asiyyah, the place where three worlds meet.

Give us this day our daily bread. Yesod of Yezirah/Da'at of Asiyyah. Where the body and psyche communicate through the Ego. The body needs impulse from the psyche and physical bread.

Forgive us our debts as we forgive our debtors. Malkhut of Asiyyah/Tiferet of Asiyyah. Emphasis on the need to let go of memory of both physical and emotional harm.

Lead us not into temptation. Yesod of Asiyyah. The Ego of the body corresponds to our base instincts and asserts its will before we have thought.

Deliver us from evil. The Malkhut of Malkhuts is the farthest Sefira from God. It is where any evil impulse we might feel could become reality.

The ending, **"for thine is the kingdom, the power and the glory, for ever and ever,"** was added by St. Paul after Jesus' time. They refer to the right-hand, the left-hand, and central column of Jacob's Ladder respectively, sending the whole prayer back to Azilut.

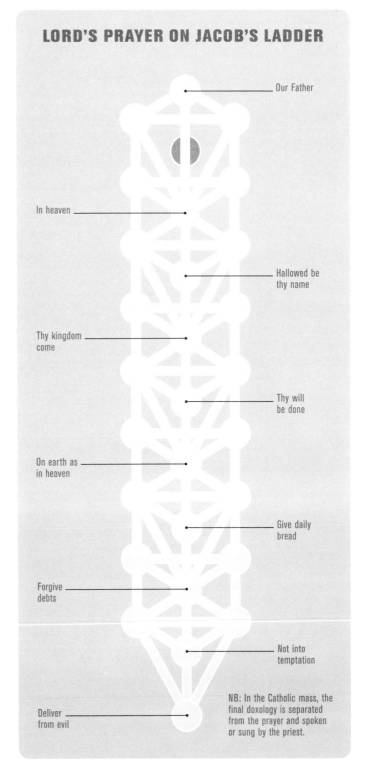

LORD'S PRAYER ON JACOB'S LADDER

- Our Father
- In heaven
- Hallowed be thy name
- Thy kingdom come
- Thy will be done
- On earth as in heaven
- Give daily bread
- Forgive debts
- Not into temptation
- Deliver from evil

NB: In the Catholic mass, the final doxology is separated from the prayer and spoken or sung by the priest.

THE CHRISTIAN COMMUNION AND THE CROSS ON THE TREE OF LIFE

✳ THE CHRISTIAN COMMUNION HAS CHANGED QUITE SIGNIFICANTLY OVER THE LAST 500 YEARS, INCLUDING THE DECISION CONCERNING THE ANGLICIZATION OF THE LATIN MASS TAKEN IN 1962. HOWEVER, ANY SERVICE THAT LIFTS OUR SOULS UP TO RECEIVE GRACE IS FORMULATED ON A STRUCTURE RECOGNIZABLE ON THE TREE OF LIFE.

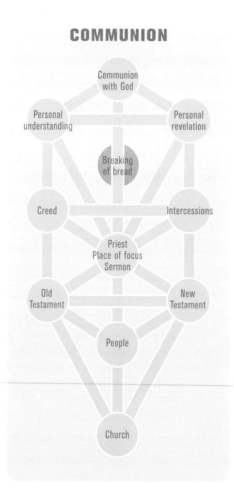

COMMUNION

It is not known whether the structure of the Mass and other spiritual services were consciously designed on the Tree of Life, but the Tree is a universal matrix that pervades the life of every one of us.

THE COMMUNION SERVICE

As with all sacred ceremonies, Malkhut represents the place where the service is held and Yesod both the people and the greeting that begins the Mass. The Act of Penitence is an acknowledgment that Yesod plays too great a role in our life, while the Old Testament (Hod) and New Testament (Nezach) readings are concerned with raising our consciousness to the level of Tiferet, where we remain for the rest of the service.

The priest then gives the sermon, which is intended to be inspirational, and we recite the Creed. This statement of belief is Gevurah—defining and discerning exactly what it is that makes up our faith.

Next comes the intercession for others (Hesed) and then the presentation of the Host.

At this point, linked to the soul triad, we call down the angelic presence of the Communion with the Sanctus and proclaim "blessed is He who comes in the name of the Lord." Nowadays both Catholic and Protestant priests face the congregation rather than acing toward the Divine. In Kabbalah this is seen as a block to the flow of energy to the higher worlds.

The Lord's Prayer is then recited and the "peace" given; this is where we greet our companions from the soul rather than the social level. The priest breaks the bread, signifying the opening of the veil (Da'at) between us and God, and the rite of communion is begun. As we partake, we draw our own understanding of the Divine (Binah) and receive whatever wisdom (Hokhmah) we are open to. At the end of the rite, the priest ends the service by sending the angelic presence back with the sacrifice. In Latin, this was the use of the words *ite missa est*—"the Mass is complete."

CROSSES OF CHRIST AND MALEFACTORS

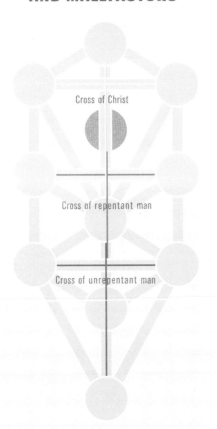

Cross of Christ

Cross of repentant man

Cross of unrepentant man

THE CROSS OF CHRIST

Christian Kabbalists see the crucifix on which Jesus of Nazareth died as the central column of the Tree of Life. The bar of the cross is the path between Hod and Nezach. In this way, the cross is seen as overcoming death (Da'at). There are two other bars, or levels, in the Tree, the Gevurah–Hesed path of the soul triad and the Hod–Nezach path between the vegetable and animal levels. These are given to the two malefactors (they are not called thieves in the Bible) who, according to the Gospel of Luke, were crucified with Jesus.

The Greek Orthodox Cross has three bars, with the bottom one tilted. Legend says that this is the cross of the unrepentant criminal. This man in Luke, Chapter 23 said, "If you are the Christ, save yourself and us," showing that he took no responsibility for whatever reason it was that he was being executed. The fallen bar on the Greek Orthodox cross shows him falling back into the cycle of everyday life—to be reincarnated to learn about responsibility. The second man rebukes him, saying, "We receive the due reward of our deeds: but this man [Jesus] has done nothing amiss," thus showing himself to be at the soul level, realizing that he had free will and that he must take responsibility for his own death. To this second man, Jesus says: "Today you shall be with me in paradise."

INAUGURATION OF THE SABBATH

✳ THIS SACRED CEREMONY IS CARRIED OUT AT DUSK EACH FRIDAY NIGHT IN THE HOMES OF JEWS THROUGHOUT THE WORLD. IT IS THE DRAWING DOWN OF THE SHEKHINAH—THE PRESENCE OF GOD OR THE FEMININE ASPECT OF GOD AND THE WORLD OF THE DIVINE—INTO THE HOME FOR THE SABBATH. IT SHOULD ONLY BE DONE WHEN THE FOLLOWING DAY WILL BE A DAY OF REST.

PREPARATION

You will need:

✡ Two candles
✡ Wine or grape juice
✡ Either one glass to share or enough glasses for all present
✡ A bowl of water, a jug, and a clean towel
✡ Two bread rolls covered with a clean cloth
✡ Salt

For the Jewish people, the Sabbath is Saturday, the "seventh day" on which God rested after creating the world. In modern times, when people often work at the weekends, you can make the Sabbath any day.

Traditionally, the woman of the house takes the part of Shekhinah and the man performs the rest of the ceremony, taking the divine essence that she has transmitted down through the worlds to Asiyyah. In a home where there is a same-sex partnership or two friends living together, one should voluntarily take the part of the sacred feminine and the other the sacred masculine.

THE FIRST PRAYER

The first part of the service represents Azilut. You can say the following prayer:

Lord of the Universe, I am about to perform the sacred duty of kindling the lights in honor of the Sabbath. Even as it is written: "And Thou shalt call the Sabbath a delight and the holy day of the Lord honorable."

And may the effect of my fulfilling this commandment be that the stream of abundant life and heavenly blessing flow in upon me and mine. That thou be gracious unto us and cause thy presence to dwell among us.

Father of mercy, O continue thy loving kindness unto me and unto my dear ones. Make me worthy to (rear my children that they) walk in the way of the righteous before thee, loyal to thy law and clinging to good deeds. Keep Thou far from us all manner of shame, grief, and care and grant that peace, light, and joy ever abide in our home. For with thee is the fountain of life; in thy light do we see light. Amen.

LIGHTING THE CANDLES

Now light the candles. Hold your hands around them as if cupping them in an embrace. Say the following prayer:

Blessed art thou O Lord our God, King of the Universe who has sanctified us by thy commandments and commanded us to kindle the Sabbath light.

POURING THE WINE

Pour the wine, which links the worlds of Azilut and Beriah. Each person holds their wine glass but does not drink yet. The next part, traditionally read by the male head of the household, represents Beriah, the world of Spirit. There are four references to God's work—three "made" and one "created." These correspond to the four worlds of Jacob's Ladder, which follow each other in the process of creation. The reference to Egypt refers both to the physical release of the Israelites from bondage and the psychological release we work for every day from the slavery of the social world and its expectations. Read the following:

And it was evening and it was morning, the sixth day. And the heaven and the earth were finished and all their hosts. And on the seventh day God had finished his work that he had made; and he rested on the seventh day from all his work that he had made. And God blessed the seventh day and he hallowed it because he rested thereon from all his work that God had created and made.

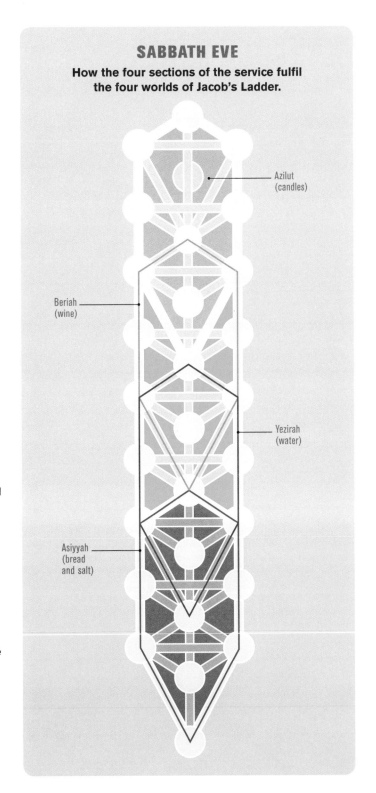

SABBATH EVE

How the four sections of the service fulfil the four worlds of Jacob's Ladder.

Azilut (candles)

Beriah (wine)

Yezirah (water)

Asiyyah (bread and salt)

Blessed art thou O Lord our God, King of the Universe, who createth the fruit of the vine. Blessed art thou O Lord our God, King of the Universe, who hast sanctified us by thy commandments and hast taken pleasure in us, and in love and favor has given us thy holy Sabbath as an inheritance. A memorial of the creation—that day being also the first of the holy convocations in remembrance of the departure from Egypt. For thou hast chosen us from among all peoples and in love and favor hast given us thy holy Sabbath as an inheritance. Blessed art thou O Lord who makes the Sabbath holy.

HAVDALAH

You will need:

✡ A plaited candle with two wicks known as a Havdalah candle—or you can hold two candles close together, so their flames overlap. (These candles represent the union of humanity and the Divine during the Sabbath and the merging of masculine and feminine both within marriage and within our own psyches.)

✡ A cup or glass of wine

✡ A box filled with spices (cinnamon, cloves and bay leaf are commonly used)

All say *"Beriah."* The people assembled drink the wine, so linking the world of Beriah to the world of Yezirah. They wash their hands, then sit and dry them. This level represents Yezirah, the watery world of the psyche, and links it by the action of sitting and drying the hands to the physical world of Asiyyah. All say:

Blessed art thou O Lord our God who hast sanctified us by thy commandments and commanded us concerning the washing of hands. Yezirah.

ASIYYAH

The next part represents Asiyyah, the physical world. Two bread rolls are used to represent the manna given in the desert, with an extra piece for the Sabbath. Lift the cover from the bread, take one bread roll in both hands and say:

Blessed art thou O Lord our God who brings forth bread from the earth.

Break the bread so that there is a piece for everyone. Salt the bread and then offer the plate to each person to take one piece. All say *"Asiyyah."* All say *"Shabbat Shalom"* (a peaceful Sabbath).

THE ENDING OF THE SABBATH

AT THE END OF THE SABBATH, AT THE SIGHT OF THE THREE STARS ON SATURDAY EVENING (OR AT DUSK IF IT IS CLOUDY), THERE IS A CEREMONY CALLED HAVDALAH, WHICH MEANS SEPARATION OR DISTINCTION. IT REPRESENTS THE RETURNING OF THE SHEKHINAH TO THE WORLD OF AZILUT FOR THE COMING WEEK.

LIGHTING THE CANDLE

Anyone in the household performs this ceremony but the fire lighting and blessing is the work of the feminine. The candle is lit without a blessing as the Shekhinah still resides in the flame from the previous night. The wine is poured. Say this prayer:

Blessed art Thou O Lord our God, King of the Universe, who creates the fruit of the vine.

BLESSING THE SPICES AND CANDLE

The cup of wine stays on the table but is not drunk yet. The spice box is opened and passed around for all to inhale to remind us of the sweetness, spice, and diversity of life during the coming week and the continual blend of physical reality (the plants) and Spirit (the scent). Say this prayer:

Blessed art Thou O Lord our God, King of the Universe, who has created varieties of spices.

We say the blessing over light, hands extended toward the candle, palms facing us and fingers bent so that the light reflects in our nails. This shows how we are reflections of the Divine and that we must honor that reflection in the work of our hands in the week. Say this prayer:

Blessed art Thou O Lord our God, King of the Universe, who creates the light of the fire.

THE HAVDALAH BLESSING

The final blessing is the Havdalah blessing itself, the blessing over the separation of different things. It is recited over the wine and acknowledges that the day of rest is over and that the time of work begins. Say this prayer:

Blessed art Thou O Lord our God, King of the Universe, who distinguishes between sacred and secular, light and darkness, Israel and the nations, the seventh day, and the six days of labor. Blessed art Thou O Lord who distinguishes between sacred and secular.

Pass the wine around for everyone to drink and then extinguish the candle in the dregs. The parting greeting at the end of the Sabbath is *Shavua tov* (have a good week).

COUNTING THE OMER

✳ THE 49 DAYS BETWEEN THE JEWISH FESTIVALS OF PASSOVER AND
SHAVUOT—THE GIVING OF THE LAW—ARE KNOWN AS THE DAYS OF THE OMER.
DURING THIS TIME, MANY KABBALISTS ACCORD EACH DAY A SPECIFIC ATTRIBUTE
BASED ON THE IDEA OF "TREES WITHIN TREES" AND THEY WILL MEDITATE ON THAT
ASPECT EACH DAY.

COUNTING THE OMER

Supernal Triad

The basis of counting the Omer is a passage in
the Book of Leviticus in which the Israelites are
instructed to count 50 days from the time of the
waving of a sheaf of corn (*omer* in Hebrew) by
a priest until the festival of Shavuot.

The idea of "trees within trees" is intended
to show the flexibility of the Tree of Life. If you
look upon the Tree of Life as a color chart, the
trees within trees are the tones and shades of
the essential hues of each attribute.

MEDITATING ON THE SEFIROTIC ATTRIBUTES

Kabbalists keep note of the Sefirotic attribute
of each day and begin with a meditation on that
attribute, focusing both on what it means to the
world and to their own lives.

The second day of the Omer, for example, the
Gevurah of Hesed, would be a time to contemplate
discipline and discernment in love. When is it loving
to say "no" to someone or when is it time to end a
relationship that is proving destructive?

The 19th day of the Omer, the Hod of
Tiferet, would be the day to consider how

you communicate yourself to others. Do you represent yourself positively or do you put yourself down when you speak about yourself to others? You could also look at how other people and nations communicate.

The 30th day, the Nezach of Yesod, would be the day to consider how to expand and bring creativity and joy into everyday repetitive processes.

The Malkhut of Malkhuts, the day before Shavuot, is a day of deep contemplation of the nature of reality and the physical experience of life. The journey of preparation for the festival has been completed.

COUNTING THE DAYS OF OMER

The Omer is counted from Hesed to Malkhut down the lightning flash (*see page 17*). As the Sefirot above Hesed are concerned with a higher level of consciousness, many Jewish festivals focus only on the seven lower Sefirot so that this practice can be carried out by the people as opposed to the rabbis.

The Omer begins on the second day of Passover with "the Hesed of Heseds." This is followed by the Gevurah of Hesed, the Tiferet of Hesed, the Nezach of Hesed, the Hod of Hesed, the Yesod of Hesed, and the Malkhut of Hesed. Then follows the Hesed of Gevurah, the Gevurah of Gevurah, the Tiferet of Gevurah, and so on down the Tree. This is a Kabbalistic exercise to demonstrate consciousness of the Tree of Life in all its aspects and to perceive the flow of Grace from the Holy One to Earth in preparation for the revelation of the Ten Commandments.

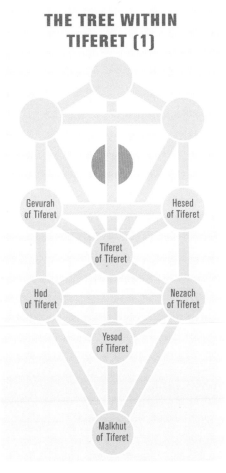

THE TREE WITHIN TIFERET (1)

Gevurah of Tiferet

Hesed of Tiferet

Tiferet of Tiferet

Hod of Tiferet

Nezach of Tiferet

Yesod of Tiferet

Malkhut of Tiferet

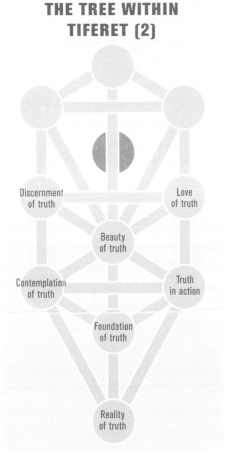

THE TREE WITHIN TIFERET (2)

Discernment of truth

Love of truth

Beauty of truth

Contemplation of truth

Truth in action

Foundation of truth

Reality of truth

CHAPTER 15

CREATING YOUR OWN RITUALS AND PRAYERS

A KABBALISTIC PRAYER USES ALL TEN SEFIROT AND CAN EITHER ASCEND OR DESCEND THE TREE, EITHER LIFTING YOUR ENERGY UP TOWARD THE DIVINE OR DRAWING THE DIVINE DOWN TO YOU. ADVANCED STUDENTS CAN ALSO USE THE LADDER AS A STRUCTURE OF PRAYER JUST AS MANY OF THE PSALMISTS IN THE BIBLE DID.

ANCIENT AND MODERN

An example of a Kabbalistic prayer by Rabbi Joseph Tzayach, a Kabbalist who lived in Jerusalem and Damascus in the 16th century. His prayer descends the Tree of Life, as does the Lord's Prayer.

Crown me (Keter)
Give me wisdom (Hokhmah)
Grant me understanding (Binah)
With the right hand of your love, make me great (Hesed)
From the terror of your judgment, protect me (Gevurah)
With your mercy, grant me beauty (Tiferet)
Watch me forever (Nezach)
Grant me beatitude from your splendor (Hod)
Make your covenant my foundation (Yesod)
Open my lips and my mouth with speak of your praise (Malkhut).

A more modern prayer from Malkhut to Keter might be:

Mother, Father Earth,
My soul is your foundation
Teach me your ways
Fill me with your fruits
Make me your link between Heaven and Earth
My left hand your justice
My right hand your mercy
As I stand before the face of God.
Guide my understanding
Show me your inspiration.
Adonai.

A very good way to "pray the Tree" is to place 11 chairs in the order of the Sefirot. You need quite a large room but this prayer can also be done on cushions or even standing up by taking a step for each Sefira. If you are placing the chairs for the Sefirot, try to ensure that those on the middle column match each other to give you an impression of balance. The chair for Da'at should be placed facing in the opposite direction from the others.

PRAYING THE TREE

Begin at Malkhut. Sit in the chair and close your eyes. Focus on your physical body and give thanks for its health and vitality.

When you are ready, move forward to the Yesod chair, sit in it, and give thanks for your family and work.

From there, move left to Hod and focus on the kinds of communication that you love—TV, movies, books, the Internet, etc. Consider how much they enhance your life and give thanks for them.

Then move right to the chair at Nezach and think of all the energizing, creative, and artistic aspects of your life, including hobbies, cooking, making love—anything that excites you. Again, give thanks.

PRAYER DESCENDING TREE (1)

PRAYER ASCENDING TREE (2)

Move forward and to the center of your Tree of Prayer to Tiferet. Focus on being the link between Heaven and Earth; experience all the levels in your body: earth, water, air, and fire, and acknowledge your link with God.

Go next to Gevurah and consider which decisions and judgments you need to make in your life right now. Then move across to Hesed and remember times when you did good things and helped others. Praise yourself for them.

Now move to Da'at, turned the other way around. Clear your mind and see what comes

to you. From there, move to Binah and focus on the concept of understanding. The affirmation "I am willing to understand" is useful here.

Next is Hokhmah—open your mind here for a flash of inspiration.

At Keter, having followed the path up the Tree, you will know yourself what to do. If you are placing the chairs for the Sefirot, try to ensure that the ones on the middle column match each other to give you an impression of balance. The chair for Da'at should be placed facing in the opposite direction from the others.

CREATING A SERVICE OF RITUAL

✳ IN THE MODERN WORLD, MANY TRADITIONAL RITES OF PASSAGE HAVE BEEN FORGOTTEN. RITUALS ARE A WONDERFUL WAY TO MARK AN IMPORTANT TIME IN YOUR LIFE WHETHER IT IS A BIRTH, PUBERTY, A NEW JOB, MARRIAGE, DIVORCE, MISCARRIAGE, A NEW INSPIRATION, RETIREMENT, OR DEATH.

BASIS FOR RITUAL

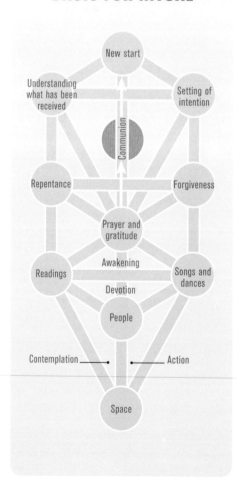

We still maintain weddings and funerals as important rituals, and the Jewish faith has joyful ceremonies known as Bar Mitzvah and Bat Mitzvah to mark the transition from childhood to adulthood. However, as the world becomes more secular, most people do not experience the beauty of a sacred ceremony to recognize some new impulse in their life.

A divorce is as important as a marriage. It is possible that some of the trauma concerned with marital breakup is caused by the failure to mark the event with a ceremony that focuses on the end of the relationship.

BASIC DIVORCE RITUAL

This ritual can be carried out alone or with friends as witnesses. Place any articles to do with the marriage, such as a ring or wedding photo, on an altar. Add a small bowl of water containing a pinch of salt. If you can, dress in your wedding outfit or another outfit that represents the marriage.

- Stand before the altar and make the Tree of Life from Malkhut to Keter with your body.
- Light two candles, for the two pillars, with the phrase: *"From Thee comes all Grace."*

• Take the wedding objects in your hands and say: *"Before God I am sorry for anything I may have done to break the vows between us. Before God I am willing to forgive anything [add the name of your former spouse] may have done to break the vows between us."*

• Dip your right hand into the water and sprinkle a few drops on the items. Say: *"Let this relationship/marriage be cleansed and healed. May these objects be cleansed and healed."*

• Blow on the items and say: *"The Breath of God now transforms these items."*

Pass the items swiftly through the flame of both candles—so swiftly that they cannot be burned! Say: *"I give this marriage/relationship back to God. It is over. It is complete."*

• Change your clothes for an outfit that reflects your new life.

• Hold your hands either side of the candles. Say: *"I dedicate my new life to spiritual growth and happiness. I Am That I Am."* (Alternatively, use another phrase that makes you feel happy.)

• Make the Tree with your body from Keter to Malkhut and blow out the candles.

What you do with the objects and clothes representing the marriage is up to you.

Tiferet also represents you in the divorce ritual. It is quite acceptable to mix and match the different levels (for example, Hod and Nezach or Gevurah and Hesed or Binah and Hokhmah) but still wise to progress up or down the Tree. You can take as much time as you like at any of the levels—whatever brings you joy and balance.

THE BASICS FOR A KABBALISTIC RITUAL

Malkhut: the space where the ritual takes place
Yesod: the people involved
Hod: the readings or contemplation
Nezach: the songs or dances
Tiferet: prayer—gratitude and requests
Gevurah: releasing of the past—asking for forgiveness if necessary
Hesed: the giving of forgiveness/acceptance of a new era
Da'at: direct communion with God
Binah: understanding of what has been received from the service
Hokhmah: setting of intention for the future
Keter: acting on the new life, new role, and new peace given by the ritual.

USING PROPS

If you want to use props for a Kabbalistic ritual, the following are good.

SEFIRA	COLOR	OBJECT
Malkhut	Soft browns and greens	Stones, rocks, pottery, wood
Yesod	Silver, pastel colors	Images of the moon, mirrors
Hod	Bright yellow	Sacred texts, much-loved books
Nezach	Bright green, pink, blue	Flowers, scarves, crystals
Tiferet	Gold, deep yellow	A picture of you looking happy, surrounded by the life you want.
Gevurah	Scarlet	A sword or knife. Image of a soldier or samurai
Hesed	Purple	An image of abundance, e.g. fruit in a cornucopia, money, a crown.
Da'at	Black, dark red	A mirror or bowl of water. Image of Archangel Gabriel
Binah	Brown, black, gray	A lock of gray hair. Image of an elder or mentor
Hokhmah	Electric blue, bright pink, or pale green	A picture of a lightning flash or an angel
Keter	Soft, silvery blue	Candle. An image of your perception of Divinity

KABBALISTIC SOLSTICE OR CHRISTMAS SERVICE

✳ ONLY THE STRUCTURE OF A KABBALAH-BASED SERVICE IS INVIOLABLE; THE CONTENTS ARE UP TO YOU. THIS IS A SUGGESTED SERVICE, BUT YOU CAN CHANGE ANY OR ALL OF THE WORDS AND PRAYERS AS ARE APPROPRIATE FOR YOU. YOU WILL FIND THAT IF ANY OF YOUR CHOICES ARE NOT "RIGHT" YOU WILL BE ADVISED FROM ABOVE!

AVINU MALKEINU

Our Father Our King

Hear our prayer

We have sinned

Have compassion

Singer and those praying

Cause hate or oppression to vanish

Help us end pestilence, famine, and war

Inscribe our names

Let the New Year be good

This service incorporates all the Sefirot. The first part is based on Malkhut, the place of worship. People contemplate their own personal understanding of the end of one year and the coming of a new one as they listen to Avinu Malkeinu, a Hebrew song sung during Rosh Hashanah (the Jewish New Year). The words in English are:

Our Father Our King,
Hear our prayer
We have sinned before thee
Have compassion upon us and
upon our children
Help us bring an end to pestilence, war,
and famine.
Cause all hate and oppression to vanish
from the Earth.
Inscribe us for blessing in the Book of Life
Let the New Year be a good year for us.

YESOD: THE PEOPLE

The Greeting. People mingle and greet their neighbors.

All say:

Peace be with you.

HOD: THE OLD TESTAMENT

In this service, all readings from the Qur'an, Bible, or any other sacred text are treated as "old" testament. All those taking part can select their own reading as relevant to them and their faith.

NEZACH: THE NEW TESTAMENT

Here, you can choose readings that are inspirational and more contemporary.

TIFERET: REMEMBRANCE

The Tree of Life: all present make the ten Sefirot of the Tree of Life with their bodies, from Malkhut to Keter and then from Keter to Malkhut.

The Statement of Faith: the following words are said by the leader of the service, then by everyone, and then contemplated in silence.
All say:

There is one presence and one power in the universe and in my life. God the omnipotent, omniscient, omnipresent.
I Am that I Am.
Amen.

GEVURAH: JUDGMENT

This is where people review the previous year, considering the mistakes they may have made or what they might have done differently with hindsight. They resolve to be more true to themselves and less led by illusion. They do this in silence for a few moments.
All say:

In the name of God and on behalf of all humanity, I ask forgiveness for all that

has been done to cause pain and the forgetting of truth in Asiyyah.

In the name of God and on behalf of all humanity, I ask forgiveness for all that has been thought to cause pain and the forgetting of truth in Yezirah.

In the name of God and on behalf of all humanity, I ask forgiveness for all that has been created to cause pain and the forgetting of truth in Beriah.

In the name of God and on behalf of all humanity I remember the perfection of Azilut.

HESED: FORGIVENESS

All say:

In the name of God and on behalf of all humanity, I forgive all actions against me in Asiyyah.

In the name of God and on behalf of all humanity, I forgive all thoughts against me in Yezirah.

In the name of God and on behalf of all humanity I forgive all creations against me in Beriah.

In the name of God and on behalf of all humanity I remember the perfection of Azilut.

In the name of God I forgive. In the name of God I AM forgiven.
Amen.

KABBALISTIC SOLSTICE OR CHRISTMAS SERVICE, continued

DA'AT: COMMUNION

The bread is broken by the leader of the service, symbolizing the drawing back of the veil between us and God the transcendent. The leader says:

Blessed art thou, God of Emanation.
Through your goodness we have this light to
guide us at the darkest time of the year.
It will become for us the symbol of new
hope, new life, and the return of the son.

Blessed art thou, God of all Creation.
Through your goodness, we have this wine
to drink, fruit of the vine and work of human
hands. It will become for us our spiritual
warmth and guidance.

Blessed art thou, God of Formation.
Through your goodness, we have this water
to cleanse us, water as old as time, filled
with your knowledge. It will become for us
our way of letting go of the past.

Blessed art thou, God of Manifestation.
Through your goodness, we have this bread
to eat, which Earth has given and human
hands have made. It will become for us the
bread of life.

Each in turn comes up to the altar, lights a candle, drinks wine, and washes hands. He or she salts, breaks, and eats bread as a representation of the four worlds in one. Whatever prayer is appropriate may be said out loud or silently.

BINAH: UNDERSTANDING

People sit in silence or enjoy background music as others complete their communion and contemplate our own personal understanding of God.

All say:

Your decrees are wonderful; therefore my
soul keeps them.
The unfolding of your words gives light;
It imparts understanding to the simple.

Almighty God
We thank you for the gift of your holy word.
May it be a lantern to our feet,
A light to our paths
And a strength to our lives.
Take us and use us
To love and serve all people
In the power of the Holy Spirit
Amen.

This prayer is an amalgam of psalm 119 and a blessing from the Christian Alternative Service Book.

HOKHMAH: REVELATION

Kaddish, the Jewish prayer for the dead, is said to mark the death of the old year and the birth of the new.

All say:

Glorified and sanctified be God's great name throughout the world that He has created according to His will. May He establish His kingdom in your lifetime and during your days, and within the life of the entire House of Israel, speedily and soon; and say, Amen.

May His great name be blessed forever and to all eternity. Blessed and praised, glorified and exalted, extolled and honored, adored, and lauded be the name of the Holy One, blessed be He, beyond all the blessings and hymns, praises, and consolations that are ever spoken in the world; and say, Amen.

"May there be abundant peace from heaven, and life, for us and for all Israel; and say, Amen.

He who creates peace in His celestial heights, may He create peace for us and for all Israel; and say, Amen.

KETER: GO OUT AND LIVE TRUTH IN THE WORLD

The fulfillment of the service and realization of the insights given. Now is the time to attempt to go out and live the teaching in the world.

OTHER HOLY READINGS

The following are sections from other holy readings that can be used:

Koran *The Table, section three, verse 47-48:*
We have ordained a law and assigned a path for each of you. Had Allah pleased, he could have made you one nation, but it is his wish to prove you by that which he has bestowed upon you.
Vie with each other in good works for to Allah, you shall all return.

Bhagavad Gita IV
The god Krishna says: However men approach me, even so do I welcome them, for the path men take from every side leads to me.

Book of Revelation *Chapter 22, verse 2.*
In the midst of the street of it and on either side of the river was there the tree of life which bear twelve manners of fruits, and yielded her fruit every month. And the leaves of the tree were for the healing of the nations.

KABBALAH A–Z

KABBALAH HAS BEEN STUDIED IN ANCIENT HEBREW AND GREEK AS WELL

AS IN LATIN AND ALL THE EUROPEAN LANGUAGES, SO THERE ARE MULTIPLE

VARIANTS ON THE SPELLING OF MANY OF THE WORDS AND TERMS USED

TO EXPLAIN THE TRADITION. KABBALAH IS VARIOUSLY SPELLED CABALA AND

QABALAH AND THE SEFIROT CAN BE SPELLED AS SEPHIROT OR SEPHIROTH.

HOKHMAH AND HESED CAN BE SPELLED CHOKHMAH AND CHESED; TIFERET

AS TIPHARETH. THERE IS NO "RIGHT" OR "WRONG" IN THIS; SIMPLY DIFFERENT

TRADITIONS. AS KABBALAH IS UPDATED AND UNDERSTOOD FOR EACH

NEW GENERATION, IN THIS A–Z WE HAVE ENDEAVORED TO USE THE MOST

APPROPRIATE, CONTEMPORARY WORDS.

KABBALAH A–Z

ACTION TRIAD

Also known as the triad of "Willful-ness," this is the triad between the Sefirot of Yesod, Nezach, and Malkhut. The action triad denotes the preferences and capabilities of each human when it comes to activities and creativity. An over-strong action triad can lead to a life lived on impulse and an underactive one to a life of torpor. This triad in balance will lead to physical fitness but not to excess. The triad is ruled by the astrological sign of Taurus which, when out of balance, will either charge like a bull at a red rag or live slumped in front of the TV. If you are a primarily active person, it is important to balance this with the feeling and thinking triads.

ADAM KADMON

Adam Kadmon is the primordial man and the divine image of God in the world of Azilut. Adam Kadmon is neither male nor female although through years of custom It is often referred to as "He" and is depicted in ancient images as a man with a long beard. It is this image that is often used to illustrate God, although God Itself is beyond the Divine World and unknowable. Every human being is a spark within the divine body of Adam Kadmon, each with its own particular destiny, whether it is to be a soldier, a medic, a farmer, a carer, an environmentalist, or any other aspect of the Divine. No spark is greater than any other and we will all return to Adam Kadmon perfected. Then the divine baby will be born.

   Adam Kadmon as the personification of God is also used as part of Christian symbology for the Christ. However, the Christ is one Sefira of Azilut not the whole of the divine world.

ALCHEMY

The science of transforming physical matter into gold in the belief that understanding this will aid comprehension of the higher worlds. In Kabbalah this is seen as a psychological process because the Sun, the astrological sign representing Tiferet, corresponds to the element of gold.

ANGEL

An angel is a cosmic being working at the Yeziratic level. Angels are not human, have no free will, and are the servants of God. They carry out all the tasks to ensure that the universe operates properly. An angel has a specific function to carry out. There are elemental angels of wind, sea, cloud, light, earth, and plants. Angels of work, laughter, play, kindness, severity, and hope work with humans and animals. Each human has its own protective angel as does each country, city, and valley. Angels do not change roles and do not grant human wishes without the permission of God. All prayers to the angelic hosts are passed up to the Holy One, and the answer given at that level is carried out by the appropriate angel.

ANIMAL TRIAD See "Awakening triad"

ARCHANGEL

An archangel is a cosmic being working at the Beriatic level. Like angels, archangels have no free will. They exist to serve God and to run the universe. The energy of an archangel is the equivalent to that of a star. Although we humans often invoke archangels, we will receive only a small part of that being's energy should it be sent to us; the full energy would destroy us.

ASIYYAH

This is the physical world where all of creation is made manifest. Asiyyah can be seen, touched, heard, tasted, and smelled and it is the only one of the four worlds in which physical "proof" can be achieved. For many humans, it is the only world that is valid, and much time and effort is put into it—including the gathering of physical possessions. Asiyyah is where "reality" lives. However, it is the most temporary and fragile of the worlds and everything in it ages and dies. In the higher worlds of concepts, thoughts, and awareness, life is eternal.

ASTROLOGY

This is the language of the stars. Until the 19th century, astronomers and astrologers were similar; the ancients observed the movements of the stars and planets together with the happenings of the time and the cycles of nature. Great churches such as the cathedrals of Bologna and Chartres had astrological clocks to help people to be aware of the cycles of the year. Astrology is a useful tool for understanding the Yeziratic Tree of Life. Our personal astrology marks the matrix of our life from birth to grave, with certain "red-flag" days that tell us whether or not we are on our destined path. However, it is purely a Yeziratic tool that can be overruled by consciousness and free will at any point.

AWAKENING TRIAD

Also known as the triad of "my will" and the "animal triad," this is the triad between the Sefirot of Hod, Tiferet, and Nezach. This triad is where each of us is capable of "waking up" to a level of awareness that sees that the world runs on certain patterns at the vegetable level.

The awakening soul can see its own place in the world and position in the tribe. It is also clear what can be done to improve that position. For those seeking spiritual growth, it is the part of the psyche that is enthralled and inspired during a seminar or workshop. However, unless the individual can rise beyond Tiferet and access the discipline of Gevurah, the effects of the workshop will be short-term and the person may sink down again into the vegetable world. Politicians, marketers, and celebrities' agents are capable of accessing this level of consciousness in order to create opportunities and also to manipulate the vegetable soul. Celebrities themselves often reach the awakening triad in their first flush of success but unless they have the discipline to recognize their success for what it is, they may resort to stimulants that will give them the feeling of awakening without discernment.

AYIN

This is absolute No-thing, the God beyond Gods, ineffable and unknowable.

AYIN SOF

This is Absolute All, or the Infinite without End, the "second stage" of the Divine in becoming knowable. It is the force that created the void or the "womb" of God to be a vessel for the light to enter in order for creation to begin.

AYIN SOF AUR

This is the endless light, the original "breath of God" that entered the void created to make all of existence possible.

Ayin, Ayin Sof, and Ayin Sof Aur all exist beyond the divine world of Azilut. The origin of the idea of sacrifice to God (which is still honored in the Christian tradition with the Communion service) derives from the idea that God sacrifices Itself daily by eternally re-creating the void and breathing life into it so that the process of creation is able to continue. The sacrifice back to God was to recognize and mirror this back to the Divine.

AZILUT

This is the perfect world of emanation where all that ever has been and ever will be exists in potential. It is in this world that the ten Sefirot of the Tree of Life were first envisioned in order to be vessels to contain the light and pass it on. It is also here that the perfect human, Adam Kadmon, resides. Here also is The Treasure House of Souls, where each human soul exists before incarnation. Azilut is a place of pure perfection. Sixteenth-century Lurianic Kabbalah taught that it was not strong enough to hold the light radiated into it from Ayin Sof Aur and that the vessels to contain the light shattered, creating an external evil force.

B.C.E.

Meaning Before Christian Era (also known as Common or Current Era), this is traditional non-denominational way of saying B.C. (Before Christ). Although both Islam and Judaism have their own traditions for logging the passing of centuries, the system based on the year zero as the reputed birth date of Jesus Christ is widely recognized.

BERIAH

Beriah is the world of creation that intertwines with Azilut above and Yezirah below. Beriah is the place of pure Spirit and the beginning of duality, including the concepts of good and evil, day and night, up and down, and male and female. It is the world of the archangels and of thought. All inspiration comes from Beriah through Yezirah. It is this world we attempt to reach through deep meditation. Any idea in Beriah is without form; it can perhaps be expressed through writing but it cannot be seen in any image or shape. It is the next world, Yezirah, which adds form. Therefore a meditation that includes visualization will access Beriah through the upper face of Yezirah so that the ideas from the higher world can be interpreted through images.

BINAH

Binah is the Sefira of understanding, ruled in the Yeziratic world by the planet Saturn. Saturn has a 29-year cycle, and it is at or around the ages of 29 and 58 that important decisions are generally made about our lives, partners, and careers. Binah is also the archetype of the grandmother—wise and practical with the wisdom of the ages. It can however be overemphatic toward boundaries or paralysis, according to your personal astrology. Saturn in Scorpio for example can lead to life being led by the book for fear of being found out to be wrong. Saturn in Cancer can be over-involved with the tribal rule of the family, while Saturn in Gemini can have contradictory and ineffective boundaries.

CABALA

This is the spelling of Kabbalah adopted by the Christian tradition.

CASSIEL

Also known as Zaphkiel, Cassiel is archangel of the Beriatic Binah and Lord of Saturn. His name means "Knowledge of God." Cassiel is petitioned on Saturdays for matters to do with home ownership, land, agriculture, or for the elderly whether human or animal.

C.E.

This stands for Christian Era, also known as Common or Current Era (to Christians, A.D. or Anno Domini, the Year of Our Lord). Although both Islam and Judaism have their own traditions for logging the passing of centuries, the system based on the year zero as the reputed birth date of Jesus Christ is widely recognized.

DA'AT

Da'at is the non-Sefira of knowledge, one of the hardest of the Sefirot to understand. It is also known as "the abyss" or "the black hole." Da'at is like a wormhole in space that leads to another reality (*see page 58*). It is the spiritual or psychological space through which information can come from another world. Each Da'at corresponds directly with the Yesod (the foundation) of the next world up. In this way, the lower world can communicate with the higher or can receive information from the higher world. The physical body communicates to the psyche if it is uncomfortable about something. This can be experienced by the reticular activating system of the brain as pain or discomfort. However, Yesod is also an aspect of the intuitive feeling triad and so can pick up a sense of unease from the body that all may not be well. It is through the Da'at of the Yeziratic world that humans perceive the Holy Spirit or their Higher Self. This spiritual impulse is formulated and honed in the Yesod of Beriah before being transmitted to Yezirah, where it may be interpreted through an image of some kind.

DUALITY

Duality consists of the opposite forces that make up creation. Without them, the endless light of creation would continue in a straight line until infinity without the boundaries needed to create form. The dualities include life and death, day and night, up and down, light and dark, and good and bad.

EGO

The human Ego is in Yezirah. The Ego is intended to be the servant of the Self, the part of us that acts on automatic so that we are free to think clearly in situations that need our full attention. The Ego is trained in humans by the age of seven, so whatever your religious, social, and family beliefs, they will be based on the teachings of your first seven years. These can be changed but only through conscious awareness and repetition.

FEELING TRIAD

Also known as the Triad of Willingness, this is the triad between the Sefirot of Hod, Yesod, and Nezach. The Feeling Triad denotes the preferences and capabilities of each human when it comes to daily feelings as opposed to deeply ingrained emotions. An over-strong feeling triad can lead to a life ruled by sentiment and an underactive one to a life of disregard for others. This triad in balance leads to an open mind and a willingness both to learn and to understand how others feel. The triad is ruled by the two

astrological signs of Gemini and Libra which, when out of balance, are either too involved with a situation or completely detached from it. Since this triad is not linked directly with the grounding force of Malkhut, it is an area of "floatiness" where much is thought or felt but very little achieved. If you are primarily a "feeler," then it is important to balance this triad with the action and thinking triads.

FOUR JOURNEYS

These are the four stages of growth experienced by the human soul on its journey back to Azilut. The first is the descent from The Treasure House of Souls to the Malkhut of Malkhuts in Asiyyah for the first incarnation. The second consists of successive lives learning how to manage, succeed in, and understand the physical, psychological, and spiritual worlds. The third is to teach and help others who are on the first and second journeys, and the fourth is to return to Azilut as a perfected soul to help complete Adam Kadmon. The second and third journeys are often taken simultaneously; whatever is learned in a particular life is passed on to others.

FREE WILL

This is the ability of human beings to make conscious decisions about who they are and what they wish to do with their lives. Most of life is lived in the repetitive cycles of nature; thoughts are repeated each day and new impulses come from the outside world. Free will exists in the soul triad (Gevurah–Hesed–Tiferet) of the Yeziratic world. To access free will, we must consciously consider a situation in order to assess its truth, its relevance to us, our possible role within it, and whether it would be kind or callous to act.

Free will carries great responsibility; it is important to be aware that much so-called "help" is actually interference in the free will of others. For example, to help a person reach a level at work for which he or she is not mentally or emotionally equipped will cause long-term discomfort, even if the individual's immediate ambition is fulfilled.

GABRIEL

Gabriel is the best-known archangel, who features in both the Bible and the Qur'an. Gabriel means "strong man of God." He resides at the Yesod of Beriah and brings messages through to humanity through the corresponding Sefira of Da'at in Yezirah. Gabriel is Lord of the Moon and all matters concerning a happy home are under his rulership. He is petitioned on Mondays.

GEMATRIA

This is a system of complex word codes that works on correspondences between the ten Sefirot and the 22 letters of the Hebrew alphabet. Many Orthodox Jews believe that this is the only valid form of Kabbalistic teaching and that it should only be available to male scholars who have deep knowledge of the Jewish faith and of Hebrew. While Gematria can be an excellent pointer to spiritual correspondences between biblical stories and teachers, it can also be a way of becoming too Hodian and paralysed in an ancient tradition.

GEVURAH

This is the Sefira of judgment, discernment, and discipline, ruled by Mars and a part of the soul triad. Gevurah is the most "unpopular" of the Sefirot because of the connotations of "judgment." An out-of-balance Gevurah is indeed judgmental and may even be cruel but an in-balance Gevurah is capable of seeing the wider picture in all events and being a focus of real justice and fairness. Gevurah should always be balanced with Hesed.

GOD, NAMES OF

Kabbalah teaches that the Absolute is unknowable and ineffable. However the great name of God, as given to Moses in the biblical Book of Exodus is "I Am That I Am." The Holy One has a name for each of the ten Sefirot of the divine world of Azilut, each of which describes the attributes of that Sefira. Through Gematria, scholars have discovered many other names for God, including the 72-letter name derived from a sequence of 72 specially arranged syllables found in the Book of Exodus (14:19–21).

HANIEL

The archangel Haniel is associated with the Beriatic Sefira of Nezach. Haniel means Grace of God. He is the Lord of Venus and is generally invoked concerning matters of the heart (although not marriage, which is the province of Michael) and domestic pets. Haniel is petitioned on Fridays.

HESED

This is the Sefira of mercy or love, part of the soul triad and ruled by the planet Jupiter. Hesed is the most "popular" of the Sefirot because it is linked to the heart and the place of unconditional love. When balanced with Gevurah, Hesed is truly unconditional, but that includes "tough love" if this is for the greater good. An unbalanced Hesed is over-merciful, which leads to overactivity and a lack of discernment.

HOD

Hod is the Sefira of reverberation and thought, ruled by the planet Mercury, messenger of the Gods. Hod is linked to three triads—the awakening, the feeling, and the contemplative. In balance, it is the ability to collect and weigh up information that can be passed on to Tiferet and Gevurah for decision making. Out of balance, it is either overintellectual or obsessed with detail.

HOKHMAH

Hokhmah is the Sefira of wisdom, inspiration, and revelation, and is ruled by Uranus. Hokhmah is linked with three triads: the supernal triad of Binah–Keter–Hokhmah that represents the Divine in humanity; the spiritual triad of Binah–Hokhmah–Tiferet, the place of mystical and spiritual revelation; and the religious triad of Hokhmah–Tiferet–Hesed that is loaded with the belief system in which the individual was raised and what he or she has come to believe about religion and God.

JACOB'S LADDER

This is the diagram of the four worlds, inspired by the design of the Tabernacle in the biblical Book of Exodus. The Tabernacle was a movable temple carried by the Israelites in the desert. It showed the cosmic design of four worlds, or elements, on which creation is based and how they interweave. Jacob's Ladder is a design of how the matrix of the universe works. It was named for the vision of the biblical Patriarch Jacob in the Book of Genesis. He saw a ladder between Divinity and the Earth with angels passing up and down it.

JUDAISM

Judaism is the religion of the writers and characters of the Old Testament of the Bible, which forms the basis for both Christianity and Islam. Jews do not follow the New Testament or the Qur'an. The Jewish people have been the main keepers of Kabbalistic knowledge for more than 3,000 years, even though the system predates Judaism.

KARMA

Karma is the principle of the Law of Attraction, which can affect individuals or nations. Whatever is put out is received back. This is often seen as a cruel or judgmental system but it is totally fair. Good Karma is as prevalent as bad Karma. The thoughts we think and the words we say are creative forces and will return to us with similar energy. If we continue with those thoughts—whether good or bad—they manifest in our life.

KETER

Keter is the highest Sefira of the Tree of Life and of Jacob's Ladder. Known as the Crown, it is ruled by the planet Neptune. The Keter of Yezirah is also the human "higher self," the Tiferet of Beriah, and the Malkhut of Azilut. It is this high level of consciousness that is attained by the Messiah. Most humans can touch it for only a few moments.

LUCIFER

Lucifer is the greatest of the archangels who, according to legend, preferred to rule in hell rather than serve in heaven. Some legends say that it was because of this decision that God took away the ability to make free-will decisions from the angelic realms. Lucifer still serves God in the role of Satan, testing the integrity of human souls as they ascend back to the holy realms.

LURIANIC KABBALAH

This system was inspired by the theory of 16th-century Kabbalist Isaac Luria that God made a mistake during creation and that the Sefirot of Azilut shattered before the light of the Divine. This theory is used to explain evil in the world as an external force caused by the shattering. The task of humanity is to repair the shattered vessels.

MERKABAH

This is probably the original name for Kabbalah. It is also known as the Work of the Chariot from the vision of Ezekiel in the Old Testament. This is the mystical Kabbalah of inner revelation attained by deep meditation in which the aspirant rises up through the four worlds of Jacob's Ladder to the level of Divinity. It can be very unsettling and even dangerous if undertaken by someone unprepared.

MALKHUT

This is the lowest Sefira of the Tree of Life and Jacob's Ladder, ruled by the planet Earth. Its name in Hebrew means Kingdom, hence Jesus of Nazareth's references to "the Kingdom of Heaven" (the Malkhut of Beriah) and "the Kingdom of God" (the Malkhut of Azilut). Each of the four worlds is fulfilled and completed in its own Malkhut. However, the word "Malkhut" generally represents the physical reality to the Kabbalist.

MENORAH

The menorah is the seven-branched candelabra created by Moses and the Israelites on God's command. It is the original model for the Tree of Life and contains all the Sefirot, the paths, and the four levels of Jacob's Ladder within it.

MESSIAH

Messiah means "the Anointed One," and is known in Islam as the Axis of the Age. The Messiah is the perfect incarnate man at Keter of Yezirah. Kabbalah teaches that there is one such person (male or female) in every generation. Most Messiahs work quietly behind the scenes but they still affect the destiny of nations by their presence and reverence. They can be of any faith.

METATRON

Metatron is the Archangel of Presence at Keter of Beriah. He is unique—according to legend he is both human and angelic. Metatron is the Spirit of the first fully realized man, Enoch, who transformed into the greatest of the archangels. Enoch is believed to have ascended into the higher realms without tasting death; this is the basis for many of the ascension teachings of the New Age.

MICHAEL

Michael is the archangel placed at the Tiferet of Beriah. He is Lord of the Sun and his name means "Like unto God." He is the watcher over humanity and can be invoked at times of crisis, although Samael is the angel of protection. Michael is also the archangel of priesthood, marriage, and legitimate ambition and is petitioned on Sundays.

MYSTICISM

Mysticism is the practice of experiencing the Divine through intuition, insight, or direct knowledge of God. Mystics look for truth beyond general reality or written texts. A mystical tradition focuses on teaching students how to do this through balancing themselves in the soul triad with the support and backup of Yesod. Once this is achieved, mystical union with Divinity can be sought safely.

NEW AGE

A term used for the late 20th-century revival, revitalization, and augmentation of old arts and sciences tied with natural healing, magic, and self-awareness. New Age encompasses health, medicine, philosophy, religion, and the occult—presented from an alternative or multicultural perspective.

NEZACH

The Sefira of eternity or action, Nezach is ruled by the planet Venus and is the aspect of both humanity and nature that kick-starts any plan or action. In nature, Nezach is balanced with Hod to start and continue the cycle of the seasons. In humanity, Nezach uses the information of Hod for appropriate action. An out of balance Nezach can lead to excess of any physical or emotional kind, including addictive behavior.

ORTHODOX

To be Orthodox means to adhere to the accepted, traditional, written version of a faith or belief. An Orthodox Jew is one who follows all 613 laws laid down in the *Torah* (the first five books of the Bible).

PEOPLE OF THE BOOK

The name given to those who follow one of the three religions based on the Bible—Judaism, Christianity, and Islam.

QABALAH

This is the spelling of Kabbalah adopted by the magical tradition.

RAPHAEL

The archangel of the Beriatic Sefira of Hod, Raphael is the great healing angel. His name means "Healer of God." Some traditions put Raphael at Tiferet and Michael at Hod but in ancient traditions it is Mercury, the ruler of Hod, who carries the caduceus—the healing staff of the gods. Raphael is therefore considered to be Lord of Mercury. He is petitioned on Wednesdays.

REINCARNATION

Reincarnation is the principle of repeating lives in order to perfect the soul. Kabbalah teaches that all human beings reincarnate in order to complete four journeys in the return to Divinity. This makes life uniformly fair; everyone has the opportunity to experience lives of happiness, love, and prosperity as well as more challenging ones. Kabbalah teaches that humans incarnate only as humans although they may live both vegetable and animal lives in a human body.

SAMAEL

Samael is the archangel of the Beriatic Gevurah and Lord of Mars. His name means "Severity of God" and he is often, mistakenly, linked to Satan because of his place in the Sefira of cosmic evil. However, evil at this level is pure destruction rather than a personal act or a temptation. Samael is petitioned on Tuesdays for help in overcoming problems and for protection from hatred, hostility, or fearful situations.

SANDALPHON

Sandalphon is the archangel at Malkhut of Beriah. He is the lower aspect of Metatron and it is through this cosmic being that Enoch and other ascended beings are able to return to Earth for particular events or missions. He is the only archangel whose name does not end in "el" (of God). Sandalphon means "co-brother."

SCHOOL OF THE SOUL

This is a specific gathering of Kabbalists who represent a particular aspect of the teaching, for example, all the members of the same spiritual soul group. Each human being belongs to a group of souls that will incarnate together several times in order to carry out particular work or to help to clear negative Karma.

SEFIRA (PLURAL SEFIROT)

The Sefirot are the lights, vessels, faces, or aspects of the Ten Divine Emanations in Azilut. They are repeated in the three lower worlds although they are generally referred to as being a part of the Yeziratic Tree of Life.

The word sefira comes from the Hebrew root "S-F-R," which can mean sphere or sapphire in English.

SHEKHINAH

This is the Divine Presence in Malkhut of Azilut and below, also referred to as "the Daughter of the Voice" and regarded as the feminine aspect of God. This is the aspect of Divinity that gives birth to souls from Azilut and receives them back after death. Shekhinah resides within the feminine in humanity, and Orthodox tradition says that a man can only access it once he is married.

SOUL

The soul is the aspect of a human being that is perpetual and survives death. Our soul is the "real" us, the person we wish to be and were meant to be. The soul resides within the soul triad and is the place from which we can operate free will.

SOUL TRIAD

This is the triad of Gevurah, Hesed, and Tiferet in Yezirah, the place unique to each human being where we individuate into our true selves. The triad is influenced by our astrological chart (Mars, Jupiter, and Tiferet) but it is also the place of free will, where we are capable of overcoming astrological and social influences through conscious choice.

TABERNACLE

The Tabernacle was the movable place of worship for the Israelites in the wilderness and the model for Jacob's Ladder. The Tabernacle formed the design of the Jewish Temple that stood in Jerusalem. Its Holy of Holies represented Azilut; the Court of the Men, Beriah; the Court of the Women, Yezirah; and the Court of the Gentiles (non-Jews), Asiyyah.

THINKING TRIAD

Also known as the triad of contemplation and the triad of "Will-lessness," this is the triad between Hod, Yesod, and Malkhut. This triad denotes the preferences and capabilities of each human when it comes to thought processes and intellect. An overstrong, active triad can lead to a life lived as a bookworm or on computers interpreting data without living in the "real world," while an underactive one can lead to a life of thoughtlessness. This triad in balance leads to intuition built on accurate information. The triad is ruled by the astrological sign of Virgo; when out of balance, it will either overanalyze everything or worry in detail. If you are a primarily passive person, it is vital to balance this triad with the feeling and action triads.

TIFERET

This is the Sefira of beauty or truth at the center of each of the four Trees of Life on Jacob's Ladder. The Yeziratic Tiferet is ruled by the Sun and is the place where three worlds meet. It is also the Keter of Asiyyah, the physical world, and the Malkhut of Beriah, the spiritual world. This is the place known in the Bible as "The Kingdom of Heaven."

TORAH

The first five books of the Bible, which contains the Law of the Israelites and is deemed deeply sacred. The word *Torah* is Hebrew for "the teaching."

TREASURE HOUSE OF SOULS

The Treasure House of Souls is the soul triad of Azilut (Gevurah–Hesed–Tiferet). According to legend, it is the place where the human soul resides until called into manifest existence. From here, the soul passes through the Yesod of Azilut to the Malkhut, known as Shekhinah, to begin the process of incarnation.

TREE OF LIFE

The Tree of Life, modeled on the menorah, is the seminal diagram of Kabbalah. This term is generally used for the psychological world of Yezirah, one of four worlds in Jacob's Ladder. Whenever it is used in any text without a specific reference to another world apart from the psychological one, it refers to Yezirah. In fact, it is equally applicable to all four worlds, as are the ten Sefirot. The original Tree of Life is the world of Azilut, which equates to the Tree of Life in the Garden of Eden. The Tree of Knowledge is the second world of Beriah, where good and evil are first created.

TRIAD

A triad is a triangle between three Sefirot. Each triad has its own physical, psychological, spiritual, or divine makeup and its emotional loading depends on the individual's personal astrology, tradition, and social mores. Each triad also corresponds to a sign of the zodiac, which governs its innate character. For example, the triad of Gevurah–Tiferet–Hod is ruled by Scorpio. This astrological sign rules secrecy, death, sex, taxes, paranoia, and spiritual transformation. The triad represents emotional pain and memories and it takes the ability of Scorpio to dig deep to uncover the secrets of inner emotions and its transformational power to overcome them.

URIEL

The archangel of the Beriatic Hokhmah, Uriel is Lord of Uranus and his name means "Light of God." Those who call upon Uriel's power must be of a sufficiently developed consciousness to work at a high level or be in such desperate need of a miracle that they are prepared to have their life transformed and re-created.

VEGETABLE TRIAD

The triad of Hod–Nezach–Malkhut, the vegetable triad contains the three triads of thinking, feeling, and action around the Sefira of Yesod. This is the level at which humans eat, have sex, reproduce, and seek both comfort and safety. It is a vital part of our makeup and corresponds to the electromagnetic systems of the physical body. Vegetable humanity is capable of living a very happy life but is ruled by social and political laws and subject to the Karma of its country and family.

YESOD

Yesod of Yezirah is also known as the foundation of the human psyche. This is because it learns and absorbs all the outside stimuli that occur in life up to the age of seven, and anything continually repeated since then. As the center of the vegetable triad, it is the focus of everyday life, and many of us live our entire lives at this level. Living in Yesod means a life ruled by the natural calls of food, sex, and the need to survive. In the more developed psyche, Yesod is the servant of Tiferet (the Self), supporting it in its free-will choices and conscious decisions. It is Yesod that gets us up in the morning, decides on our breakfast, chooses our clothing, and gets us to work. It runs our everyday life without question. Only when something new or unexpected happens is it at a temporary loss. This is why a calamity or crisis is known as the "wake-up call," when Yesod gives up its control over the psyche and surrenders to the higher power of the Self.

YEZIRAH

Yezirah is the psychological world of emotions, soul, and angels, the world traditionally known as The Tree of Life. It contains all levels of human existence from the vegetable level, through animal and human levels to the spiritual and Divine, demonstrating that we are all capable of the highest and the lowest of thoughts and actions.

ZADKIEL

Also known as Sachiel, Zadkiel is the archangel of the Beriatic Hesed and Lord of Jupiter. His name means "Benevolence of God." He is invoked on Thursdays in matters concerning finance, earnings, recovery of debt, legal matters, or authority.

ZIMZUM

This is the contraction within the Absolute to allow the void into which existence was able to come into being.

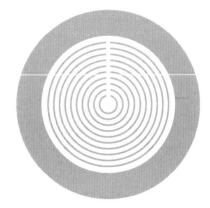

INDEX

ACKNOWLEDGMENTS

The author gratefully acknowledges Z'ev ben Shimon Halevi, Dr. David Goddard, Peter Dickinson, Adam Simmonds, and Michael Hattwick MD.

PICTURE ACKNOWLEDGMENTS

The publisher would like to thank the following organizations and individuals for their kind permission to reproduce the photographs and illustrations in this book. Every effort has been made to acknowledge the pictures, however we apologize if there are any unintentional omissions.

akg-images: 33, 56, 98, 105 right, 127, 173; Rabatti-Domingie: 183; Eric Lessing: 139.

Art Archive/Eileen Tweedy: 103.

Suzanne Bosman: 38, 152, 219.

Bridgeman Art Library/Bibliothèque Nationale, Paris, France: 37.

Corbis/Bettmann: 76; Chris Hellier: 134, 170.

Professor Keith Critchlow: 179 left.

Getty Images/Bridgeman Art Library: 9.

Z'ev ben Shimon Halevi: 7, 8, 15, 100, 102, 129, 187.

Clay Holden and The John Dee Publication Project. © 2007. All rights reserved: 146.

Jupiter Images: 22, 32, 34, 41, 47, 54, 88, 97, 129, 130, 133, 172, 184, 195, 198.

The Lordprice Collection: 167.

Nova Development Corp.: 171.

TopFoto: 86; Fortean: 62, 175; Fotomas: 36, 125; The Print Collector/HIP: 145; Ann Ronan Picture Library/HIP: 126; Roger-Viollet: 105 left; Charles Walker: 30, 153, 161; World History Archive: 110.

US Games Systems Inc.: 97, 162, 163. (Illustrations from the Universal Waite Tarot Deck® reproduced by permission of U.S. Games Systems, Inc., Stamford, CT 06902 USA. Copyright ©1990 by U.S. Games Systems, Inc. Further reproduction prohibited. The Universal Waite Tarot Deck® is a registered trademark of U.S. Games Systems, Inc.)